# Praise for *The Power of Teacher Teams*

" . . . *as text for collective work in schools, this book could substantially change the way we organize and support teacher teams."*

—from the foreword by Richard F. Elmore
Gregory R. Anrig Professor of Educational Leadership
Harvard Graduate School of Education

*Tools ready-to-use! A required resource for principals, teacher leaders, instructional coaches and professional development facilitators. Troen and Boles make teaming practice public so that we can begin to do the same across our schools.*

—Barbara Crock
Founding Principal, University of Chicago Charter School, Woodlawn Campus
Director, Chicago School Leadership, The New Teacher Center

*Change through collaboration occurs when school leaders and teachers meet consistently to talk about student learning and teaching design and hold each other accountable. As a principal practitioner dedicated to adult learning and professional growth, I treasure the gems scattered throughout this salient book.*

—Gerardo J. Martinez
Principal, Edward Devotion School
Brookline, MA

*A powerful book that offers practical advice grounded in research . . . the case studies can assist superintendents, curriculum/staff developers, teacher leaders, and principals in implementing effective, school-based instructional teams.*

—Christine M. Johns
Superintendent of Schools
Utica Community Schools, MI

*At a time when teacher effectiveness is under attack nationwide, Boles and Troen add a fresh perspective to the conversation. Through a thoughtful use of theoretical analysis and "in the trenches" case studies, the authors admonish America that if we are truly interested in restoring our prominence in the world through a first-rate educational system, then our strategies for improving teacher effectiveness must also include parallel strategies for improving schools' team effectiveness.*

—Irvin Scott
Chief Academic Officer
Boston Public Schools, MA

*Finally, a book written in user-friendly language that explains the value of educators working in teams to improve student achievement! It's as if the authors are there in team meetings with you, clearly explaining how to avoid and correct the many problems of teacher teams— showing team members how to self-identify areas of strength and weakness, leading to greater team efficacy. Educators who read this book will be able to use its cases and guides to case analysis to solve the challenges they face in their own schools.*

—Marguerite Izzo
Language Arts Teacher
2007 New York State Teacher of the Year
Howard T. Herber Middle School, Malverne, NY

*. . . an incredible gold mine of ideas, strategies, practices, and advice, rooted in a conceptual frame that is both accessible and engaging!* The Power of Teacher Teams *is must reading for teachers, principals and policy makers who care passionately about transforming our schools for teachers and their students.*

—Ann Lieberman
Senior Scholar
Stanford University, CA

*Troen and Boles give us a concrete image of how collective educational practice can be focused on the instructional core of schooling. Their portrait of teacher teams is an important contribution to our understanding of how teaching is learned and will be useful for both practice and analysis.*

—Magdalene Lampert
George Herbert Mead Collegiate Professor of Education
University of Michigan

*The authors identify the real-life challenges of teaming and collaboration that teachers and principals face each and every day. They provide cases that describe the everyday experiences of working in teams, and then present tools that professionals will find extremely useful in aligning their efforts around improving student learning.*

—Jeff Ronnenberg, Superintendent
Spring Lake Park Schools District
Spring Lake Park, MN

# The Power of
# TEACHER
# TEAMS

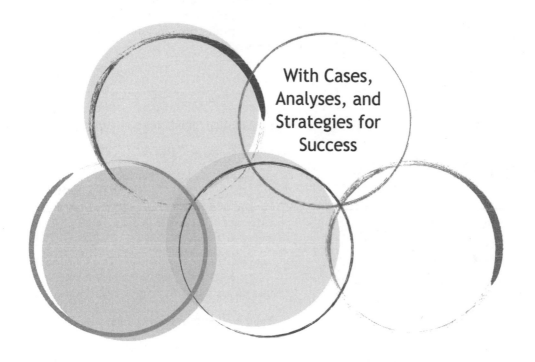

With Cases,
Analyses, and
Strategies for
Success

## VIVIAN TROEN | KATHERINE C. BOLES

Foreword by Richard F. Elmore

A JOINT PUBLICATION

CORWIN
A SAGE Company

*learningforward*

**CORWIN**
A SAGE Company

FOR INFORMATION:

Corwin

A SAGE Company

2455 Teller Road

Thousand Oaks, California 91320

(800) 233-9936

Fax: (800) 417-2466

www.corwin.com

SAGE Ltd.

1 Oliver's Yard

55 City Road

London EC1Y 1SP

United Kingdom

SAGE India Pvt. Ltd.

B 1/I 1 Mohan Cooperative Industrial Area

Mathura Road, New Delhi 110 044

India

SAGE Asia-Pacific Pte. Ltd.

33 Pekin Street #02-01

Far East Square

Singapore 048763

Acquisitions Editor:  Dan Alpert

Associate Editor:  Megan Bedell

Editorial Assistant:  Sarah Bartlett

Production Editor:  Libby Larson

Copy Editor:  Sarah J. Duffy

Typesetter:  C&M Digitals (P) Ltd.

Proofreader:  Christina West

Indexer:  Diggs Publication Services

Cover Designer:  Scott van Atta

Permissions Editor:  Karen Ehrmann

Copyright © 2012 by Corwin

Printed in the United States of America.

*Library of Congress Cataloging-in-Publication Data*

Troen, Vivian, 1940-

The power of teacher teams: with cases, analyses, and strategies for success/Vivian Troen, Katherine C. Boles; foreword by Richard F. Elmore.

p. cm.

"Joint Publication With Learning Forward."

Includes bibliographical references and index.

ISBN 978-1-4129-9133-9 (paper w/cd)

1. Teaching teams 2. Teaching teams— Case studies. I. Boles, Katherine. II. Title.

LB1029.T4T76 2012
371.14'8—dc23

This book is printed on acid-free paper.

15 16 17 18 19 10 9 8 7 6 5 4

# Contents

**On Companion CD-ROM**

**Cases**
    Case 9. Is It "Take Us to Our Leader" or
        "We Can Do It Ourselves"?
    Case 10. Managing From the Middle

**On Companion DVD**

**Video Cases**
    Video Case 1. A 3rd-Grade Team Meets
        to Examine Student Work
    Video Case 2. A 5th-Grade Team Meets to
        Follow Up on a Professional Development Workshop
    Video Case 3. A 9th-Grade Physics Team Meets to Plan
        Interventions for Underperforming Students
    Video Case 4. A High School History Department Meets to
        Develop Consistent Grading Criteria

*In the course of our 30-plus years of teaching and writing, we have met hundreds of teachers, principals, policymakers, and legislators who every day struggle with what we believe is the most important question faced by a participatory democracy: how can we make schools and teaching better for the education of our children?*

*This book is dedicated to them, in the hope that it may help to answer that question.*

# Photo Credits

# List of Figures

**NOTE: All figures are available as full-size reproducibles on the companion CD-ROM and at www.corwin.com/ teacherteams**

## Case 6

## Case 7

## Case 8

## On Companion CD-ROM

## Case 9

## Case 10

## Video Case 1

# Foreword

*Richard F. Elmore*

*"This book could substantially change the way we organize and support teacher teams."*

As part of my professional practice, I routinely observe teacher teams at work, in addition to observing teachers and students at work in classrooms. As recently as eight or ten years ago, it would have been rare to find a school with designated grade-level or content teams, much less dedicated common planning time for team members to meet and work together. Now, virtually every school I visit has some kind of team structure and a regular schedule of team meetings. That's the good news. The bad news is that only about one in ten teacher teams that I observe functions at a level that would result in any improvement of instructional practice and student learning in the classroom. I have observed all the dysfunctions of teacher teamwork described in this book, and many more. Yet I continue to be an ardent advocate of teacher teams. Why?

The answer is that there is no other way to improve instructional practice at scale in schools than to organize groups of adult learners to work on problems of instructional practice and to weave those groups into an organization-wide strategy of improvement. The evidence is clear on this point. Relational trust among teachers, and between administrators and teachers, is positively related to student performance in schools, and trust is constructed through face-to-face collaborative work. Collective efficacy, or the degree to which adults believe that working together on common tasks improves the quality of their work and its influence on student learning, is positively related to student performance in schools. The performance of organizations in general is related to the existence of high-functioning teams, and the primary source of *organizational* learning—that adoption and implementation of practices that lead directly to improvements in performance—is the team structure. Team learning predicts performance more than individual learning in organizations. So when you step back from particular schools and look at the overall evidence, there is no doubt that high-functioning teams are the route to school improvement.[1] The problem is that most schools, in my experience, don't actually know how to make teams work for the benefit of the organization. Why?

The major culprit is the default culture of U.S. schooling. Schools have traditionally been organized as highly atomized "egg-crate" organizations, and teaching has traditionally been defined as an individual, rather than a collective, practice. We now know—and have known for at least 40 years—that changing the structure of an organization does not automatically change its culture, much less its practice or performance. Introducing teams into a school, by itself, does not transform the culture of that school from a radically atomized one into a coherent one. Yet we persist in the belief that if we just get the structure right, the practice will follow. Wrong. Wrong. Wrong. How many more generations of educators will hurtle over this cliff before we recognize that this is a losing proposition?

The solution lies in deliberately changing the practice to fit the structure, rather than changing the structure on the bet that it will change the practice. As a general rule, we should never put people in a new structure without first modeling the practice that goes with that structure and without explicitly addressing the changes in actual behavior that are required to make the structure work. Changes in culture *follow* changes in practice, rather than vice versa. We are routinely dumping teachers into team structures without any preparation for the actual work it takes to make collective decisions about team practice. We glorify teamwork, as if it were an end in itself, without examining its actual impact on practice or on the learning that is required to do the work. And then we wonder why the teaching that follows the team meeting looks an awful lot like the teaching we saw before the team meeting.

What Vivian Troen and Kitty Boles have done in this book is to begin the process of drawing educators into the practice of teamwork that goes with the structure of teamwork. The narrative chapters of the book lay out a framework for the practice of teamwork that provides the rationale and general guidelines for the work. The case studies raise penetrating questions about the problems that arise as teams develop. It is at once a hard-nosed, realistic look at how teams actually function and, in the spirit of their previous work together, an essentially optimistic book. They believe, as I do, that the future of work in schools lies in powerful face-to-face relationships among teachers. Taken seriously, as a text for collective work in schools, this book could substantially change the way we organize and support teacher teams.

There are at least three themes in this work that connect to the broader context of research on teamwork and that are worth underscoring for readers who are new to the work. First, there are huge differences between novices and experts in matters of practice. The differences, we now know, are not just in the quantity of knowledge that experts have, but in their ability to discern patterns and their fluency in diagnosing and solving problems.[2] By definition, no matter how "experienced" teachers are in their classrooms, they will enter teamwork almost exclusively as novices. Novices need expert guidance and support to develop their practice, and teamwork requires both behavioral and cognitive coaching in order to make the transition from novice to proficient to fluent. Putting people in teams without expert support is not only unlikely to produce the benefits of teamwork, it is likely to reinforce the negative patterns it is designed to change.

Second, team structures without an overall strategy of improvement at the school level will not result in any measurable improvement of practice. Troen and Boles speak clearly about the role that school leaders need to play in designing and supporting teamwork. Leadership is not just making structures work, it is also putting the work of those structures into a central narrative that connects structures, processes, and purposes in ways that people in the organization can understand. This narrative can be called a "strategy." If people in the organization don't understand how the pieces of the whole fit together to form a common storyline, then "collective work" of any kind will be directionless.

Finally, Troen and Boles make a point of stressing that effective teamwork requires teacher team members to be responsible, or accountable, to each other for their work. In my experience, this is the toughest problem American educators face in school improvement. Teachers who have been socialized to the default culture are reluctant to give up control of their individual practice in the interest of collective improvement. Without this movement from individual to collective responsibility, school improvement typically stalls and stagnates. The structure of teamwork provides the occasion for the development of collective responsibility; the practice of teamwork provides collective responsibility itself.

—Richard F. Elmore
Gregory R. Anrig Professor of Educational Leadership
Harvard Graduate School of Education

# Acknowledgments

The many teachers with whom we have worked over the years are the true heroes of our teacher team adventure. Those elementary, middle, and high school teachers opened their classrooms and their team meetings to us. They worked with us to implement our ideas in real-life teams and helped us refine our ideas in helpful, constructive ways.

Teachers in large schools and small, in big cities and in rural towns—schools public and independent; Native American reservation schools; schools in faraway places such as Singapore, Japan, Germany, South Africa, England, Australia, and Greece; they are all a part of this book. Our thanks go to all those tireless practitioners, and their principals, heads of school, superintendents and others who were brave enough to take the risks that allowed us to test our ideas and pilot our cases and activities. We have promised to protect their anonymity, but we continue to sing their praises because of their willingness to put themselves and their practice up for observation and analysis. They welcomed us without reservation and with great warmth, and were willing to have their practice videoed for a wide audience—stepping beyond their culture, which traditionally has been hidden from outside view.

We remember with great appreciation our original teacher team at the Edward Devotion Elementary School in Brookline, Massachusetts, a team that we helped form in the mid-1980s, and to our fearless, indomitable, and ever-supportive principal, Jerry Kaplan. Gretchen Albertini, Steve Brady, Jack DeLong, Martha Farlow, Bill Gardner, Betsy Kellogg, Betsy Lake, Jim Swaim, and the late JoAnne Rostler, we remember you.

Through the years our work has been informed by the wise counsel and constructive criticism and support of Karen Worth, the professor at Wheelock College who listened closely to us when we first brought our ideas of collaboration and teacher teams to Wheelock in 1986. She continued to watch over us as we progressed through our goal of creating a college-school partnership (one of the first Professional Development Schools in the country), and gave us invaluable feedback on the first drafts of this book.

Barbara Neufeld made an indelible mark on our work as teachers and consultants. We thank her for giving us invaluable research instruction when we needed it and for sharing warmth, laughs, great dinners, and much love.

Lee Teitel's case studies on PDSs inspired us as we worked with teacher teams, and his friendship sustained us through many a rough period. He was always there when we had a question about our PDS or about our team, and we are indebted to him for all his support.

Special thanks are due to our colleague Sharon Feiman-Nemser, director of the Mandel Center at Brandeis University, for her ongoing mentorship, her creative ideas that helped us with the activities in our Guides to Case Analysis, and her inspirational leadership in the field of teacher education.

Spencer Foundation grants have supported us through many of the projects that led up to this book, and we are indebted to the wisdom and support of Patricia Albjerg Graham and Lauren Young at Spencer. As teachers themselves, they understood our passion for the power of teacher teams.

We want to thank the many faculty and staff at the Harvard Graduate School of Education who helped us in our journey to this book's publication. Faculty members Kay Merseth and Susan Moore Johnson gave us their wise advice; Harvard's librarians promptly responded whenever we needed books, articles, references, and links to electronic resources, and amazed us with their kindness and competence. And the skill of Gino Beniamino and Susan Eppling of the Learning Technology Center enabled us to create the videos on our DVD. In addition, masters students in Harvard's School Leadership Program worked in schools with teacher teams, helped write cases for this book, and enthusiastically joined in our teacher team research. Doctoral students Candice Bocala, Susan Henry, Monica Ng and Marcia Russell provided us with their methodological prowess and fine analytical skills.

Katherine Bassett and our colleagues at the Teacher Leadership Exploratory Consortium at Educational Testing Service helped us hone our thinking about teacher leaders, and JoEllen Killion of the National Staff Development Council/Learning Forward, not only made the first suggestion that we write a book focused on team cases, but also helped connect us to Corwin.

And what would we have done without Dan Alpert, our shepherd and guide at Corwin? He gave us his frank and detailed comments and showed us how to improve our ideas. He was critical when he needed to be—and supportive at all times. And, we would be greatly remiss if we did not acknowledge the work of an often unsung hero, the production editor—in our case, Libby Larson, whose superhuman scrupulous attention to detail was always unflagging.

For people who might wonder how these things just happen, the creative genius behind the design and production of the companion DVD and CD-ROM is Pip Clews.

As we neared the end of our journey to this book's publication we reconnected and learned from Susan Szachowicz, a long-time colleague, now the principal of Brockton High School in Massachusetts, who has effectively worked with groups of high school teachers to turn a large, once-failing large urban high school into a model of excellence that has garnered wide and well-deserved acclaim.

We thank Kitty's husband, Barney Brawer, a Boston elementary school principal, for his unflagging support and willingness to listen to nascent ideas and give us critical feedback from a principal's perspective. His reactions helped make our book more balanced and more cognizant of the important work of the principal in school-change initiatives. Barney invented the "Islands" exercise we present in this book, and we thank him for that valuable contribution.

And last, we owe an enormous debt of gratitude to Vivian's husband, Paul Wesel, who throughout our 30 years of collaboration has been even more than a text editor, researcher, materials organizer, ideas tester, schedule keeper, coffee provider, and energy-inducer—a dear friend and ever supportive fan and champion. Paul is a stalwart, level-headed counselor, a wise colleague, and we believe it is fair to say that without his many and varied contributions this book would likely never have come into being.

We could not have done our work—either in writing or teaching—without the people we've acknowledged here, and many others besides. Teachers should never work alone, and that is the message. There is strength, power and joy in collaboration and we hope through our work we can continue to demonstrate the power of teacher teams.

## Publisher's Acknowledgments

Corwin gratefully acknowledges the contributions of the following reviewers:

Patricia Bowman, Adjunct Professor
University of California, Los Angeles
Los Angeles, CA

Thelma A. Davis, Principal
Robert Lunt Elementary School
Las Vegas, NV

Nancy Drake, Consultant
Student Assistance and Community of Practice
Maine Department of Education
Machias, ME

Cathy Galland, Curriculum Director
Republic R-III Schools
Republic, MO

Pam Houfek, Director of Professional Development
  and Teacher Evaluation
Sarasota County Public Schools
Sarasota, FL

Catherine Menard, Curriculum Director
MSAD #31
Howland, ME

Fernando Nuñez, Director of Professional Development
Isaac School District #5
Phoenix, AZ

Jeff Ronnenberg, Superintendent
Spring Lake Park School District
Spring Lake Park, MN

Marion E. Woods, Director of Elementary
  Professional Development
Little Rock School District
Little Rock, AR

# About the Authors

Considered authorities on the subjects of teacher education, teacher leadership, and professional development schools, Vivian Troen and Katherine C. Boles deliver workshops on teacher teams and teacher leadership, speak at conferences and seminars, and regularly consult with schools and school districts in the United States and internationally. As classroom teachers, they founded one of the nation's first professional development schools to link colleges and public schools in partnerships for the preservice education of teachers as well as the ongoing professional development of veteran teachers.

They are the authors of *Who's Teaching Your Children: Why the Teacher Crisis Is Worse Than You Think and What Can Be Done About It* (Yale University Press, 2003) as well as numerous articles and book chapters on teachers and teaching. Most recently they have joined national leaders of professional organizations of educators, state education agencies, and universities in the Teacher Leadership Exploratory Consortium, convened by the Educational Testing Service to develop model national standards for teacher leadership.

Troen codirects the Induction Partnership Initiative at Brandeis University, guiding schools in developing the capacity to support new teachers. She also leads school administrators in regularly scheduled online, networked seminars investigating a wide range of issues surrounding induction practices and professional development for new and experienced teachers.

Boles is a senior lecturer on education and faculty director of the Learning and Teaching Master's Degree Program at the Harvard Graduate School of Education. She received her doctorate from Harvard, and her courses examine the latest research on school reform, teacher education, teacher teams, and new forms of teacher leadership.

# 1

# Read This First

*I never let my schooling interfere with my education.*

—Mark Twain

## Our Shared Legacy

A book about school reform—and teacher teaming is indeed a major and vital reform—should not plunge into an explanation of how to successfully implement that reform without a nod to the historical context that compels it. We need to know something about the forces that made schools and teaching what they are today.

If you were to visit classrooms all over the world, as we have, you might be surprised to see the same model of an American classroom replicated in a remote village along the Amazon River as exists in Paris, and in Shanghai, and in a thatched-roof schoolhouse in Botswana. How did that happen? Where did that model come from, and what does it tell us about how we teach children?

The schooling of American citizens began with the revolutionary idea that a democratic society and the economic engine that makes it possible to thrive are built on the foundation of an educated populace. Reading. Writing. Arithmetic. How best to distribute those skills among a widespread and mostly agricultural populace? In the 18th century the answer was the one-room schoolhouse. A bunch of children of all ages were squeezed into small, drafty, poorly heated buildings and taught by an unregulated corps of almost exclusively male schoolmasters, many of whom were only a few steps ahead of their students. And yet, to a certain extent, it worked. For a brief period in our country's history, this model fulfilled its purpose. The American genius for innovation had proven itself, almost overnight.

And then, almost overnight, a confluence of related events radically transformed America and with it the landscape of education. In the mid-19th century the powerful forces of rapid industrialization combined with waves of arriving immigrants to result in major population shifts and explosions. New cities erupted where before there were only small towns or villages. Established cities like New York, Chicago, Boston, and Baltimore overflowed, challenging their capacity to house, feed, employ, and educate the swelling masses.

Advances in technology meant fewer hands were needed on the farm. While successful farmers whose lives were made easier by agricultural technology stayed on the farms, droves of farmers and other workers from rural areas moved to the cities, attracted by the burgeoning number of jobs in factories and mills. But this new stream of rural and foreign workers caused problems for industrialists; the arriving workers were mostly unskilled, semi-literate at best, and unaccustomed to the kind of work demanded by industry. What was good enough for the farm was not good enough to meet the needs of the new economy.

One-Room Schoolhouse

Urgently needed to transform this human resource into a well-prepared workforce were a whole new form of schools and a different cadre of teachers along with them. Already at hand were two factors that made this transformation possible. One was the ready availability of young women who could both read and write and were no longer needed for farm work. The other was the innovation introduced by Horace Mann in Boston, Massachusetts, of the graded-classroom school building, created on the industrial model of mass production. The era of the one-room schoolhouse was essentially over.

Quickly, large school buildings were constructed—graded classrooms, where children of the same age were grouped together, greatly simplifying both instruction and discipline. The large number of women who arrived to teach were pleased to enter this newly feminized profession, and teaching was transformed from a male-dominated enterprise to a "woman's 'true' profession."[1] The assembly line, used so successfully in industry, was easily transported to this new model of schools and teaching. School boards, which were committees of business and professional elites, were modeled after corporate boards of directors. The power to administer school systems was put into the hands of professionally trained school *superintendents* (a term borrowed from the railroads, which were considered to be the acme of efficient industrial organization).

Early Graded Classroom

## A Culture of Isolation and Egalitarianism

And thus, although teaching was the entryway to a meaningful and respected vocation for women, this newfound "profession" brought with it an inescapable resemblance to factory work. Factory workers were interchangeable employees, hired to do an assembly-line piece of work, laboring alone at looms or workstations, receiving a product in an unfinished state, improving it, and passing it on to the next worker along the line. So it was with teachers, solo practitioners of their craft, self-reliant and autonomous, working in isolation with minimal supervision.

What evolved from this worklife condition was a powerful school culture in which teachers neither sought advice nor offered to give one another counsel or support. Seeking help was considered an admission of incompetence. This led to the evolution of a cultural norm that held all teachers to be equally accomplished—no teacher could risk appearing to be smarter or more skilled without subtle (and sometimes overt) rebuke from fellow workers. In turn, this culture made true accountability all but impossible.

Over the years, professional development for teachers has been partly an attempt to correct some of the deleterious effects of this culture, but much of what passes for professional development has been shown to be ineffective. Sent to workshops to compensate for the drawbacks of their isolation and to "correct" the inadequacies of their teaching, teachers might return to the classrooms energized with new knowledge and ideas, but school culture soon defeats what they may have learned on their own. Without school-based support and reinforcement, teachers' attempts at self-improvement have often proved futile.

## The Move Toward Collaboration

The pervasive view that public education in America is in trouble dates back at least to 1983 with the publication of *A Nation at Risk: The Imperative for Educational Reform*,[2] which described American education as a system "being eroded by a rising tide of mediocrity." Thereupon followed a flurry—one could even call it a landslide—of proposed reforms to remedy the problems laid out in the report. It has taken quite a while, however, for educators, administrators, policymakers, and other would-be reformers to come around, and warm to, the idea of teacher teaming. Yes, they now acknowledge, the old solo-practitioner model is out of step in a world in which doctors work in teams and rely heavily on current and meaningful professional development to improve their practice, where novice attorneys are routinely assigned mentors, where computers and automobiles are designed by collaborators in highly skilled work groups, and where even the tradition-bound military has embraced teamwork as the key to battlefield success.

Conceptually, at least, the notion of teachers collaborating in teams has arrived. But in the words of an old English proverb, "there's many a slip 'twixt the cup and the lip." In practice, creating successful teacher teams is much harder than it looks. It is complex and difficult work for those not knowledgeable about the process. Even the definition of what constitutes "success" is not universally agreed upon.

Yet we must have teacher teams. More and more states, districts, and individual schools—both public and private—are insisting on it as the way toward improved teaching and learning. The educational model of teachers collaborating in teams, if it has not already arrived in your school, is certainly the wave of the future.

This book is designed to help you surf rather than paddle.

# 2

# Get Ready for Better Teams

*Talent wins games, teamwork wins championships.*

—Michael Jordan

## Why Teacher Teams?

Bottom line: if you're not currently involved in teacher teaming there's a pretty good chance that you will be soon. And it isn't just because the U.S. Department of Education has proclaimed that teachers' professional development is to be conducted among learning teams of educators including teacher, paraprofessional, and other instructional staff at the schools.

The most powerful argument for teacher teaming is that educationally, for all involved, it's a very good idea. When teachers work together in *successful* teams, they get group assistance with problem solving; together they examine student work, address issues of class management, learn a new curriculum, provide support for new teachers, and give veteran teachers roles as mentors. And they have an opportunity to observe each other at work in order to improve their own practice. What teachers are unable to accomplish alone, or only with great difficulty, they can accomplish more successfully in a team.

There's also enough very good data to indicate that teachers who work in teams get more enjoyment and self-fulfillment from teaching[1] as they see their own practice improve, and along with increased job satisfaction comes the increased likelihood of a longer career in teaching.[2] Perhaps the most compelling reason of all: when teachers collaborate, their students do better.[3] That is, when teachers' expressed goal is to improve instruction. And that story is at the heart of this book.

## Why This Book?

The concept of teacher teaming is relatively new in the history of education, and while the idea of teams sounds simple and easy to implement, teachers have never been taught how to collaborate in teams *for the express purpose of improving instruction.* This is mostly uncharted territory, and teacher teams generally fail in this regard. Remarkably, even though schools struggle mightily to create more effective teacher teams, they have few reliable resources to help guide their efforts.

It is not widely acknowledged that to get the most out of their teams, teachers, teacher leaders, and coaches/facilitators need to learn *specific teaming skills* in order to be able to turn collaborating groups of teachers into well-functioning instructional teams that *improve children's learning.* To be successful as teams, they must first be able to discuss and understand the intricacies and tensions of teacher teamwork. They must then be able to assess and reflect on the level of work for their team so that the team meets what must be their ultimate goals: better teaching and better student outcomes.

As educators who each have over 30 years' experience as classroom teachers, university faculty, educational researchers, and consultants, we have seen, time and time again, the efforts of frustrated teacher teams who work hard shoveling sand against the tide, only to see their efforts bear meager results. As you will discover, this need not be.

Inside this book you will find the tools and the techniques to uncover and address realistically the true, bedrock issues of teaching and learning. You will discover the attributes of productive teams while learning how to avoid the pitfalls that beset teams that are dysfunctional.

Principals, the unsung key players in team development, must occupy a central role in the success of teacher teams. They will find guidelines, methods, and tips on how to support the development and maintenance of teacher team effectiveness.

Furthering the confluence of theory and practice, this book's teaching cases illuminate the key concepts that lead to principles of good practice.

## Why Cases?

The heart of the book is the cases. These are the most fun to read and, if you're like most of us, you will be tempted to skip the preliminary chapters ("I'll read those later, when I have time") and head straight for the (hopefully) entertaining stories. Okay, you can skim the cases first. But we would urge you to come back to read the preliminary chapters that are critical to an understanding of *how* to read the cases and how to get the most value out of them.

The study of cases is a powerful pedagogical tool long employed in the education of physicians, attorneys, therapists, and scientists as well as in business schools and studies in economics, public policy, and law enforcement. Using cases, teachers—like other professionals—can develop skills in analytical thinking and reflective judgment by reading and discussing complex, real-life scenarios. Cases can provide a rich basis for developing problem-solving and decision-making skills. As a medium for analyzing the work of teaching teams, cases can demonstrate both the problems and the possibilities of teaming situations. The protocol-driven discussions that follow the presentation of a case often lead teachers to specific, teacher-initiated methodologies that improve the work of their team. By providing them with real-life dilemmas that test their thinking, cases make theory come alive for teachers, challenging them to devise their own solutions. Cases are empowering, allowing teachers to engage in constructing their own professional development.

The cases in this book were developed by educational researchers, by classroom teachers, by doctoral students who worked on a grant-funded team research project, and by teacher leaders and school administrators from around the country whose work we came to know and admire.

The names of the teachers and schools identified in each case are fictional, but the people and situations they describe are drawn from real events, observations, and in-the-trenches research. Some of the dialogues are compiled and paraphrased; some are taken verbatim from teachers' conversations. Each case, through the lens of a particular team's struggles, addresses one or more fundamental conditions that underlie teams' dilemmas. Each case offers opportunities to analyze situations that are organizational, cultural, political, or pedagogical in nature. These cases can guide you toward teasing out specific strategies you can employ in order to improve your own team's functioning, and the study questions given at the end of every case are carefully constructed to strengthen your understanding of how teacher teams should function if they are to be successful.

## It Isn't *Extra* Work, It's *The* Work

We give workshops in creating and maintaining successful teacher teams. Inevitably, when the reality of the work begins to sink in, someone will say, "We already know there's a problem with our team. Just tell us what to do!"

Well, things are rarely that simple, but here are some words of encouragement. First of all, if you're on a team you're already working pretty hard. The problem with your team isn't about lack of effort, it's about inefficient or misdirected effort.

"But we don't have time for this!" you may reply. Yes, you do. If you're on a team, you're already spending the time, just not efficiently.

That isn't to say that this is all going to be easy; the work is not a walk in the park. You will have to refocus. Wrestle with difficult precepts and redirected efforts, gain new insights and understandings, and cope with changing attitudes and behaviors. But if you want to put a final end to painful struggles that don't lead to successful outcomes, that is what you have to do.

And here is the best part—you *can* make a difference in your teaching, and your students *can* improve their learnings and, yes, even their test scores. That will make it worth the effort.

# 3

# What Makes a Good Team, What Makes a Team Good?

> *It's easy to get the players. It's getting them to play together that's the tough part.*
>
> —Casey Stengel

## Why Teams (Typically) Fail

Perhaps use of the word *fail* is a bit strong—after all, most teams are able to accomplish *some* of their stated goals, even if those goals are to figure out such low-level tasks as organizing field trips and planning bulletin board displays that represent the work of the team's students. It's easy to be successful if your expectations are low. However, what we mean by failure is the *inability to achieve the higher-level goals of improving teaching and learning*. The work of the team should include building content, pedagogical, and teaming skills such as

- increasing teachers' ability to assess student work using protocols for looking at student work and then implementing strategies developed during focused discussion of the student work,

- providing team members with new teaching strategies that engage students more deeply in the content while giving students the skills to learn critical thinking, and
- enlarging these strategies through observation of other teachers and the use of lesson study.

## The Complexities of Collaboration Are Untaught

While the concept of teachers collaborating in teams to improve school performance is not new, teams rarely live up to the hype that accompanies them. While teacher teams may get started with energy and enthusiasm, team members most often lack the skills, tools, and support structures that would allow them to orchestrate significant pedagogical and curriculum changes through the collaborative work of the team. Also, principals generally lack the time and preparation to properly guide and supervise teacher teams (they haven't been taught how to do it, either), and the feeling that no one is really in charge is pervasive. Consequently, neither the school nor the teachers themselves see changes in their practice or in the work of their students.

A term from the field of psychology, *groupthink,* coined by social psychologist Irving Janis,[1] might aptly be applied to teachers in teams. Groupthink kicks in when all members of a group have been initiated into the status quo culture, when the members are similar in background and training and when there are no clear rules for decision making. The group tends to dismiss or ignore alternative ways of doing things and tends to feel that others' opinions are not necessarily valuable. Members are under pressure not to express arguments against any of the group's views. Members of the group censor themselves so that consensus is achieved, and there is a veneer of unanimity.

Since teachers are a congenial bunch, caring very much about what others think of them and that everyone gets along, they gravitate easily into the culture of groupthink. No one's feelings should be hurt, and conflicts are to be avoided. Of course, this condition can exist whether there is a team leader or not; the key is to have *effective* team leadership.

## Effective Teacher Leadership Is Missing

Is there a team leader? Should there be a team leader? Who is the team leader and what are the limits of her or his authority? Which team member, for example, has the authority to make sure teachers arrive on time, or that teachers come prepared to their meetings, or that assigned tasks are carried out in a timely fashion?

The cultural foundation of teaching—teacher autonomy—can prevent teachers from accepting another teacher's authority. And without a clear understanding of the benefits of consistent team leadership and team roles, the team will too often continue to meet unproductively.

"Let's share leadership" is often another way for individual teachers to avoid stepping into leadership roles and attempting to assert authority. Should a teacher be brave enough to do so (such as trying to solve the problem of other team members not fulfilling their commitments), the automatic response is generally "Who are you to tell me what to do?" Usually this is unspoken, since passive-aggressive is the modus operandi of teachers who have been conditioned to reject all forms of school reforms they find onerous or unpalatable. Assuming leadership is a risk most teachers are reluctant to take.

NOTE: For more on the components of effective team leadership, see Case 3: Can't Follow the Leader.

## The Need for Expertise Is Ignored or Misunderstood

When teachers arrive in the classroom right out of college or from whatever teacher preparation program they've attended, the expectation is that they come fully formed—that they know everything they need to know in order to be good teachers. There are, of course, induction initiatives in many schools (the movement is growing), but truly effective mentoring and induction are still the rarity. Add that to the fact that most professional development is generally inadequate to deal with the real-life problems of classroom teachers. So, should a teacher attempt to reach out for help or support, the message that is sent is "She's in trouble," not "How can I help?" Given that, teachers are disinclined to admit in a group of their peers that perhaps there is a problem or condition they can't solve by themselves—one that calls for outside expertise. Even in those instances when a principal insists that visits by a math coach or ELL (English language learner) specialist be included in team meetings, teacher teams are often at a loss as to how best to incorporate their expertise. In most teacher teams, the expertise made available by drop-in coaches is underutilized.

## Pitfalls Are Unrecognized or Poorly Addressed

The commonly held belief that teacher teams by themselves should automatically be highly functioning groups simply because they are "all good teachers" means that teams are rarely if ever trained in the basic skills of team facilitation, such as time management, goal setting, development of team norms, and conflict resolution. This allows them to fall into any number of the pitfalls listed here:

- Teachers are given common planning time for team meetings but lack the facilitation skills necessary to use their time effectively.
- Teachers and principals believe that experience equals expertise; so while teams frequently lack internal expertise, they are reluctant to look outside the team for support.
- Teachers are reluctant to exert leadership or assume leadership roles.
- Teachers choose to team around issues that are peripheral rather than central to their daily teaching.
- "Good working relationships" are seen as the key to team success; the content of teaching and learning has less emphasis.
- The team has no clear purpose or goals; team members may speak of issues like increased collegiality or mutual support, but rarely do they engage in instructional talk that would significantly change teaching and learning.
- Putting necessary structures in place is undervalued.
- Most teachers have no vision of what constitutes effective teaming, and they have few models to learn from.

## Team Members Give Up When They Don't Get Along

It is a truly unpleasant experience to be given orders such as "You are a team and you *have* to work together" when you deeply dislike one or more of the people in your group. So unpleasant, in fact, that team functionality flies out the window and all energies are expended in just meeting with other people who are impossible to get along with anyhow. This has caused the downfall of many a team and the early grey hairs of many a principal. It's a tough problem, and there are no easy solutions. (However, there are ways to have difficult conversations, and we suggest another book titled just that: *Difficult Conversations*.[2] For further insights, see also Case 1: The Neutral Zone: Handling Interpersonal Dynamics on Teams.)

## There Are No Consequences for Poor (Individual or Team) Performance

Now we're at the place where the rubber hits the road, as they say. At the end of the day, in a team whose members aren't accountable to one another for the collective work of the group, you can screw up royally, blow off your assignments and commitments, and only your teammates (and your students) pay the price. And you don't even have to be a bad person. You can even be a great teacher—on your own—encultured to be completely autonomous and beholden to practically no one as you go about your everyday teacher life, unencumbered by any notions of team accountability. Just keep the principal happy (you're mostly unsupervised anyway) and the parents happy (just tell them their kids are doing fine), and you can keep on teaching—working very hard, of course—just the way you always have, and always will.

That's the reality—*nobody can tell you what to do.* And if they do, you don't really have to do it anyway. Because in a typical team, just like in a regular teacher's life, aside from the test scores there is no real accountability.

To be sure, test scores are extremely important in a teacher's life and they loom large; however, they are a yardstick that belongs to one teacher alone—a measure of *personal* accountability. Team accountability, on the other hand, means that every teacher on the team is accountable for every student's success, and in that regard many teams fail to live up.

# The Five Conditions of Effective Teacher Teams

Our research has shown that very few teacher teams can truly be called effective in every sense. The reasons for this are many and vary from school to school, but too often teams are mandated by central office and implemented by school principals whose knowledge of the complexities of team building is minimal at best. Groups of teachers are put together, generally by grade level or subject matter, and simply told that they are now a team and must work collaboratively. In those situations, most teams lack the tools and resources as well as effective team attributes that are needed in order to make them successful. Anyone who wants to upgrade the performance of teaching teams needs to understand not only these factors but also how to implement strategies necessary to ensure team success.

We've developed a framework for evaluating the effectiveness of teams (Figure 3.1), and we look at each team we investigate using five criteria, or conditions. Within each condition, of course, are several levels of development that determine where a team's overall effectiveness lies along a broad spectrum.

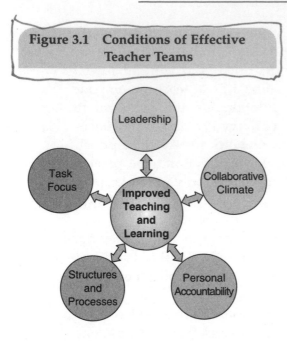

Figure 3.1    Conditions of Effective
Teacher Teams

## Task Focus

Is the team's task well defined and articulated, and does it focus on improving student learning? The lowest level of development would indicate that the team focuses most of its energies and attention on logistics, or that its goals are not well defined. Or, more critically, that its goals do not have student learning at their center, and that their focus is driven by crises or pressing school needs. At the highest level of achievement, the team's focus is proactive and team meetings are directed toward improving the planning and measuring of student progress. Team conversations are dialogues that help team members develop new understandings about teaching and learning. It should also be understood that one of the team's goals must be to *commit* to the idea that teacher learning is an ongoing process in and of itself, and that this learning directly contributes to student achievement.

## Leadership

Does the team encourage leadership by all its members? A low level of achievement in the area of leadership occurs when leadership roles are assumed reluctantly, or forced upon a member, or assumed by the strongest or most vocal person on the team. A higher level of functioning occurs when potential leadership roles are distributed so that they are available to all team members in one way or another, and at one time or another. In high-functioning teacher teams, both novice and veteran teachers are empowered to take risks, and individual teacher instructional expertise is valued and utilized by all team members.

## Collaborative Climate

Does the team promote a working environment that generates trust, communication, and synergy? It's easy to avoid conflicts by never confronting serious issues and to achieve harmony by simply allowing only the more dominant members to have a voice in conversations. Yet successful teams do not shy away from conflict; rather, they understand that there are benefits to be gained from conflict resolution. Teams have to find ways to legitimately and strategically make critiques within the team.

Recent research has shown that teams that collaborate successfully have been shown to demonstrate a higher level of "collective intelligence." A study led by a professor at the MIT Sloan School of Management and reported in the journal *Science*[3] shows that small teams of people display a collective intelligence that has little to do with the intelligence of individual members or even the intelligence of the group's smartest member. This collective intelligence is, however, strongly correlated with "the equality in distribution of conversational turn-taking." In other words, the collective intelligence of a team depends on shared conversations about the team's tasks.

## Personal Accountability

Is there an expectation of performance improvement for both the team and the individual? Is there any *articulated* expectation of accountability? Do team members fail to complete tasks or deliver unacceptable levels of quality? In a team that is functioning at mid-level, you might expect variable quality, with some assigned tasks completed well. In those teams, individuals may hold themselves accountable, but there is no process in place to hold individuals accountable for accomplishing team goals. In the highest-level teams, all members complete tasks effectively, the team holds all members accountable for their performance, and all members share responsibility for the team's success and for the success of all students within the purview of the entire team.

## Structures and Processes

Does the team determine ways to work together to achieve agreed-upon goals? Can the team articulate its structure and the team processes it uses to accomplish its goals? A team cannot function well if its goals are poorly defined or if articulated goals are arrived at merely to satisfy low expectations of the team's abilities to affect student learning. Does the team apportion resources effectively to accomplish its goals? Does the team know how to access and enlist outside expertise? Highly effective teams have a process for deciding if certain tasks are best accomplished by individuals or by the group, and the team *continuously* adapts plans and processes to ensure that the team's focus is on students' learning needs.

A detailed Teacher-Teaming Continuum Assessment that can help evaluate the effectiveness of a team can be found in Chapter 5. Team participants investigate the team's work using the above five conditions as an assessment tool. Within each condition are several levels of development that can help a team assess its overall effectiveness along a broad continuum.

## Talking the Talk, Walking the Walk: Connecting Curriculum and Instruction

Combining curriculum (the *what* we teach) and instruction (the *how* we teach) is at the heart of any work in schools. This has been true from the days of the one-room schoolhouse when children brought their own reading materials to school, to the current day as textbook companies blanket the country with an innumerable variety of texts representing a broad spectrum of teaching philosophies, content, methodologies, and even political points of view. Since the late 19th century, when textbooks began to be published for specific grade levels and subject areas, teachers' influence over content and pedagogy has varied greatly, as have the range of schools' and teachers' approaches to curriculum and instruction.

At one end of the spectrum are schools where individual teachers faithfully follow the "teacher's guides" that accompany most textbooks and use pacing guides to keep on track with the curriculum. In other schools, teachers flip through the pages of the guides, highlighting what they want to emphasize and using their discretion with how they use the rest. Elsewhere, teachers are encouraged to elaborate on curriculum, using the curriculum to support rather than direct instruction. These schools and school districts believe that teachers should be participants in molding and shaping curriculum, encouraging their students to think critically, assessing material, and delving more deeply into the curriculum's content.

Increasingly, though, whatever the individual school or district's philosophy on curriculum and instruction, the teacher team is being looked to as a means to deliver curriculum more effectively, increase teachers' productivity, and foster improved instruction. The team is seen to be the place where professional development strategies, learned at the school or district level, can be enacted collaboratively and more efficiently. Teacher teams are now expected to be the solution to our schools' constant quest to dramatically improve the delivery of curriculum and instruction.

Conditions for instructional improvement and students' academic achievement are strengthened when teachers engage in meaningful collaborative professional development activities—the kinds of activities that could be the centerpiece of teacher teams. Such activities include collective questioning and analysis of teaching practices, deep discussion of curriculum, joint work in lesson planning, and observation and discussion of colleagues' teaching. Central to all of these professional development efforts for curricular and instructional improvement is the "instructional talk" of teachers.

With the clear message that the primary work of every teaching team is to improve curriculum and instruction—to affect the instructional core (see Figure 3.2)—the imperative of teacher team instructional talk has taken on additional weight. In addition, as leadership among school players has been *distributed* and new formal and informal teacher leadership roles for teachers have emerged, it has become increasingly likely that instructional talk will be an important part of team work.

**The instructional core consists of the relationship between students and teachers in the presence of content.** Anything you do that does not result in an observable effect on this relationship is wasted time and resources.[4] In other words, teaming initiatives and activities that do not address improvements in teaching practice, the type of content given to students, or the role that students play in their own learning do not affect the instructional core and are therefore ineffective in helping the team reach its goals.

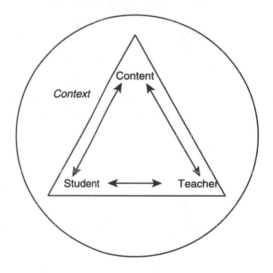

Figure 3.2   The Instructional Core

## The Importance of Instructional Talk

Examined closely, teachers' understanding of what they may call "instructional talk" frequently refers to informal discussions of curriculum implementation, a recounting of a teacher's experiences with delivering particular lessons, informal talk about children's experiences with curriculum, and discussions of children's learning and behavior. This does not meet the criteria of instructional talk because it lacks the critical dimension of an examination of lessons and curriculum and rarely includes the expectation that teachers will

- observe and critique the work of their peers;
- discuss, assess and revise lessons taught by team members based on student results; and
- hold each other accountable for the learning of all the team's students.

Instructional talk demands the use of *records of practice*—tangible artifacts such as teachers' journals, student work, videotapes, lesson plans, and assessments. Only artifacts can produce tangible evidence of changes made in teaching practice and student learning.

How to engage in meaningful instructional talk is almost never taught to teachers, and they therefore lack the skills that could enable them to use their team meetings and other team interactions to improve their curriculum and instruction with any form or depth. Thus, despite schools' and school districts' eagerness to stress the importance of teacher teams, the potential positive impact on instruction through effective teamwork has been underrealized.

Yet it has been demonstrated that well-supported, well-structured instructional talk in teacher team meetings can improve curriculum and instruction.[5] Preceded by appropriate training in team development and meeting facilitation, well-prepared teacher teams achieve more efficient and academically focused meetings and utilize other team-building skills. These skills are essential to teachers as they shift team meetings from unfocused conversations to meetings in which high-level instructional talk and analytical discussions target curriculum and instruction.

## Connecting Instructional Talk to Classroom Planning and Practice

Teams support the improvement of classroom instruction and student achievement when they do the following:

- Focus on instruction
- Connect instruction to curriculum
- Connect instructional talk to classroom practice by:
  - Using assessment data
  - Working collaboratively on lesson plans
  - Conducting classroom observations

Instructional talk provides the scaffolding for teachers to assume responsibility for curriculum analysis, learning a curriculum that extends beyond the curriculum-as-given, supporting each other in intellectual risk taking, taking on peer observation in a systematic and well-trained fashion, and mentoring novice teachers. These rich professional development opportunities, supported by instructional talk, can be factored into the team's structure and schedule, and serve to raise the level of the team's work together.

## Promoting Accountability Through Instructional Talk

Studies have shown that successful schools are most likely to be environments in which teachers are engaged in frequent, continuous, and increasingly concrete and precise talk about teaching *practice* . . . building a shared language adequate to the complexity of teaching, capable of distinguishing one practice and its virtues from another and capable of integrating large bodies of practice into distinct and sensible perspectives on the business of teaching. Teachers and administrators in successful schools observe each other teach; they plan, design, research, evaluate, and prepare teaching materials together.[6]

When interviewed by researchers, teachers who have been given the benefit of team training in how to conduct an instructional conversation emphasize what they've learned from watching one another teach. Teachers want to hold themselves accountable for the work they do, but the definition of *accountability* is often based on unclear standards, a lack of rigorous curriculum, and the absence of meaningful supervision and evaluation.

The team that focuses on the quality of instructional talk will include and implement more content-specific professional development as part of its agenda, leading often to a heightened sense of accountability. Creation of a regular schedule of peer/group observations is also a means of improving curriculum and instruction, and the inclusion of special education teachers along with other specialists, such as those in language arts and math, provides an essential and rewarding growth experience for both classroom teachers and specialists. Collectively or singly, these actions help promote and support team accountability.

But achieving accountability in teacher teams is even more complicated than it appears. Mutual accountability within the team varies according to the type of task being undertaken; accountability for logistical and management items and accountability for the team's instructional agenda are two very different beasts. Teams are most successful when it comes to mutual accountability for *noninstructional tasks*. Team members understand the more immediate, concrete, and visible consequences of not completing tasks such as scheduling field trips or setting up bulletin boards. They generally have little experience in, and are more reluctant to perform the more difficult, sustained work on *instructional tasks* at a high and efficient level. Teachers resist assuming responsibility for, and holding each other accountable for, completing instructional tasks.[7]

This underscores the necessity for effective team leadership, which is discussed in more detail in Chapter 4. In "leadership-impaired" teams, teachers charged with holding themselves accountable for instructional tasks are unprepared to do so, unable to implement team decisions on curriculum and pedagogy, and unable to hold others on the team accountable as well.

When teachers, working in teams, recognize the value of teacher leadership, engage in systematic high-level instructional talk, and have the opportunity to improve practices collaboratively and in concrete forms, they develop team loyalty, trust, and new feelings of responsibility and accountability. The collective team is responsible to each other and for all the team's students. The result is improved teaching and learning.

## Using Team Meetings
## to Improve Instructional Practice

Data analysis, currently touted as the best new way to improve instruction (and raise test scores) can be used to excellent effect in the teacher team. When teachers learn how best to analyze their standardized achievement data, they can better understand their students' learning and use their own teaching expertise to develop student improvement plans. Supplemented by other evidence (student work, behavior analysis) as well as assessments that can be developed and administered collectively by the team, data *can* become the tools they were meant to be—but only if such data lead to strategies for effective teacher-student interventions.

Team meetings that examine student work, or use other protocols to monitor and assure that teachers focus on curriculum and instruction, should be conducted on an ongoing basis throughout the year. The team should engage in implementing longer-term professional development tools as well, such as rounds and lesson study, as it determines its yearly accountability goals.

### Rounds

In a story about collaboration among medical doctors, reported in the *New York Times* science pages,[8] 23 heart surgeons in Maine, New

Hampshire, and Vermont agreed to observe each other regularly in the operating room and share their knowledge, insights, and approaches. Two years later, the death rate among their patients had fallen an astonishing 25 percent. Merely by emphasizing teamwork and communication instead of functioning as solitary practitioners, all the doctors had brought about significant changes in their individual and institutional practices.

For teachers who, like heart surgeons, have traditionally worked as isolated professionals, the experience holds a powerful lesson. If our goal is to lower the "death rate" of young minds and see them thrive, it is obvious that we can do it better by collaborating than by working alone.

The practice of rounds promotes collaboration through the sharing of successful practice. Like doctors making hospital rounds, and lawyers collaborating to provide feedback as they build a case, teachers in schools all over the country, public and private alike, have begun to purposefully probe the rich evidence at hand for what it can reveal about how teachers can better teach and students can better learn.

The similarity between medical rounds and teaching rounds is that they are both intended to *make practice public*. While medical practice has been public (within the profession) for some time, teaching practice has not.

During rounds, teachers teach individual lessons while other teachers observe. Through rounds, more experienced practitioners can pass on knowledge and experience to the less experienced. Rounds encourages teachers to observe, discuss, and analyze teaching, which, in turn, allows them to create strategies to improve their own teaching.

There are several different models of rounds, but all have these intended goals and benefits: an increased focus on student learning, the sharing of successful practice, the development of strategies for problem solving, and a platform of support for both novice and veteran teachers.

**Disclaimer:** What we provide here is merely an overview of rounds, and we caution the reader that rounds is not an easy, do-it-yourself project for the uninitiated. It's a complex process that does require acquiring skills (possibly by coaching) that must be learned in order to do well and accomplish its intended purposes. For further reading, we suggest a book we use often when coaching teachers and teacher leaders on rounds in schools: *Instructional Rounds in Education*.[9] It is not written primarily for teachers, but its precepts are adaptable for teachers, and it provides a wealth of background information on the basic foundations of rounds.

## Lesson Study

Another pathway for collaboration is lesson study, a professional development process in which teachers systematically examine their practice with the goal of increasing content knowledge and improving pedagogy. This examination centers on teachers working collaboratively on a small number of "study lessons." Working on these study lessons involves planning, teaching, observing, and critiquing the lessons. To provide focus and direction to this work, teachers select an overarching goal and a related research question that they want to explore. This research question then serves to guide their work on all the study lessons.

Working on a study lesson looks something like this:

- Teachers jointly draw up a detailed plan for the lesson, which one of the teachers uses to teach the lesson in a real classroom (as other group members observe the lesson).
- The group then comes together to discuss their observations of the lesson, and based on their observations collaboratively revises the lesson.
- Another teacher implements the revised lesson in a second classroom, while group members again observe.
- The group comes together once more to discuss the observed instruction. Finally, the teachers produce a report of what their study lessons have taught them, particularly with respect to their research question, and the lesson can become an anchor lesson for that grade level or department.

It is essential to note that lesson study is professional development, *not lesson development.* Its goal is to develop lifelong learners by supporting teachers as independent thinkers and problem solvers and by giving them—as does rounds—the opportunity to reflect deeply about their practice.

By examining work together, teachers look for variability across classes and discuss what might explain greater-than-expected differences. Discussions of these differences lead to questions and sometimes difficult conversations about classrooms and teaching.

# 4

# Instructional Leadership

## Principals and Teacher Leaders

*Teams that lack open conflict are dying entities.*

—Thomas Harvey & Bonita Drolet

## Throw Out Your Old Org. Chart

Remember the "good old days" when the principal sat on the top of a purely hierarchical, top-down organizational chart with all "his" or "her" teachers arranged in a neat row at the bottom? Well, those days are pretty much over, or will be very soon. States, districts and schools all over the country are busily engaged in creating—and implementing— new models of distributed leadership in which "the successful school leader more closely resembles an orchestra conductor than a virtuoso soloist."[1]

Because let's face it—no matter who you are in the food chain, the challenge of school reform is far too difficult and complex for any single individual, and a framework of distributed leadership that harnesses the power of principals, teachers and teacher leaders is driven by the understanding that *all* members of the school community have knowledge and expertise that can benefit the school. This doesn't mean dividing up jobs among multiple players, but engaging school faculty and staff as co-participants. Power is not a zero-sum game, a fact borne out by the tons of research that reveals how school leaders who share responsibility and create opportunities for leadership throughout their school are far more successful in achieving goals of improved student learning.[2]

School leaders must work together with teachers to influence the school culture, policies and practices in a positive manner that supports student learning. Teacher leaders have the ability to exercise considerable influence over instructional practice among their peers, as they lead from the classroom. They often have critical content and pedagogical knowledge that their principals may not possess. If we want schools to be laboratories of innovation that are able to tackle the significant challenges they face, school leaders and teacher leaders must work together to identify, replicate and scale up programs and practices deemed effective in raising student achievement. Principals must feel secure in these new structures, and teachers and teacher leaders have to see real value in each other's work. Teams are the perfect venue for them to do so.

## The Principal as Instructional Leader

Educators now generally understand and appreciate the potential value of teachers working together, collaboratively, in teams. However, the pressure on principals and heads of schools to quickly achieve the benefits of teaming often results in teachers being put together in a grouping of one kind or another and someone saying

> "Poof! You're a team! Okay—now work together!"

This is generally followed by something like

> "You are all great teachers, I know you'll be a great team, now meet regularly and I'm here if you need help."

Try to imagine a hang-gliding instructor attempting to teach a new student by strapping a glider wing onto her back, pushing her off a cliff and calling out (as the hapless victim plunges earthward), "Call me if you need me!" And then reflecting on the crash by saying, "Hmmm . . . I wonder what she should have done differently."

We may laugh, but this is often what school administrators do to teacher teams. Yet there is abundant evidence that without the active, informed participation of the principal or head of school, no strategies in the world will be successful in building and sustaining effective teacher teams.

## The Principal Articulates a Vision for the School

There's no hotter seat in all of education than the principal's, nor one more closely examined by professional researchers who, after decades of research, agree that, by gosh, principals can make a difference in school improvement and student achievement. Overwhelmingly, the data point to a need for instructional leadership from principals who pay close attention to curriculum and teaching.[3]

Without the principal's vision, all that occurs in the school will be transitory. Nothing—and we really mean nothing—can become long-lasting in a school without the initial and continued support of the principal.

## The Principal Emphasizes the Importance of Collaboration

There is a tension here. School culture requires that we put a lot of emphasis on people getting along, avoiding confrontation and having things run smoothly. But in "real" teams there is, most importantly, professional work to be done. As we point out elsewhere in this book, collegiality is not the same as collaboration, and the principal who seeks to build productive teacher teams understands the difference.

## The Principal Actively Engages in Team Development

Teams are developed through a rigorous process that takes knowledge, understanding, energy and commitment—and the right set of tools and guidance. Unless principals are on board with teachers working in teams that focus on instruction, the idea of effective teaming is just an unfulfilled desire. In order to survive and thrive, *every* form of professional development *must* have the full support and advocacy of the principal or school head.

Principals invest in team development by

- providing adequate time,
- providing necessary support,
- providing teaming skill development, and
- connecting teacher teams to curriculum and instruction.

## Team-Building Tips for Principals

1. Build capacity first: make development of the team a top priority. Don't assume a team will work well together on its own.

2. Set specific, doable goals and priorities for the team.

3. Work collaboratively with teachers to create a team learning plan. One of the team's goals—often neglected in teacher teams—must be the goal of improving practice (which includes "de-privatizing" teaching).

4. Make sure the team's activities are aligned with its goals.

5. Identify and tackle barriers to performance.

6. Communicate clearly and honestly to help team members survive conflict and develop confidence in themselves and their leader.

7. Focus more of the team's meeting time on instruction rather than logistics.

8. Grow other leaders.

9. Honor individual and team success.

If you want a relatively easy (admittedly, not very deep) snapshot of how teams are doing *generally*, here's a suggestion. Make copies of the Team Development Checklist (Figure 4.1), and distribute them

### Figure 4.1 Team Development Checklist

| Teaming Practice | Strongly agree | Somewhat agree | Somewhat disagree | Strongly disagree |
|---|---|---|---|---|
| 1. Team members talk about teaching. | | | | |
| 2. Team members observe colleagues teach and help one another improve their practice. | | | | |
| 3. Team members plan, design, research and evaluate materials collaboratively. | | | | |
| 4. Teachers hold each other accountable for improving their practice. | | | | |

among your teams. Tell them you'll be dropping in (at a few specified times) to gauge how they're doing in these specific areas. This is *not* a game of "gotcha!" where you're trying to surprise teachers and catch them with their guard down. And it's also *not* a "let's put on a good act for the principal" game either. Emphasize to teams that your objective is to uncover areas where they may need your support. And get ready to provide it.

## Teacher Leadership

We have emphasized, over and over, that teachers in teams cannot be successful without the active participation of principals. But the opposite is also true:

*Principals cannot be successful without the collaborative support of teachers—specifically, teacher leaders.*

### What's a Teacher Leader?

For any school initiative to be successful, teachers need to be involved, and the need to engage teachers in leadership roles is critical—particularly in leadership roles focused on instructional improvement. Yet within top-down structures, there are limited opportunities for teachers to effect meaningful change outside their classrooms. What is needed is the creation of expanded opportunities, a framework to guide practice and the support to do so. This impulse, to provide meaningful avenues for teachers to exert leadership, is guided by the notion that teacher leaders are required in order to professionalize the practice of teaching in these ways:

- Acknowledging that teaching has a recognized knowledge base
- Demanding rigorous training and certification of team members
- Fostering a culture of consulting and collaboration in the workplace
- Systematically indoctrinating and "enculturing" new members
- Requiring that continuous, regular learning be built into the work cycle
- Ensuring high public accountability and taking full responsibility for student improvement
- Internally maintaining high standards of practice
- Making autonomous decisions guided by an agreed-upon set of rules and guidelines[4]

All teachers have the *potential* to exercise leadership in their schools and profession, whether informally or formally. But what, exactly, is a *teacher leader*?

We all like nicely packaged, easy-to-grasp, simple definitions. But concise, all-purpose definitions of teacher leadership are elusive since there is considerable variation in what people mean by the concept, how teacher leadership is implemented and what people believe it can accomplish.[5] Defining teacher leadership and the roles and responsibilities we want teacher leaders to assume is not a straightforward task. Our job descriptions of potential teacher-leader roles in a team structure are therefore necessarily derived from an admitted bias that bends toward teacher and principal empowerment in the cause of improved student and teacher learning. And since you've just read (above) how the principal's role in that regard might best be supported in a *distributed leadership* context, we are going to describe a framework in which both principals and teacher teams would benefit from certain forms of teacher leadership.

Teacher leadership differs from formally established roles such as principal, director of curriculum or pupil services director. Teachers become leaders in their schools by being respected by their peers, being continuous learners, being approachable and using skills and influences to improve the educational practice of their peers. They model effective practices, exercise their influence in formal and informal contexts and support collaborative team structures within their schools. They work in collaboration with principals and other school administrators by facilitating improvements in instruction and promoting practices among their peers that produce improved student learning outcomes.[6]

An examination of teacher leadership in practice reveals some commonalities and patterns in the responsibilities of teacher leaders. Teacher leaders are most often engaged in activities related to

- developing curriculum,
- selecting instructional models and materials,
- planning and/or leading professional development activities,
- mentoring and coaching other teachers, and
- making building-level decisions, including school budgets.[7]

## Teacher Leaders in a Team Context

Teacher leadership is a concept that finds a ready home in the context of teacher teams, but what we've talked about so far in terms of teacher leadership need not take place on a formal basis. Indeed, most teacher leadership is carried out by exceptional teachers whose talent and proclivity for leadership propel them into roles for which there is no niche on the school's organization chart. But creating formalized teacher leadership roles within schools can be a powerful strategy to promote teaching as a dynamic profession with innovative opportunities to effect positive change for teachers, students and the school community. The teacher team provides the ideal venue for those roles.

## Inside-Outside: Teacher Leaders and Team Leaders

Team leaders are, in effect, teacher leaders who have specific team responsibilities and function mainly inside the team; other teacher leaders can operate inside the team, outside the team or both. Indeed, the performance of these many roles can and should play an integral and powerful part in the scope and reach of an effective teacher team.

### The Team Leader

The team leader, a form of teacher leadership assumed by one member of a teacher team, takes on responsibility for leading team members, championing the team's power and looking beyond the team's instructional base. The team leader must have a set of skills that enable her or him to direct the team's movement, focus the team on its goals and norms, encourage individual leadership and work effectively and collaboratively with colleagues both within and outside the team to re-culture the school and teaching. Teacher team leaders can operate in many diverse contexts, formal and informal, in the classroom, outside the classroom, in school settings and outside school settings. They can work closely with the principal to develop and implement effective mechanisms of support for teams.

### Other Forms of Teacher Leadership

The teacher team provides a perfect structure in which teacher leadership and teacher leaders can flourish. With team facilitation roles differentiated within the team, ample room and opportunity for teachers to exercise different forms of leadership can open up simultaneously and more effectively.

Many members of teams can exercise leadership by using the team as a vehicle to develop, maintain and share their own pedagogical expertise; other team members may find that their interests lie in observing other teachers teach, giving them feedback and reflecting within the team.

In addition, the team can provide fertile ground for an array of other formal teacher leader roles. Such roles will not interest all team members. These roles, newly emerging or long-established and now supported by the new national recognition of the importance of differentiated, enhanced roles for teachers, can enable teacher leaders to grow in a number of specific ways.

### Facilitating Peer Coaching

Peer coaching is a process by which two or more colleagues work together to share pedagogical knowledge and increase their technical repertoire. Peer coaching doesn't just "happen," of course. It is scheduled and supported by the teacher leader, who is in turn responsible to the principal for accomplishing peer coaching initiatives.

That means formalizing a way in which people can get together as colleagues to help each other out. In peer coaching, the focus is on the teacher as a learner. Teachers reflect on current practices, build new teaching skills, improve instructional strategies and match teaching strategies to individual differences that exist among children. Peer coaching provides teachers with opportunities to try out new ideas or different approaches and discuss the results with a colleague.

Peer coaching creates an environment in which school people can collaborate as "critical friends" who examine in a nonjudgmental fashion one another's practice and help improve it. Peer coaching allows teachers to share successful practices in a forum for addressing instructional problems. The end result of peer coaching, in addition to improving the practice of teaching, is ending the school culture in which every teacher must struggle alone through the early years (and even the later years) of practice with a frustrating and often defeating trial-and-error method of learning.

### Facilitating Rounds

We've talked elsewhere in this book (Chapter 3) about rounds as a strategy for connecting curriculum to instruction. But *facilitating* rounds (which can be thought of as a more complicated version of peer coaching) is a perfect job for a teacher leader. After all, rounds, like every other initiative we've described, doesn't just happen—it has to be facilitated.

### Integrating Meaningful Professional Development

In most states physicians are required to take a certain number of hours of continuing medical education each year in order to maintain their certification. In theory, teachers get recertified in much the same way—by taking courses relevant to their practice. In reality, however, teachers are often allowed to take courses that have nothing to do with education or teaching. And when education is the subject of their study, their professional development does not build on what teachers already know. Rather, the emphasis is on correcting presumed deficiencies, "fixing" what the teacher is doing wrong. Professional development is mostly remedial instruction. Rarely do seminars and workshops of this kind improve practice over the long run. And when professional development is delivered at a higher level, whatever may have been learned quickly fades back in the classroom, where new understandings go unsupported and are pushed aside by the urgencies of real life.

By providing the necessary tools and resources, however, teacher leaders can help facilitate the incorporation of meaningful professional development into the daily schedule of the workplace. Teacher leaders can guide and support the transferring of skills and knowledge gained outside the classroom into team members' classrooms, where they become integral to teaching practice.

### Incorporating Teacher Research

In the education world, educational research is most often conducted from above, by experts who may or may not ever have been classroom teachers themselves and whose findings get published in journals that are rarely read by teachers. Teachers don't read educational research because, frankly, most of it isn't *for* teachers, it's *about* teachers, and teachers just don't connect with it.

But educational research *done by teachers* recognizes that the practitioner's wisdom is a valid source of knowledge about teaching, validating the voices of teachers and raising the level of professional development from remedial to professional. Teacher researchers working within the team can define their own research questions and embark on the process of collecting and analyzing data with the express purpose of improving teaching and learning in their classrooms.

This is an area rich with opportunity for teacher leaders to help *create knowledge* for other teachers to read about teaching and learning, to nurture those conditions under which research by teachers can flourish so that research becomes an integral part of the school's norms.

Figure 4.2   Principal-Leader-Team
             Relationship

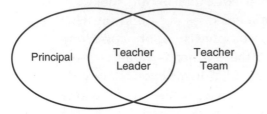

The teacher leader is a supportive resource
for both principal and teacher team.

# This Could Be the Beginning of a Beautiful Relationship

If you wanted to film the interactions between the principal, the teacher leader and the teacher team, it wouldn't be an action flick (although there's certainly potential for drama). It would be the story of a *relationship*—a successful collaboration between allies who may have had a stormy past but who now see the many benefits of working together for mutual self-interest. In the ideal plot setting, the principal, teacher leader and teacher team are a multitalented cast of characters harmoniously engaged in an epic enterprise of great importance, with the teacher leader at the center of the action (see Figure 4.2). It's a script worth writing.

# 5

# Team Development and Strategies for Success

*If you give people the right tools, and they use their abilities, they will develop things in ways that will surprise you beyond what you expected.*

—Bill Gates

## We Have to Stop Meeting Like This!

How often have you left a meeting and said to yourself (or someone else):

> "Well *that* was a total waste of time! Why are our meetings so ineffective, so unproductive? We just meet and meet and meet without ever getting anything done!"

Maybe now is the time to make a commitment to stop having those deadly, unproductive meetings that go nowhere.

How can your team engage productively in meetings that *are* the work rather than *about* the work and/or *peripheral* to the work? First, there needs to be an acknowledgment that just like teaching, teaming is a learned skill that comes with knowledge, practice, and patience. If you know this, your first step is accomplished. The purpose of this section is to show you how to do it.

To begin, we'll suggest an organizational model for a successful team—including team norms and roles for team members. People have to know what they're supposed to do in order to work together efficiently. But having done that, the work is still not finished.

Remember what Richard Elmore points out in the Foreword to this book. Changing the structure of an organization, by itself, does not transform the culture of that organization. What we have to do is deliberately change the practice to accommodate the structure. The rest of this chapter is devoted to that ambitious enterprise.

## Establish Team Norms

*Materials:* Chart paper, markers

Norms are behavioral guidelines that signify ways of being together and learning from one another. They help participants think about how to treat each other's ideas and how to push one's own thinking.

It is more likely that teams will support norms if team members are part of developing them; the time spent in the beginning is worthwhile in order to establish a supportive, trustful, and collaborative culture in which sometimes difficult conversations can take place. (Remember that every time a new teacher joins the team, it is a different team, with different team dynamics, and the norms should be revisited.)

### As a Team, Brainstorm Norms for Successful Team Work

Some norms will probably include: starting and ending on time; respectful listening; maintaining confidentiality; giving space and time to quieter voices; pausing before responding; not interrupting; supporting open and honest discussions.

Team members should ask each other how the group might ensure that these norms are met. The norms become an empty document if they are not monitored.

### An Example of Team Norms

COMMUNICATION

- Listen—without interrupting.
- Stay focused and avoid tangents.
- Ask questions.
- Maintain a sense of humor.
- In group conversations, make "pass" an option.
- Limit distractions:
    - Cell phones off
    - No sidebar conversations
    - No class work
- Be aware of your "air time."

RELATIONSHIP

- Don't shoot down others' ideas.
- Support active and full participation by all members.
- Assume good intentions.
- Embrace mistakes as opportunities.

TEAMING

- Use colleagues as resources.
- Make sure roles are meaningful.
- Be a team player.
- Distribute responsibility with awareness.
- Recognize the importance of individual and team accountability.
- Keep discussions confidential.

GUIDELINES

- Lay out clear expectations/overview.
- Handle conflicts when they arise (early work of teams).
- Create clear, measurable team goals.
- Evaluate team meetings.
- Maintain team records of accomplishments.
- Include a wrap-up at team meetings.

## Appoint Specific Roles to Team Members

1. *Facilitator*—Keeps the team's focus on agenda items, prevents side conversations, and makes sure that all voices are heard, with room for each person's reactions, interpretations, conjectures, and analyses. The facilitator is not necessarily the team leader, but plays a vital role in keeping team meeting efficiency at a high level. While it may not be the job of the facilitator to provide all the materials, agendas, and other items necessary for the meeting, it is the facilitator who assumes responsibility for making sure those things get done.

2. *Timekeeper*—Assumes responsibility for maintaining the meeting's momentum by providing appropriate time-checks for the facilitator, keeps meeting on track, makes sure meetings begin and end on time.

3. *Note-taker*—Uses the meeting agenda as a guide. The note-taker writes down team members' suggestions and comments, records decisions made by the team, and sends the notes to the team for discussion and preparation for the next team meeting. (Note: A laptop computer is a particularly useful tool for the

note-taker. With the agenda document on the screen, notes can be typed directly into the agenda, enabling the note-taker to quickly finalize the notes and send them to team members for prompt review.)

4. *Norms/Process Checker*—Maintains team norms during meetings and reflects people's behavior back to them. At the end of the meeting, asks the group to choose a debriefing question from the list below, checks with the group about the success of the meeting, and encourages each participant to reflect on and answer the question aloud.

*A Norms-Checker Debriefing*

- Was the agenda clear? Did we follow it? Did we accomplish our goals for this meeting?
- Has today's team conversation helped us think about how we work with students and, if so, in what ways? If not, why not?
- Was practice shared in concrete, accessible ways during this team meeting?
- Did all members have the opportunity to share their views, and did we actively listen to one another?
- What questions emerged for us as a result of today's team conversation?
- Did we hold each other accountable for work we said we would do at our last meeting?
- Did we end the meeting with a clear direction of where we go from here?

## Acknowledge Team-Meeting "Sore Spots" and Take Steps to Avoid or Cure Them

Now that your structure is solid, you can begin to address the next job: your team's culture. The road to A-Plus Superior team meetings is never a smooth one, but with hard work and enormous effort, most of the problems that confront teams are universal and can be solved once they are recognized and acknowledged. Here's what to look for.

*Sore Spot: Teachers don't value the potential of meetings to inform their work.*

Evidence: Teachers arrive late, leave early, doodle or text during a meeting.

Interventions: Make sure that for every meeting there are:

1. Clear goals (Not too many, however, and prioritize! If everything is important, nothing is important.)

2. A structured agenda

3. Role delineation

4. All materials necessary *for* the meeting are *at* the meeting (not left behind in the classroom or at the copy machine)

5. An End-of-Meeting Summary (Figure 5.1) and a Meeting Action Plan (Figure 5.2)

6. A *short* debriefing session

**Figure 5.1     Worksheet—End-of-Meeting Agenda Summary**

| What were the agenda items discussed? | What decisions were reached? |
|---|---|
| 1. | |
| 2. | |
| 3. | |

**Figure 5.2     Worksheet—Meeting Action Plan**

| What is to be accomplished? (List action steps.) | Who is responsible? | When will action be complete? |
|---|---|---|
| 1. | | |
| 2. | | |
| 3. | | |

*Sore Spot: There are more sidebars than focused discussions.*

Evidence: Lack of attention to agenda items

Interventions: Make sure there is:

1. A person appointed to be the "Stick-to-the-Agenda Police" or a facilitator

2. An agenda template that lists the meeting topics, who will lead that section of the meeting, how long each section will take, and expected outcomes

3. A "parking lot" for creative ideas that emerge but are off topic (a board of Post-It notes or chart paper); but watch out: don't let the parking lot become a black hole

*Sore Spot: The team consistently avoids conflict at all costs (a.k.a. "the school culture of nice").*

Evidence: Members don't address conflicts because they believe that conflicts are anathema to smooth team functioning. Issues caused by bad team behaviors remain unresolved, even though organizational behavior research[1] indicates that under certain

The Parking Lot Takes Shape

circumstances, conflict can benefit groups. It is important to differentiate between conflicts that are the result of interpersonal relationships and conflicts that are about the work. Artificial harmony does not support team efficacy. There is a difference between *collegiality*, which is simply a cooperative relationship between colleagues, and *collaboration*, which means working, collectively and successfully, to get the work done.

Interventions: Promote a team environment that:

1. Promotes mutual trust and creates comfort zone in which team members feel safe enough to call out other members' unproductive behaviors.

2. Prevents rigid adherence to protocols from smothering the expression of new ideas. (While team focus is important, appropriate leeway should be given for outlier comments to be heard.)

3. Encourages team members to directly express their ideas, positions, and feelings coupled with learning how to listen, react, and integrate different points of view. (To encourage this, teams can designate a devil's advocate or naysayer or agree to a norm that no important decisions are to be finalized before contrary points of view are aired and discussed.)

*Sore Spot: Individual needs outweigh team success.*

Evidence: There is avoidance of accountability and inattention to results. Teams discuss issues using protocols but spend too much time commiserating about the individual's problems and don't make decisions about what to do about the issues or how to follow up and hold each other accountable for actions. At other times, the team's decisions are overruled by administration or ignored by team members.

Interventions: Make sure the team:

1. Spends time initially to develop a compelling purpose for the team to which all members are committed.

2. Reaches clear agreement with administrators about the purview of the team and what decisions the team is able to make.

*Sore Spot: People get stuck in their patterns; therefore, meetings don't get better.*

Evidence: Meeting after meeting, agenda items pile up. Some agenda items always get pushed aside. Some people don't contribute while others do the work. Productivity is low. Ad infinitum.

Intervention: If you haven't already done so, appoint a norms/process checker as described in the "Appoint Specific Roles" section earlier in this chapter. If the role exists but hasn't been effectively implemented, it may be time for the team to revisit the norms and/or the questions listed as part of the norms/process checker role.

*Sore Spot: Meetings end without a wrap-up and an action plan.*

Evidence: Self-evident

Interventions: All meetings must end with:

1. A formal review of what agenda issues were tackled and the results of any decisions reached. A handy form to track these, kept by a meeting log keeper, might look like Figure 5.1.

2. A what/who/when Meeting Action Plan (Figure 5.2), with assigned responsibilities. Ideally, these can be generated on the computer at the meeting, projected for everyone to see, and can be distributed to all members at meeting's end.

3. A debriefing discussion that includes an evaluation of how we did during the meeting. Were we productive? This ritual

gives team members an opportunity to say what didn't work and how they can improve. In addition to maintaining the norms, the norms checker asks a question to allow each team member to check in at the end of the meeting.

This routine gives team members an opportunity to help the observer get "up on a balcony"[2] so they can gain a distanced perspective. Five minutes of every meeting should be allowed for this kind of processing.

## Learn by Example

While the sore spots listed above may seem easy to understand, they are not always easy to uncover in real life. People's group behaviors are more often subtle than obvious, which is why we've included two very important sets of learning tools in this book: teaching cases and video cases (see Chapter 6 for a brief synopsis of each).

With your team, read the cases and study them carefully. See if you can tease out the underlying causes of each team's problems. Read the section on how to use the videos, and then watch them with an eye toward identifying how "teaming potholes" and meeting sore spots play out in real-life situations.

If you apply even some of the things you've learned in this section, you will be absolutely amazed at what you and your team will be able to accomplish at meetings. We've seen it happen, and we know it can happen for you.

## Don't Bite Off More Than You Can Chew

Your team has done all of the above and is now a well-oiled machine—ready to tackle anything on its plate. But be cautious. Even if your team is now composed of superheroes in the teaming business, the reality is that you simply cannot do everything.

Remember that meetings should probably never last much longer than 90 minutes (with a break); efficiency drops off sharply after that. Given the overwhelming amount of stuff you have to watch out for, as evidenced above, getting the real work done in the time available is a mighty challenge.

You have to be brutally realistic about setting goals and defining those tasks you've decided to take on. If you don't, your hard work will be for naught as your team sinks slowly, and painfully, into the swamp of irrelevance. The team has to prioritize, reach agreement, and set its aspirations and expectations accordingly.

Be rigorous in creating the agenda, holding team members accountable, and focusing on the work at hand.

# Tips and Tools for Maintenance, Survival, and Success

You could say that this entire book, from end to end, is filled with tools and tips for building and maintaining successful teacher teams. And we hope that you find this to be true. In addition, however, here are six additional strategies—you could call them "team tune-ups"— that will add strength and depth to your growing knowledge and expertise in the ongoing teacher teaming enterprise:

   I. Improve your team's communication skills.

   II. Fine-tune your team's effectiveness.

   III. Move your team to its next stage of development.

   IV. Get your new principal on board.

   V. Connect your team with your school.

   VI. Leverage your "what I know now."

## i. Improve Your Team's Communication Skills

*Overview*

Good teaching can be defined in many ways, but there is no question that part of that definition includes a willingness to collaborate with colleagues around shared goals and standards. *Especially* in a team setting.

Yet not everyone plays well with others, and sometimes there may even be good reasons for resisting mandates or going against the flow when it comes to mandates and teamwork. The challenge for teams is to figure out how to bring everyone together regardless of the personality and ego differences that emerge when colleagues resist the requirements of teamwork. Let's face it—nobody's difficult all of the time (and everybody's difficult some of the time). How do we reinforce the most positive behaviors?

Here's a communication-building activity that may help raise teachers' consciousnesses of the way they communicate in groups. The purpose of this activity, which can be facilitated by whoever is leading the team meeting, is to bring out each team member's best behaviors and most productive efforts during team meetings.

*Activity*

> ### Materials Needed
>
> Enough printed copies of the Observation Worksheet (Figure 5.3) to distribute to each meeting participant.
>
> Full-size reproducibles of worksheets and handouts are available on the companion CD-ROM.

### Step 1

What are you good at in groups? Team members write down five things they believe they do during team meetings that help facilitate communication. For example: "I help the team stay focused." "I support the ideas of other members of my team." "I take personal responsibility for the success of the team."

What are you *not* very good at? Team members then write down five things they do, or don't do, in team meetings that probably hinder good communications. For example: "I'm probably not a good listener." "I talk too much during meetings and don't give others a place in the discussion." "I stick to one point of view; I tend to be inflexible."

### Step 2

Team members engage in a role-play. Each person is either a role-player or an observer. If it's a small team, then outsiders should be recruited as observers. Choose your own scenario or use the following:

> It's been proposed that there be a Staff Member of the Month award in your school. You are all on a committee to discuss the merits of the idea and come up with criteria for making such an award.

Each person in the role-play tosses a coin. If you get heads, you'll exhibit positive behavior; tails, you'll exhibit negative behavior. Keep your role secret.

If possible, have an observer for each team member who's a role-player or at least two observers for the activity. The observers will keep notes, using the Observation Worksheet (Figure 5.3), and comment later on what team members said and how it impacted the meeting.

### Step 3

Both observers and role-players answer these questions: Which behaviors were effective? In what ways? Which hindered? In what ways?

*Step 4*

In a two-minute write-up after the role-play, role-players answer the following prompt: "As I think about our next team meeting, my first thoughts are. . . ." After the two-minute write-up, role-players read what they wrote and underline main ideas as if they were reading someone else's paper. Teammates share their main ideas.

**Figure 5.3  Worksheet—Observation Worksheet**

| Behaviors that advance team effectiveness | Behaviors that hinder team effectiveness |
|---|---|
|  |  |

*Step 5*

Follow-up: At the next meeting, do a quick recap of the *"a-has"* from the last meeting. Then have all members think about their roles in the team meeting.

1. As a speaker—some people think before they speak, and some speak before they think. Which do you do?

2. As a listener—this is the most demanding role on a team, and it involves more than just hearing. What listening skills do you use?

3. As an observer—of yourself and your team. What is your participation? Are you closing others out or bringing people in?

*Step 6*

The two-minute team write-up: How effective was the meeting? What roles did people play?

The team shares its responses, with a view toward gaining further insights into how to strengthen the team through improved communication and an understanding of how to avoid negative roles.

## II. Fine-Tune Your Team's Effectiveness

### Overview

We've developed a framework for evaluating the effectiveness of teams, using five criteria, or conditions, with some natural overlap (see Chapter 3 and Case 8). Within each condition are several levels of development that determine where a team's overall effectiveness lies along a broad spectrum, or continuum. The Teacher Teaming

Continuum Assessment (Figure 5.4) is both a conceptual and practical tool designed to prompt team self-assessment and reflection, deepen understanding of teaming, and support the development of effective teams. It encourages teacher teams to *examine what is* and *envision what might be.*

Using the Continuum Assessment can be a rich learning experience that helps teams recognize what they do well, uncover challenges that they face, set priorities, and develop action steps that will strengthen their team. The Continuum Assessment prompts a team to evaluate itself in each of the five conditions of effective teams:

- Task focus
- Leadership
- Collaborative climate
- Personal responsibility
- Structures and processes

Be careful, though. If a team were to attempt this entire two-part team tune-up by examining all five conditions in one meeting, the task would be formidable and overwhelmingly time-consuming. It is better to go deep and slow rather than shallow and fast. We recommend that a team, after looking at the Continuum Assessment, select no more than one or two of the conditions to concentrate on in the first meeting, depending on available time. Parts 1 and 2 of this activity should take about 45 minutes each.

*Activity*

---

### Materials Needed for This Activity

Materials needed: Enough printed copies of the following to distribute to all team members:

- Teacher Teaming Continuum Assessment Worksheet
- Team Continuum Action Plan Worksheet (if you plan to use this instead of chart paper)
- Team Continuum Action Plan
- Two colors of index cards
- Chart paper and markers

Full-size reproducibles of worksheets and handouts are available on the companion CD-ROM.

**Figure 5.4** Worksheet—Teacher-Teaming Continuum Assessment

| | A Framework for Evaluating the Effectiveness of Teams | | |
|---|---|---|---|
| Condition | Not present | Developing | Well underway |
| **Task Focus**<br><br>*Is the team's task well defined and articulated, and does it focus on improving student learning?* | • Team's focus is driven by crisis within the team or pressing school needs.<br>• Team devotes over 50% of meeting time to logistics (e.g., field trips, other events, parent/teacher conferences), leaving little time for issues pertaining to curriculum, pedagogy, and student learning.<br>• Team goals are not established or don't have student learning at the center; goals are not specific, attainable, or results oriented.<br>• Team dialogue and exchange are rare or infrequent.<br>• Team members do not adopt the team task as part of their larger teaching purpose. | • Team's focus is sometimes proactive, but the task is often undermined by reacting to crises or pressing school needs.<br>• Team devotes 30%–50% of meeting time to logistics.<br>• Team has identified some goals that focus on student learning; some goals are specific, attainable, and results oriented.<br>• Team dialogue and exchange foster collaborative sharing of classroom activities and resources. | • Team goals are challenging; focused on curriculum, instruction, and student learning; and specific, attainable, and results oriented.<br>• Team's focus is proactive, concentrating on assessment and future planning; little time is spent reacting to crises or school needs that do not relate to the team.<br>• Team devotes a maximum of 20% of meeting time to logistical issues.<br>• Team dialogue and exchange develop new team understandings about teaching and learning. |
| Evidence | • | • | |
| **Leadership**<br><br>*Does the team encourage leadership by all its members?* | • One team member tends to assume leadership (or is deferred to) on a regular basis.<br>• Team members do not initiate new leadership activities or roles on their own.<br>• Team has not developed skills in deciding whether a task is best done as a team or individually.<br>• Team members maintain their individual entrepreneurial status that seems like "parallel play." | • Team leadership is rotated among team members but without clear purpose; leadership and facilitation skills have not yet been taught to team members, and the team recognizes its need to improve these skills.<br>• Team encourages its members to assume new leadership roles but does not think strategically about how these roles will affect and improve the team.<br>• Team is working on, but has not yet achieved, the goal of distributing leadership in a manner that results in team improvements. | • Team members distribute leadership functions in a purposeful and strategic way (e.g., expertise in areas of curriculum and instruction).<br>• Team leadership is rotated with an explicit goal of developing leadership skills for all team members. (In some cases team leaders are designated.)<br>• All team members can provide a common description of how leadership works on their team.<br>• Team members are supported as they assume new, as well as established, leadership functions. |

*(Continued)*

47

(Continued)

| Condition | Not present | Developing | Well underway |
|---|---|---|---|
| | | | • Team leader ensures that each meeting agenda is planned, facilitated, and communicated.<br>• Team communicates and networks with other teams and the administration, and seeks outside resources. |
| Evidence | • | • | • |
| **Collaborative Climate**<br><br>*Does the team promote a working environment that generates trust, communication and synergy?* | • Team members do not identify or make use of other teammates' strengths; new ideas are routinely defeated.<br>• Team conflicts are ignored or denied. Team members avoid handling conflict, don't recognize when it might be productive for the group.<br>• Norms of listening and participating have not been established (e.g., acknowledging, probing, summarizing). | • Some team members identify strengths of individuals, but the team does not utilize the strengths strategically to advance the goals of the team.<br>• New ideas from team members are encouraged, but processes are not in place to ensure action steps are tied to agreed-upon ideas.<br>• Team conflicts are identified but inconsistently dealt with due to lack of skills or processes.<br>• Norms of listening are implicit, and team members occasionally uphold them. | • Team performance is measured by assessing collective work products.<br>• Team acknowledges each member's strengths and creates a shared understanding of strategic ways each individual contributes.<br>• Team uses processes that value diverse perspectives in order to develop team understandings and solutions. Each voice is heard and valued.<br>• Conflicts within the team are brought to the team for resolution. The team employs a conflict resolution process that solves the problems and promotes collaboration and collegiality.<br>• Team has established and upholds norms of effective listening.<br>• In addition to internal collaboration, the team networks and communicates with other teams and the administration, and seeks outside resources. |

(Continued)

| Condition | Not present | Developing | Well underway |
|---|---|---|---|
| Evidence | • | • | • |
| **Personal Responsibility**<br><br>*Is there an expectation of performance improvement for both the team and the individual?* | • Team members are often late and/or come unprepared to meetings.<br>• Team members give feedback that is frequently critical and negative.<br>• Team members fail to complete tasks in a timely manner, or quality is unacceptable to the team.<br>• Team members are most concerned with personal agendas.<br>• Team members have articulated no expectations of accountability. | • Team members are sometimes late and sometimes come unprepared.<br>• Team members focus on problems they have with others' viewpoints and sometimes give ideas for improvement.<br>• Team members complete some assigned tasks, not always according to the agreed-upon schedule; quality varies.<br>• Team members are somewhat concerned with team success.<br>• Many team members hold themselves accountable individually, but no group-level process is in place. | • Team members are punctual and come prepared to all team meetings.<br>• Team members give both positive comments and constructive feedback for improvement.<br>• Team members complete tasks effectively and on schedule.<br>• Team members place highest priority on team success.<br>• Team members hold individual members accountable for their performance and for results. |
| Evidence | • | • | • |
| **Structures and Processes**<br><br>*Does the team establish ways to work together and achieve agreed upon goals?* | • Team lacks many effective meeting practices. Meetings lack clear goals for student learning, agendas, and documentation.<br>• Meetings do not begin on time, and/or time management is not evident.<br>• Team does not focus on student needs until adult needs have been accommodated.<br>• Team has not developed skills for deciding whether tasks are best done as a team or individually. | • Team has developed some explicit goals for student learning and has expectations that appeal to most team members.<br>• Team is developing effective meeting practices. Meetings have some, but not all, of the elements important to productive meetings.<br>• Team tries to adapt plans to student needs but sometimes fails because of poor skills or lack of consensus.<br>• Team is developing skills in determining whether tasks are best done as a team or individually. | • Team has well-defined goals and expectations focused on student learning.<br>• Team continuously adapts plans to meet the needs of its students.<br>• Team follows effective meeting practices (e.g., clear objectives, agenda, stays on task, appropriate time management, appropriate documentation).<br>• Team has a process for deciding whether tasks are best done as a team or individually. |
| Evidence | • | • | • |

*Part 1—Self-Assessment and Reflection (45 minutes)*

*Step 1*

Make sure your team has a facilitator. Also, designate a note-taker who will record the major discussion points that will be used later in Part 2.

*Step 2*

Give each of the participants a copy of the Teacher Teaming Continuum Assessment.

*Step 3*

Start by explaining that the Continuum Assessment has three purposes:

- To help your team assess its strengths, challenges, and progress
- To deepen team members' understanding of the potential of teacher teams
- To aid in planning for stronger teaming

Explain that it is not unusual for members of the same team to find themselves at different places on the continuum regarding different practices.

*Step 4*

Briefly review the five conditions (left-hand column), and select two of them to analyze. Consider a condition that is not your strength. In our experience task focus is a good place to begin.

*Step 5*

Ask participants to read the one or two conditions that the team selected. While reading they should circle the description from each row that they think best describes the team's current practice and jot down evidence in the space provided.

*Step 6*

Taking one condition at a time, each person shares where he or she located the team and the evidence he or she considered when making those choices. Encourage anyone making general statements to provide evidence. Discuss areas where participants disagree.

(While coming to agreement is not necessarily a goal, discussing these areas of disagreement may deepen everyone's understanding of the practice and your team's strengths and challenges.)

### Step 7

Collect and save all the Continuum Assessments filled out by team members, along with the notes on the conversation, so that you can compare them the next time you review this category.

### Part 2—Team Condition: Assessment and Planning (15 minutes)

This tune-up activity is designed to give each team member an opportunity to contribute ideas (somewhat anonymously, to guard feelings and personalities) about the evidence uncovered in Part 1 regarding the one or two conditions chosen for assessment. These ideas will be expressed either as Problems or as Positives. The goal is to work toward an action plan that addresses the major issues discussed in order to strengthen the team. Don't overlook the bullets that have not been circled in any column. They may be indicators of potential problems that you can highlight in the following activity.

### Step 1

Pass out copies of the notes taken by the note-taker in Part 1, along with copies of the Teacher Teaming Continuum Assessment containing written evidence.

### Step 2

Pass out two differently colored 3x5 index cards, four of each color, to each participant. Tell people that one color is for Problems, the other color for Positives. Participants will write down one idea on each card: four problems, four positives.

*Important:* To keep the discussion on track, the ideas expressed on the cards must focus *only* on the condition(s) chosen for discussion in Part 1 and should reference, at least in part, the evidence uncovered in Part 1.

Card 1: What is difficult, challenging, risky, untenable, or problematic about (name of condition)? For example, in Task Focus you might have a goal that is "challenging, focused on curriculum, specific, and attainable." However, the goal does not meet all of the criteria because it is not "focused on instruction" or "results-oriented." In that case, you might write on your card, "We need to be more results-oriented and, therefore, look more at student work."

Card 2: What is important, rewarding, enriching, stimulating, satisfying about (name of condition)?

**Figure 5.5    Worksheet—Team Continuum Action Plan (Part 1)**

| | |
|---|---|
| What would be different in your team if you made progress on the conditions discussed? | |
| What gets in the way of progress on these conditions? | |
| What strategies might you use to make progress? | |
| What action steps need to be taken? Who will take them? When? (This information can be transferred to the next step.) | |

**Figure 5.6    Worksheet—Team Continuum Action Plan (Part 2)**

| What is to be accomplished? (List action steps.) | Who is responsible? | When will action be complete? |
|---|---|---|
| 1. | | |
| 2. | | |
| 3. | | |
| 4. | | |

## Step 3

Collect the cards, shuffle them so that they are all randomly mixed, then pass them back to the group. Each person, in turn, will read one idea aloud from one card, whatever the color. As each idea is read, record the responses on chart paper, using two columns, one for each category: Problems and Positives. Use another piece of chart paper to synthesize the ideas.

## Step 4

When done, distribute copies of the Worksheet—Team Continuum Action Plan (Figure 5.5) to each team member and give each 5 minutes to fill it out, or post these on chart paper and fill in responses, as provided orally.

## Step 5

Have the note-taker record information in the Team Continuum Action Plan (Figure 5.6). You're already familiar with this format from Figure 5.2.

You and your team should use this two-part team tune-up for each of the five conditions—say, choosing one or to work on every sixth to eighth team meeting. Of course, filling out the Action Plan is only the first step. Next comes implementation, which should be the subject of your next meeting following this team tune-up.

## III. Move Your Team to Its Next Stage of Development

### Overview

**Forming—Storming—Norming—Performing**[3] is a model of team development that identifies the phases that are necessary and essential in order for the team to grow, face up to challenges, tackle problems, find solutions, plan work, and deliver results. In this model, it is understood that for any team to reach the final, high-performing stage, it must first successfully meet and resolve the challenges presented in the first three stages of development (see Figure 5.7).

In many cases, for example, teams get stuck in the Forming stage because, well, it's comfortable and offers few challenges. Or they attempt to skip lightly over the Storming stage—it's just too difficult, and the required norms of trust, collaboration, and conflict resolution go against the embedded school "culture of nice," which does its best to avoid confrontations of any kind. Yet it is precisely the act of going through this stage and its processes that enable the team to mature, build trust, and prepare for the skill development that will occur in the Norming stage.

Ultimately, to become truly successful, any team must go through each stage to become a Performing team. And it remains a fact of life that when new members are added (or others subtracted), teams often have to cycle back to revisit issues previously resolved.

### The Four Common Stages of Team Development

#### Forming (Testing)

- Polite
- Impersonal
- Watchful
- Guarded

#### Storming (Infighting)

- Controlling conflicts
- Confronting people
- Opting out
- Experiencing difficulties
- Feeling stuck

#### Norming (Getting organized)

- Developing skills
- Establishing procedures

**Figure 5.7  Stages of Team Development**

| 1. Forming | 2. Storming | 3. Norming | 4. Performing |
|---|---|---|---|
| | | **Indicators** | |
| • Teachers get to know one another and where they stand on classroom issues; they share personal information.<br>• Team goals are identified.<br>• Teachers begin to share ideas of practice, comment on student progress, and offer each other suggestions.<br>• Teachers begin to take on roles and assume responsibility for tasks. | • Different ideas compete for attention; members confront each other's ideas and perspectives, may express frustration at lack of progress.<br>• Team struggles to determine what model of leadership is acceptable.<br>• Issues of team accountability and individual accountability arise.<br>• Team works to establish roles, goals, and responsibilities.<br>• Team develops strategies that build trust and help to focus on tasks. | • Team goals are accepted, and a mutual plan for meeting objectives is in place.<br>• Strategies for conflict resolution are developed; team members take responsibility for meeting team goals.<br>• Dissatisfaction is replaced by trust, support, and respect.<br>• Members are comfortable in their roles.<br>• Team leader keeps team moving productively.<br>• Team exhibits ambition to achieve goals. | • Work of the team is almost entirely focused on the improvement of teaching practice and student performance.<br>• Teachers have become interdependent, recognizing that each team member is responsible for all the team's students.<br>• Problems of leadership and individual and team accountability are successfully addressed.<br>• Strategies for conflict resolution assure smoothly functioning teamwork.<br>• Collaboration and communication are at a high level.<br>• Team members handle the decision-making process with little or no supervision. |
| | | **Challenges** | |
| • There is an initial lack of trust.<br>• Discussions focus on logistics rather than instruction.<br>• Team lacks strategies for dealing with difficult issues; high value is placed on conflict avoidance.<br>• Reluctance to assume team leadership results in lack of focus on goals.<br>• Teachers still see themselves as independent practitioners rather than team members. | • Members can express anger or resentment toward authority; conflicts can be contentious and painful.<br>• If tolerance, patience, and trust are not established, team will not be able to move forward.<br>• Lack of leadership and accountability will stymie growth and prevent moving to the next stage of development. | • Team members may find it hard to adapt if one teacher leaves or another joins the team; strategies for mentoring of new team members may not be in place.<br>• Some team members may be reluctant to give up their strongly held beliefs in order to benefit team functioning. | • Changes in leadership or administration challenge team norms and dynamics and could cause the team to revert to Storming stage of development. |

- Giving feedback
- Confronting issues

### Performing (Mature closeness)

- Resourceful
- Flexible
- Open
- Effective
- Close and supportive

### Activity[4]

The objective is to identify the present stage of the teamwork model that your team is currently operating in so it can take the right steps to move to its next stage of development.

---

### Materials Needed

Enough printed copies of the following to distribute to all team members:

- Teamwork Questionnaire
- Team Development Score Sheet

Full-size reproducibles of worksheets and handouts are available on the companion CD-ROM.

---

### Step 1

The Teamwork Questionnaire (Figure 5.8) contains statements about teamwork. Next to each question, indicate how often your team displays each behavior by using the scoring system explained on the questionnaire.

### Step 2

Complete the Team Development Score Sheet (Figure 5.9). Next to each survey item, write in the score that you gave to that item on the Teamwork Questionnaire. When you have entered all the scores, total each of the four columns.

The Teamwork Questionnaire is designed to help you assess what stage your team normally operates in. The lowest score possible for a stage is 8 (for Almost never) while the highest score possible for a stage is 40 (for Almost always).

## Figure 5.8   Worksheet—Teamwork Questionnaire

*Directions:* This questionnaire contains statements about teamwork. Next to each question, indicate how often your team displays each behavior by using the following scoring system:

**1 = Almost never, 2 = Seldom, 3 = Occasionally, 4 = Frequently, 5 = Almost always**

1. _____ We try to have set procedures or protocols to ensure that things are orderly and run smoothly (e.g., minimize interruptions, everyone gets the opportunity to have a say).

2. _____ We are quick to get on with the task at hand and do not spend too much time in the planning stage.

3. _____ Our team feels that we are all in it together and share responsibilities for the team's success or failure.

4. _____ We have thorough procedures for agreeing on our objectives and planning the way we will perform our tasks.

5. _____ Team members are afraid, or do not like, to ask others for help.

6. _____ We take our team's goals and objectives literally and assume a shared understanding.

7. _____ The team leader, or facilitator, tries to keep order and contributes to the task at hand.

8. _____ We do not have fixed procedures; we make them up as the task or project progresses.

9. _____ We generate lots of ideas, but we do not use many because we fail to listen to them and reject them without fully understanding them.

10. _____ Team members do not fully trust the other members and closely monitor others who are working on a specific task.

11. _____ The team leader, or facilitator, ensures that we follow the procedures, do not argue, do not interrupt, and keep to the point.

12. _____ We enjoy working together; we have a fun and productive time.

13. _____ We have accepted each other as members of the team.

14. _____ The team leader is democratic and collaborative.

15. _____ We are trying to define the goal and what tasks need to be accomplished.

16. _____ Many of the team members have their own ideas about the process, and personal agendas are rampant.

17. _____ We fully accept each other's strengths and weaknesses.

18. _____ We assign specific roles to team members (e.g., team leader, facilitator, time-keeper, note-taker)

19. _____ We try to achieve harmony by avoiding conflict.

20. _____ The tasks are very different from what we imagined and seem very difficult to accomplish.

21. _____ There are many abstract discussions of the concepts and issues; some members get impatient with these discussions.

22. _____ We are able to work through group problems.

23. _____ We argue a lot even though we agree on the real issues.

24. _____ The team is often tempted to go above and beyond the original scope of the project.

25. _____ We express criticism of others constructively.

26. _____ There is a close attachment to the team.

27. _____ It seems as if little is being accomplished with the project's goals.

28. _____ The goals we have established seem unrealistic.

29. _____ Although we are not fully sure of the project's goals and issues, we are excited and proud to be on the team.

30. _____ We often share personal problems with each other.

31. _____ There is a lot of resistance to the tasks at hand and to quality improvement approaches.

32. _____ We get a lot of work done.

**Figure 5.9   Worksheet—Team Development Score Sheet**

**Directions:** Next to each survey item numbered below, write in the score that you gave to that item on the Teamwork Questionnaire. When you have entered all the scores, total each of the four columns.

| Forming Stage  Item Score | Storming Stage  Item Score | Norming Stage  Item Score | Performing Stage  Item Score |
|---|---|---|---|
| 1. ___ | 2. ___ | 4. ___ | 3. ___ |
| 5. ___ | 7. ___ | 6. ___ | 8. ___ |
| 10. ___ | 9 ___ | 11. ___ | 12. ___ |
| 15 ___ | 16. ___ | 13. ___ | 14. ___ |
| 18. ___ | 20. ___ | 19. ___ | 17. ___ |
| 21. ___ | 23. ___ | 24. ___ | 22. ___ |
| 27. ___ | 28. ___ | 25. ___ | 26. ___ |
| 29. ___ | 31. ___ | 30. ___ | 32. ___ |
| Total _____ | Total _____ | Total _____ | Total _____ |

The highest total score indicates which stage of development you perceive your team to be operating in. If the highest score and lowest score are close to the same, you are probably going through a transition phase, except in the following circumstances:

- If you score high in both the Forming and Storming stages, then you are in the Storming stage.
- If you score high in both the Norming and Performing stages, then you are in the Performing stage.

If there is only a small difference between three or four scores, this indicates that you have no clear perception of the way your team operates, the team's performance is highly variable, or you are in the Storming stage (this stage can be extremely volatile with high and low points).

*Step 3*

Now that you know where you are, move on.[5] This is an exercise for the team leader or facilitator whose team has assessed which stage their team is in. What do you do next? Here are some strategies you can begin to employ that will help your team keep developing, no matter what stage you're in. Because even if you've reached the Performing stage, you're never really "done."

### Stage 1: Forming—The Undeveloped Team

- Facilitate "getting to know you" exercises, stimulating greater personal knowledge.
- Demonstrate openness by example.
- Invite members to share their concerns and problems.
- Encourage consideration of individual strengths and weaknesses.
- Make team activities enjoyable.

### Stage 2: Storming—The Experimenting Team

- Encourage greater openness.
- Begin to involve team members in review of team performance.
- Build bridges between individuals.
- Allow conflicts to surface.
- Question decision-making and problem-solving methods.
- Find opportunities to experiment.
- Encourage individual team members to air their grievances.
- Seek common ground.
- Give a high level of support.

### Stage 3: Norming—The Consolidating Team

- Develop problem-solving skills.
- Develop decision-making strategies.
- Develop individual skills.
- Develop a capacity for the team to compensate for individual weaknesses.
- Encourage people to share strengths.
- Celebrate successes.
- Clarify objectives.
- Regularly review performance, and plan improvements in team functioning.
- Give moderate support.

### Stage 4: Performing—The Mature Team

- Build bridges with other teams.
- Experiment with different forms of leadership.

- Allow leadership to change with the needs of the task.
- Clarify values.
- Consider the possibilities of enhanced inputs into the organization.
- Encourage informal communications.
- Fight insularity.
- Expose team functioning to external scrutiny.
- Give minimal support.

The important thing to remember is that team interactions and behaviors are dynamic—they remain constantly fluid as situations change, such as the addition and subtraction of team members, a new administration or curriculum, or other challenges to team stability. The objective is to put into place those procedures and protocols that help guard against slipping backward insofar as possible and, when that happens, to know how to adjust and move forward once again.

## IV. Get Your New Principal on Board

### Overview

It's a fact of life. If you're a teacher with almost any kind of longevity, you probably have seen more than one principal come and go. And what do new principals want to do? Of course the new broom sweeps clean, as they say, and one thing a new principal wants to do upon arrival is to assert authority by claiming ownership of new ideas, new curricula, and new initiatives. Uh-oh. How do you protect the hard work you and your team have already invested?

### Your Strategy

Well, the good news is this: new principals want to demonstrate their support for teachers. What you and your team have to do is give the principal the opportunity she or he really needs to show that support. And you have to do this quickly.

Be proactive. You have to get your new principal on board early in the game, and a good way to do this is to create a well-prepared (but not too long or overly produced) PowerPoint presentation that gives your principal important (and compelling) information about your team.

Think specifically about what you want your presentation to convey to the principal. Decide who will speak, when (during which slide), and how long the presentation will take. All principals value their time, so a presentation of about 10 minutes (adding 5 minutes for questions) is long enough.

*Activity*

### Step 1

*Developing your presentation:* You're all teachers. You know that preparation is 90% of the battle. Here are some tips.

1. Make your PowerPoint as simple as possible. Each slide should contain very few words, but communicate the main points you want to get across.

   - The principal should view the PowerPoint only as a guide, with the team filling in the details. Don't repeat what's on each slide. Use the words on the slide as a reinforcement of what you're saying. This will add power to the presentation.
   - Make sure that team members have a formal or informal script so that everyone knows what the others will be saying.

2. Create no more than 8–10 slides.

3. Examples of slides might be:

   - An introductory slide naming the grade level or department and stating the team's purpose
   - A slide listing the team's goals for the year in abbreviated fashion
   - A list of the norms that guide the team's work
   - Three slides that delineate—one each—a single important accomplishment of the team so far, indicating that the team is meeting its goals
   - A slide that indicates one or two new challenging but doable goals the team has set for itself
   - A final slide that invites the principal to join in the task or—if you prefer, and it seems more appropriate with this principal—an inspirational quote

4. Do a timed run-through of the presentation before you meet with the principal, and stick to your goal of *short*. Plan on the whole meeting lasting under 30 minutes.

### Step 2

*During the meeting:* Make sure to invite the principal to ask clarifying questions, and emphasize that her or his questions are welcome throughout the presentation—and at the end of the presentation.

### Step 3

*Ending the meeting:* Give the principal a copy of the PowerPoint in handout form.

Again, make sure you've left enough time for questions from the principal, and make it very clear that you would greatly appreciate it if she or he could find the time to attend one of your team meetings.

Also leave time to arrange a set of meeting dates with the principal for the entire year so that she or he recognizes your serious desire to keep her or him apprised of your team's progress.

Without being proactive, your relationship with the principal could be in jeopardy. Your taking the initiative will go a long way toward starting the year on a solid footing and reassuring the principal of your instructional goals (something every principal wishes that every team would have!).

## V. Connect Your Team With Your School

*Overview*

A problem voiced by both principals and teams is that the school and the teams that work within the school structure do not feel connected; each feels isolated from the other. Everyone knows there are teams around—grade-level teams or other configurations—but if teams work in isolation, who bothers to stay in touch, to communicate in any meaningful way exactly what individual teams are doing?

Here's a presentation protocol given to us by an elementary school principal[6] who uses it with his school's teacher teams to give schoolwide presentations so that all team members feel they have at least an idea of, and even a stake in, what's going on inside the teams. The school faculty then feel connected to their teams, and the teams feel more connected to each other. There's the added benefit of teams learning from one another and strengthening team accountability as well.

*Activity*

*Content*

1. Your presentation should describe your team's goal and the process of implementing it. The presentation will describe how the Instructional Core (see Figure 5.10) relates to the goal:
   - How has the content of learning changed or been modified?
   - What has changed about the role of the teacher in relation to the content and students?
   - What has changed about the role of the students in relation to the content and the teacher?

2. Your presentation should show student work or assessment results as evidence.

**Figure 5.10    The Instructional Core**

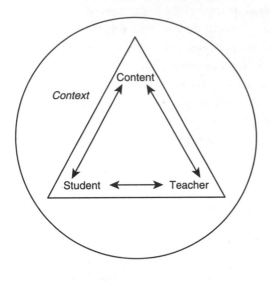

3. Your presentation should include a reflection on your learning as teachers:
   - What did you learn working as a team?
   - Has "instructional talk" increased in your team as a result of working with the goal? If so, how?
   - What might you do differently next time?

*Form*

   - The presentation should last approximately 8–12 minutes.
   - Materials should be presented in an organized way.
   - The presentation should engage the faculty in a variety of ways (listening, seeing, etc.).
   - Time should be included for faculty members' questions.

*Impact*

   - An engaged faculty audience
   - A more fully informed faculty
   - Faculty, acting as critical colleagues, offering feedback to the team

Ideally, principals, faculty, and teams will schedule regular team presentations to strengthen school-team connections. Principals could also facilitate team presentations to parents and PTOs.

## VI. Leverage Your "What I Know Now"

*Overview*

This is an assessment activity for either individual or multiple teams. It can work well at the end of the school year to support some reflective conversation for your team or a number of teams that might want to work together for this meeting. This activity allows team members to look back over the year and acknowledge the learning and support they provided one another on the team. The first two prompts (see Figure 5.11) focus on individual learnings achieved; the last two prompts are intended to help focus next year's plans.

*Activity*

+--------------------------------------------------------------+
| **Materials Needed**                                         |
+--------------------------------------------------------------+
| Chart paper, markers, and enough printed copies of the following to distribute to all team members: |
|                                                              |
|   • "What I Know Now" Chart Prompts                          |
|                                                              |
| Full-size reproducibles of worksheets and handouts are available on the companion CD-ROM. |
+--------------------------------------------------------------+

*Step 1*

Post four pieces of chart paper—a different piece of paper for each of the boxes in Figure 5.11. This activity can be facilitated as a "Carousel Brainstorm," a good strategy for generating large numbers of responses to questions or issues, and a way to get everyone involved in the generation of ideas. Each participant contributes one idea for each of the prompts.

**Figure 5.11   Worksheet—"What I Know Now" Chart Prompts**

| I used to think . . . , but now I think . . . | What I know now that I wish I knew when we began our team |
|---|---|
| What I still wish I knew | What I wish my team members knew |

*Step 2*

Starting at different charts, either as individuals or in small groups (depending on the size of the group), rotate from prompt to prompt. As you approach a new chart, read what is already written on it and put a check (√) next to the idea if you agree, an (X) if you disagree, or a question mark (?) if you need clarification.

*Step 3*

Together the team looks at each chart, clarifying any items that have question marks and highlighting areas of disagreement. The last two may provide a focus for future team work, either collective study or new processes or . . . fill in your own. These charts can provide a good record of where teams were, where they are at the end of the year, and where they are going in thinking about their own learning and the needs of team members. The activity also can help integrate new members to the team.

Now, save these charts for next year and use them at your opening team meeting as a way to address traditional jitters that most teachers face at the beginning of every school year. The "What I Know Now" chart can be especially useful in providing direction for the team so it doesn't make the same mistakes all over again. What's more, it will get the new year off to a good start by having the team wondering together:

"What will we know next year at this time that we wish we knew now?"

# 6

# Teaching Cases

*Storytelling is the most powerful way to put ideas into the world.*

—Robert McAfee Brown

## Cases and Guides to Case Analysis

For decades, case studies have been used as a valuable teaching tool in the fields of medicine, law, and business—and only more recently in education. In the credo of Harvard Business School, which pioneered the use of case studies, "Wisdom can't be told":

> Teaching cases—also known as case studies—are narratives designed to serve as the basis for classroom discussion. Cases don't offer their own analysis. Instead, they are meant to test the ability . . . to apply theory . . . to a "real-world" situation.
> Cases . . . present ambiguous situations in which protagonists face difficult questions. A good case teacher aims to shape a discussion in which there is a high quality of analysis—not a single right answer.[1]

That's why we feel that the combination of cases and their accompanying Guides to Case Analysis are the meat and potatoes of this book. In both you will find numerous connections to theory and practice. In

65

the Guides to Case Analysis, we urge you to pay particular attention to the sections labeled Exploring the Dilemma and Reflect and Connect. Closely following both sections will help ground your discussions in relevant established theory and deepen your understanding of the underlying factors affecting the dynamics of teacher teams.

The Guides to Case Analysis present a variety of study and discussion options—so many, in fact, that when you look at the (estimated) times needed for engaging in the activities and exercises, you will find yourself scratching your head and exclaiming, "We can't possibly do all this at once!"

And you can't. These are not one-shot deals designed to be squeezed into a single team meeting. There is enough resource material there to allow you to revisit cases and their guides to analysis time and time again, perhaps finding new insights each time you and your team delve ever more deeply into the opportunities presented.

If we could give you the one most important piece of advice, it would be this: remember the Boy Scout motto, and **be prepared**. These cases will prove more valuable to you the more you take the time and effort to prepare thoroughly beforehand.

## What the Cases Are About

### Case 1. The Neutral Zone: Handling Interpersonal Dynamics on Teams

A novice teacher is caught between two factions in the team. There is weak communication and little trust among the members of the team, and the novice must decide how she will align herself to become an accepted member of the team.

### Case 2. Surface Collaboration or Dynamic Interdependence?

This team devises team norms and plans agendas but has difficulty keeping to its agendas. Outside experts regularly override meeting agendas, logistics trumps teaching and learning, and curricular topics most important to the teachers and students are continually postponed. Everyone on the team is frustrated.

### Case 3. Can't Follow the Leader

A departing teacher coach/team leader attempts to teach the new designated team leader how to facilitate team meetings and move the team's curricular work forward. Using a gradual-release model, the leader finds that when she steps back, team members lose focus and fail to delve deeply into instructional topics. She wonders what she should be doing differently to pass on the leadership of the team.

### Case 4. Good Intentions Aren't Enough

A math team must coordinate its established curriculum so that all Algebra II classes are teaching the same lessons in the same time frame. Dissension occurs when the department chair praises the alignment work of two teachers and asks the other teachers to learn from them. This work is challenged by a newer member of the team who believes that students can move more quickly and go more deeply into the curriculum. No decision is reached on how to proceed.

### Case 5. A Principal's Dilemma: The Challenge of Change

A principal and an assistant principal learn about and attempt to implement a team structure in their elementary school. Given minimal team training, team leaders are designated, but other members balk at the leadership attempts of their designated team leaders, preferring the autonomy that preceded this team model.

### Case 6. How Far We've Come

A principal has established high-functioning teams at her school and now must present this six-year developmental process to the School Board. She describes how each of the teams has developed, and she wonders how to convey the change process to the Board, and if the successful structure can be replicated or even if it will continue after she leaves the school.

### Case 7. A Vague Destination, No Compass or Map

A teacher in the 2nd-grade team is chosen by the school administration to become the team's leader and work on improving the team's reading instruction. The other teachers resist her leadership efforts. The principal wants the team leader to observe the team's teachers and give them feedback, but the teachers are reluctant to be observed; in fact, they resist all of her leadership efforts. The team leader feels helpless and ready to give up her leadership role.

### Case 8. The Team That's "Practically Beloved"

A middle school cross-area team, considered highly successful by the school principal, receives its standardized test scores, which are surprisingly low. The principal demands that the team develop an action plan that will improve the achievement of all its students. Some teachers are ready for the task; others balk at having to work on a common plan with their teammates. The team leader wonders how she can convince the entire team to work together and feel responsible for all of its students.

## Case Themes

When you first read these cases—and it is not necessary to read them all in sequence—just select the three or four that you think are most relevant and are most likely to help your team right now. Each case has a major theme—there are seven in all (see Figure 6.1)—and some of these themes apply to more than one case.

Use Figure 6.1 as a guide to find which cases contain which themes. Be strategic about choosing the most appropriate cases. The far left column lists the five conditions of effective teams, and the rest of the chart indicates which is *most* applicable to each particular case—although, in reality, cases may explore other conditions as well.

# Video Cases and Their Guides to Analysis

**(These are all on the DVD included with this book.)**
Video can be a powerful teaching and learning tool, and it is underutilized in the work of teacher teams. By filming real teacher teams in action, we learned a lot about the power and potential of teacher teams as well as the challenges teachers in teams face as they grapple with the dilemmas and the issues that arise in just about *every* kind of team.

When teachers allow their practice to be video recorded, the results can

- help to "make teaching public," transforming teaching from a solo practice to one that is subject to peer review;
- provide a platform for critical analyses of teaching practice in real-life classroom situations;
- uncover how teachers collaborate (and where they don't) as they work through the difficulty of improving their teaming skills in order to improve teaching and learning;
- help teachers and teams develop a common language about their practice so that they may have more substantive and meaningful conversations; and
- represent *a spectrum of endeavors*—insights into the difficult and complex work of teaming and classroom teaching.

Figure 6.1   Case Themes

| Exploring a Condition of Effective Teams | Case Theme | Case 1 Grade 3 Interpersonal dynamics | Case 2 Grade 5 Mutual accountability | Case 3 Middle School Building leadership capacity | Case 4 High School Math A divided department | Case 5 Pre-K to Grade 6 Resistance to principal leadership | Case 6 K–8 All Teams Effective team conditions | Case 7 Grade 2 Resistance to teacher leadership | Case 8 Middle School A divided team |
|---|---|---|---|---|---|---|---|---|---|
| Task Focus | The team curriculum: instructionally focused conversations to improve student learning | X | X |  | X |  | X |  |  |
| Personal Accountability | Interdependence and accountability; collective responsibility | X |  |  | X |  | X |  | X |
| Leadership | Team leadership as opposed to egalitarianism and individual leadership roles for teachers |  | X | X | X | X | X | X | X |
| Structures and Processes I | Building team knowledge and skills ("team tune-ups," professional development, networking) |  |  | X |  |  | X | X |  |
| Structures and Processes II | The role of the principal (or department head) as a champion of involvement structures |  |  |  |  | X | X | X | X |
| Collaborative Climate I | Teacher autonomy vs. team coherence and alignment of curriculum | X | X |  | X | X | X | X | X |
| Collaborative Climate II | Promoting a working environment that generates trust, communication, and synergy | X |  |  |  |  |  |  | X |

Unlike the written cases, the videos are the cases themselves. Watch each video carefully and analytically. And in preparation for the Guides to Analysis, watch each once again. Then dig into the Guides to Analysis and become amazed at what you'll discover.

It is here that we have to acknowledge the principals, teachers, and teams who took the plunge and allowed us to video their practice. In a guarded culture only now opening itself up to public view, this notion can be pretty unnerving, and we salute the brave souls who took the risk and gave us access to their classrooms, team meetings, and personal reflections.

## What the Video Cases Are About

### Video Case 1. A 3rd-Grade Team Meets to Examine Student Work

A team examines the writing of a student using a version of the Looking at Student Work Protocol. The team follows the correct guidelines of the protocol, looking at aspects of the student's writing, and analyzes the student's writing and the instructional practices of the teachers. The question emerges: how could the team have delved more deeply into the work?

### Video Case 2. A 5th-Grade Team Meets to Follow Up on a Professional Development Workshop

The teachers explore the issue of how to go beyond professional development workshops and use team meetings to implement new strategies. The teachers have attended a workshop on guided reading. In this meeting they discuss what they learned from that workshop and how it might change their practice. They also raise questions and discuss the challenges of implementing a new strategy.

### Video Case 3. A 9th-Grade Physics Team Meets to Plan Interventions for Underperforming Students

This team meeting is co-facilitated by the team leader and the special education teacher (who is a fully integrated member of the team). The team discusses students' midterm exam grades, highlighting students who received Ds and Fs on their exams, and uses the meeting to develop interventions that will improve the learning of low-performing students and all other students.

*Video Case 4. A High School History
Department Meets to Develop Consistent Grading Criteria*

This department meeting, facilitated by the chair, considers how to make the criteria for grading students' written work more explicit and consistent. The teachers use an Essay Checklist to assess an essay written by students in one class. They read and give grades to five essays from the same assignment. For the meeting discussion, they focus their analysis on Editorial 1, noting specific reasons for the grade they gave and focusing on the quality of the student work.

## Okay, One Last Word

Before you go plunging into the following cases, we'd like to leave you with this final thought. Over the past 30 years we've enjoyed (mostly) a thrilling roller coaster ride through the tunnels and over the mountains of what the teaching profession has offered to us—and we have been willing actors in some of its shining moments as well as its darkest days. We wouldn't want to change any of it. But we are smiling now because we believe that we have (honestly and truly) begun to sense the winds of change on our fevered brows.

Teachers working in teams—as professionals willing to engage in the process of looking at their practice and changing it for the better through collaboration with their fellow teachers—are going to change the face of education in America—and then the world. We hope you will be part of it.

# Cases

## CASE 1. The Neutral Zone: Handling Interpersonal Dynamics on Teams

Key Concept: A Collaborative Climate Promotes a Working Environment That Generates Trust, Communication, and Synergy

## A New Teacher Caught in the Middle

Standing nervously in the hallway between the two classrooms, Lia Del Rios balanced the plastic Tupperware container filled with last night's pasta salad in one hand and her teacher's manual for the new *Explorations* reading program in the other. To her right, she could see Tanya Owen and Kathy Mason already eating lunch, laughing over something humorous one of their 3rd-grade students had done earlier that morning. Two large, shiny boxes filled with *Explorations* materials sat at Kathy's feet. To Lia's left, fellow first-year teacher Andrew Weitz was pulling up a chair next to Marie Ellington's desk.

In September, Andrew and Lia had eaten lunch together frequently to discuss the trials and tribulations of first-year teaching, but now it was November, Andrew was struggling, and he had begun eating his lunch in Marie's classroom to ask her advice. In that moment, Lia caught the end of Marie's words to Andrew: " . . . just don't let Kathy catch you doing it. Ever since she came back from that workshop, she's so 'by the book,' you know."

Indecisive, Lia stood in the middle and debated whether she would go talk to Kathy and Tanya. She knew that they would ask her to advocate for the new assessment plan that accompanied *Explorations*. Kathy and Tanya needed Lia's support because Marie, the most veteran teacher on the 3rd-grade team, had already commented that she had neither interest nor time to give a weekly reading assessment to all the students in her class. Her response had been met with Kathy's stony stare. Tanya had pursed her lips and said they would continue the conversation next time. Thinking over what had happened last week, Lia knew that she'd need to say something today at the team meeting, which was in exactly one hour. She hoped that she would know what to do before then.

## Southeast Elementary School

Lia had joined the staff of Southeast Elementary School directly after graduating from college with her degree in elementary education.

Southeast is an urban elementary school for students in Kindergarten through 5th grade, all of whom are African American, reflecting the demographics of the surrounding neighborhoods. Sixty-five percent of the students qualify for free or reduced-price lunches. The facility recently underwent an extensive renovation, due in large part to a partnership forged with a charter school opening next door—the gym and playground were modernized and expanded to allow sharing of the space between the two schools, and new shelves and lighting had been installed in all the freshly painted classrooms.

Southeast was in the stage of "corrective action" by the district, having failed to make AYP (Adequate Yearly Progress) in both reading and mathematics for the past two years[1] (see Figure C1.1).

Although the school improved its mathematics scores in the past year, students were still struggling schoolwide in reading. Southeast continued to be labeled "a school in need of improvement," and according to the district expectations it had to implement the school improvement plans created by the principal and the School Leadership Committee (SLC). As part of the improvement plan mandated by the district, the school had to demonstrate that it was using benchmark assessments to monitor student progress on performance measures over multiple points throughout the year (Figure C1.2).

**Figure C1.1  Exhibit 1: Southeast Elementary School State Test Results**

|         | 2007 % proficient | 2008 % proficient | 2009 % proficient |
|---------|-------------------|-------------------|-------------------|
| Reading | 29                | 20                | 22                |
| Math    | 26                | 34                | 35                |

Last spring, Principal Markus Garrison requested that the teachers begin thinking about how to examine student data. The SLC convened a series of meetings and, at the meeting in early October, SLC member Kathy proposed the use of weekly progress monitoring assessments in reading.[2] Holding up the materials, Kathy had said, "At the *Explorations* workshop, they told us that the most effective form of quick reading assessment is a one-minute timed test that measures rate and accuracy. You can give this fluency check to students at the end of every week and track students' progress over time."

Kathy passed out a set of materials from the *Explorations* reading intervention program, which had gained some recent press for successfully turning around reading achievement in other urban districts. Other SLC members quickly became excited about the clear, straightforward presentation of the assessment, since *Explorations* kits came with different leveled reading passages, tracking charts, and annotated scoring manuals. Principal Garrison requested that the

### Figure C1.2    Exhibit 2: School Improvement Process

**Corrective Action for Schools**

If, after two years of undergoing school improvement, implementing a school improvement plan, and receiving extensive technical assistance, a school still does not make AYP, the SEA and LEA* must identify it for corrective action. Identifying a school for corrective action signals the LEA's intention to take greater control of the school's management and to have a more direct hand in its decision making. This identification signifies that the application of traditional school improvement methods and strategies has been unsuccessful and that more radical action is needed to improve learning conditions for all students. Taking corrective action is designed to increase substantially the likelihood that all students enrolled in the school will meet or exceed the state's proficient levels of achievement.

**What are the responsibilities of the LEA when the SEA and LEA identify a school for corrective action?**
If the SEA and LEA identify a school for corrective action, the LEA must:

- Continue to ensure that all students have the option to transfer,
- Continue to ensure that supplemental educational services are available to eligible students in the school,
- Continue to provide or provide for technical assistance to the school.

In addition, the LEA must take at least one of the following corrective actions:

- Institute a new curriculum grounded in scientifically based research and provide appropriate professional development to support its implementation;
- Extend the length of the school year or school day;
- Replace the school staff who are deemed relevant to the school not making adequate progress;
- Significantly decrease management authority at the school;
- Restructure the internal organization of the school;
- Appoint one or more outside experts to advise the school (1) how to revise and strengthen the improvement plan it created while in school improvement status and (2) how to address the specific issues underlying the school's continued inability to make AYP.

*AYP = Adequate Yearly Progress; SEA = State Education Agency (state department of education); LEA = Local Education Agency (school district).

SLC present the idea to the grade-level teams and asked for at least two teams to volunteer to pilot the process for tracking data. Kathy told the SLC, "I'm confident that my team will quickly be on board. I'll talk to Tanya about putting this on our agenda for the week."

## The Team Meeting

Tanya ripped the still-warm copies of the team's agenda from the photocopier as they were shooting out, walked briskly out of the teachers lounge, and climbed the steps to her classroom, where they held team meetings. A sixteen-year veteran teacher, Tanya was the team's official meeting facilitator by default. At the beginning of the year, Tanya had revealed to Lia how she had been chosen facilitator.

"At the end of last year," Tanya had said, "our previous team leader left the school, and Kathy and Marie argued for months over who was more qualified to lead the team. Kathy's only a fifth-year teacher but she's got a master's degree and is certified as a reading specialist. Since she joined Southeast, she's been taking every leadership position available, including chairing the staff social committee and volunteering to draft curriculum maps! Just last year, Markus appointed her to the School Leadership Committee. On the other hand, Marie has twenty years of experience, which makes her the most senior, but I just don't think she knows what she's doing anymore. I never see her doing *any-thing* with those students. So much has changed about curriculum since she started—I really wonder if she's *teaching* or if she's just giving out worksheets! In the end, Markus figured the only way to solve this was to prevent either one of them from getting chosen and to make *me* the team leader, so I facilitate the meetings. But really," added Tanya, "I just make the agendas. I never wanted this role to begin with!"

On the day of the team meeting, Tanya entered her room, laid out the agendas meticulously around her center cluster of desks, and brought her lukewarm cup of coffee over to the group. The other 3rd-grade teachers came in one at a time. Kathy was the first to arrive, bringing with her an open lesson planner, a pile of spelling tests, and a bag of leftover Halloween candy. Andrew and Lia came in together, talking about how they could more effectively monitor student behavior in the bathrooms. Tanya noticed how tired Andrew looked, and she reflected on how Andrew's life must be so different since he left his first job as an assistant at one of the city's law firms to join an alternative certification program. Now, he was teaching eight-year-olds during the day and going to education classes at night.

Kathy looked around the room and sighed. "Where's Marie? It's almost 10 minutes past."

"I think she's dropping her kids off at the gym—the P.E. teacher is late, as usual," Andrew said.

"No, I just saw her go into the teachers lounge. Maybe she has to copy some homework," Lia offered.

Kathy frowned. "That's not good. She has to be here for team meetings; it's a rule. This is the fourth time she's been late. She arrives at 8:00 with the kids and walks out when the bell rings at 3:00. She should be coming earlier or staying after school if she needs to do extra prep work. Can someone go get . . ."

At that moment, Marie opened the door to the classroom, carrying a stack of papers and a steaming cup of coffee. Without a word, she sat down at the cluster of desks and began stapling packets together. Tanya paused for a moment, cleared her throat, and began the meeting. "OK, you all have today's agenda. Let's not forget to talk about the parent newsletter before we leave today. The thing I'd like to start with is something from Markus. He needs teams to volunteer to pilot this new program for tracking data. It's part of our school improvement plan and we have to start implementing pieces of it this year so the district office can see that we're in compliance. I know that you all give weekly spelling tests and the end-of-story tests in reading, but we are going to have to do something more. Kathy has just returned from some professional development and she has a great idea that has already been cleared by the SLC. Kathy?"

Kathy looked excited as she brought up the *Explorations* kit from its resting place at her feet and put it on the desk. She explained, "This is a new intervention program that several other districts are already adopting. It's designed to work with our current reading program, so we'll still be reading out of the basal reader, but we'll also be pulling students who are falling behind and using these supplemental texts. There are leveled short stories and worksheets, all in the kit. The thing I'd really like you to pay attention to is the progress monitoring part. Each week, we could test *all* of our students using their one-minute timed reading test. Each student reads the same passage, and we listen to them read and mark their mistakes. Then we count up the mistakes and subtract from their total words per minute, and you have their score. There are 'target' scores for each season, fall, winter, and spring. The kit comes with computer software, where you will go in every week and input student scores into the program—then it generates this *really nice* graph, and you can see the kids who are scoring on target are green, approaching the target is yellow, and below the target is red. I'm really excited about this because it will give us a weekly measure of student reading progress, and we can see how we're doing as a team!" Kathy sat down and looked around the table.

Lia noticed that the room felt unusually quiet, then she noticed that Marie had stopped stapling packets and was staring at Kathy with a crease in the center of her forehead.

"You mean to say," Marie began, "that in addition to my Friday spelling test and all my story tests, I have to sit with *each* kid and listen to them read for one minute *every week*? Who has time to do that? And who is going to watch the rest of the class while I'm sitting with one kid at a time? Those kids will be all over the place, and you know it. That's why I always take my class outside on Fridays—they need some time to run around."

"Well," Kathy responded in a low voice, "You could always do it when they're playing . . ."

". . . and miss watching them on the equipment! If one of them gets hurt, I'm liable. No, thank you!" Marie scoffed.

"Actually," Kathy continued, "there is no reason why your class has to go outside on Friday afternoons—it makes my students really jealous because we're still inside and they see your class outside."

"You know that it's their reward. I always promise them longer Friday recess if they get enough class points," said Marie.

Tanya interrupted; she knew that this was another longstanding debate between Kathy and Marie that she felt would sidetrack the conversation. "The point is: we have to do something to show that we are monitoring student progress, and this is the best idea the SLC has come up with for reading. I really think our team should volunteer for the pilot. If it works, everyone will have to implement it next year anyway. This will also allow us to be more consistent across the team. We'll be able to see how everyone's class is doing, and we can talk about it."

"Don't we already do this, when we give those baseline reading tests in the beginning of the year?" Andrew asked.

"No, that's *completely* different. That's the pre-test that tests basic reading comprehension and vocabulary, and we'll give the post-test in the spring. This is a test of fluency. It's a straightforward miscue analysis," Kathy said matter-of-factly.

Andrew looked nervous. "What is a 'miscue analysis'?"

Kathy looked at him. "Didn't they teach you how to do that in your methods class? You look at a copy of the text as the students read out loud, and you write their errors exactly as they are over the words they said wrong. You can determine where students are having trouble by looking at their mistakes."

"They haven't gone over that yet," Andrew said in a flat voice.

"I know what level my students are on without having to track it every week," Marie insisted. "You just watch them in class and you can tell—why waste time doing this on Fridays when we already test and drill these kids to death? Besides, this is so much paperwork. If you give me a teacher's aide, I can have her do it—but of course, I don't get an aide! They always give them to the new teachers."

"I really think we need to get on the same page about this," Tanya said firmly. "If we're all doing the same thing, we can see which students need help in certain areas. Then maybe we can split our students between the classes for reading—for example, I can take the kids who need help with single-word decoding, and Lia can take the ones who are OK to go on to chapter books and work on comprehension."

Marie shook her head. "You know that I have a routine that already works for my class. We do 15 minutes of word work, 15 minutes of vocabulary, and 30 minutes of the story from the textbook. These kids need stability so they know what to expect. If you start moving them between classrooms, you're just asking for chaos. So I'm against this whole thing—it just seems like we're making needless work."

Tanya looked at the clock. "OK. We have other agenda items, and I can tell that we're going to have to wait and decide this at the next meeting. I just want to remind you that Markus and the SLC are already behind this, so I think it just makes sense for us to volunteer."

## Weighing Both Sides

"You were quiet today in the meeting," Andrew said to Lia as they walked back to their classrooms. "What do you think about this whole 'progress monitoring' thing?"

"I don't know," Lia admitted. "I think it does sound like a lot of work, but it would be nice to track my students' scores. It would be interesting to see the numbers over time. I learned how to do a running record and miscue analysis in my program, but I haven't used it since I started teaching."

"I am just so lost right now," he sighed. "It's too much. We have one program for spelling, one program for vocabulary, a basal reader, and now this? I can barely just figure out what to teach the next day. My arms are tired from carrying all those teacher manuals home at night. I think Marie has it down—her classroom runs so efficiently. Her students are quiet, she does the same thing every day, and because she has the routine she doesn't have to change much every week. I've been trying to copy her routine with my class. I've had enough of this unpredictability!"

"But don't you think that we should be looking at student data?" Lia asked.

Andrew replied, "I am actually really nervous about all those scores being so public. I mean, you'll be able to see whose students are doing well, and whose aren't! What if I'm doing something wrong in teaching reading? Everyone will know . . ."

Lia opened the door to her classroom and they both entered. Once the door had closed again, Andrew admitted quietly, "I suppose Kathy and Tanya do know what they're talking about, but I just get so defensive in meetings. Kathy makes me feel like I don't know anything. Like today, when I didn't know what a miscue analysis was— she has that tone of voice like she's talking to a 3rd-grader, and it's so condescending. So I just stop listening."

"I know what you mean," Lia agreed. "It seems like we spend more time in meetings just being talked *at* than actually talking *about* anything. I've stopped talking because I don't see the point; it seems like they've already made up their minds. They have their little club of two, and Marie will disagree with them, but I'm not really on her side either. It just bothers me that they seem to have come up with this plan all on their own and then they present it to us like it's not even a choice. Why doesn't someone ask for *our* opinions?"

"It's because Kathy and Tanya don't really want to hear anyone's opinions but their own," Andrew said. "I think Marie has it right— just get your own classroom under control and don't worry about anyone else's business."

## In the Middle

Lia stood in the hallway and felt torn: she could advocate against the program because she knew it would add another responsibility to her overburdened schedule, or she could do something that she knew might be good for her instruction. She could hear Tanya and Kathy in the room to her right. Lia had spent some time reading the *Explorations* teacher's manual, and she had some concerns about how well the program would align with their already full reading agenda. Still, she had a feeling that Kathy and Tanya would simply announce that the 3rd-grade team would pilot the assessments without even hearing everyone else's opinions. Lia was tired of being silent, but she saw no use getting into arguments in team meetings.

To her left, Andrew and Marie were getting out their lunches. Andrew's classroom instruction was beginning to look a lot like Marie's, and Lia didn't think Marie was a particularly strong teacher, but Andrew seemed to value her advice. Lia wondered, if she began spending time with Andrew and Marie, would Tanya and Kathy stop taking her seriously altogether?

Not for the first time, Lia wondered why no one had warned her that there was so much politics on the 3rd-grade team. It almost seemed as if the battle lines had been drawn before she had ever been hired at the school, and she was simply standing in the line of fire. "No wonder Andrew calls this hallway 'the neutral zone,'" she muttered to herself as she made her decision and walked into the room. She would try to talk to Kathy and Tanya.

*************************************************************************

# CASE 1—Guide to Analysis

## The Neutral Zone: Handling Interpersonal Dynamics on Teams

**Key Concept: A Collaborative Climate Promotes a Working Environment That Generates Trust, Communication, and Synergy**

This case recognizes the complexity of teacher collaboration. Collaboration does not mean having to reach consensus; it does not mean disagreements are forbidden; it does not mean going along with the crowd.[3] But there cannot be collaboration without some mechanisms in place for conflict resolution.

---

### Your Facilitator

**Wait!** It would be very, very difficult to gain any appreciable benefit from your expenditure of time and energy by attempting to conduct this analysis and its series of exercises without a facilitator. You *need* to appoint someone (it can be a team member) as a designated facilitator. This is not necessarily your team leader. This person will not be your "boss." But this person *will* be responsible for:

- Copying and distributing to all participants copies of the Case and Case Analysis and all handouts
- Organizing role-plays (appointing time keepers and observers, where indicated)
- Moving the process along and staying on track

**Psst! Facilitators:** Read all the activity directions as if they applied to you.
**Psst! Team members:** You, too.

---

### Materials Needed

Enough printed copies to distribute the following to all team members:

- The Case and Guide to Analysis
- (optional) Handout—Southeast Elementary School State Test Results
- (optional) Handout—School Improvement Process
- Handout—Difficult Conversations
- Worksheet—Preparation Notes for Role-Play: Lia
- Worksheet—Preparation Notes for Role-Play: Others
- Worksheet—Preparation Notes for Team Conversation Activity
- Chart paper and markers

Full-size reproducibles of worksheets and handouts are available on the companion CD-ROM.

# A. Analyzing the Case

## Step 1: Read the Case (20 minutes)

Distribute the teaching case, and have all team members read it through, underlining or highlighting pieces of information that they think are significant to understanding the case.

## Step 2: Establish the Facts of the Case (10–15 minutes)

As a whole group, make a list on chart paper of the significant *facts* of the teaching case. Include what you know about each team member. Try to withhold judgment, inferences, or evaluation, and come to agreement about what happened.

Just the Facts!

**Very Important:** When we say *facts* we mean just that—you must stick to the facts ONLY. There is a huge temptation, when analyzing other teachers' interactions, for teachers to voice *opinions* such as "She talks too much during the meeting" or "She's not a very good teacher." These are not *facts,* and negative comments such as these are counterproductive. The group should consciously steer away from such comments and instead either ask questions such as "Does she allow other voices to be heard?" or offer statements based on *evidence* such as "She says _____, but then she does _____."

> If teachers feel they will be attacked for opening up their practice for other teachers to view, they simply will not do it. Making practice public is a risky proposition, and part of your challenge as a case analyst is to pretend that the teachers you are talking about are right there in the room with you.

### Step 3: Case Analysis Questions (10 minutes)

Discuss the following questions. For each question, identify the evidence that leads to your response.

- How would you describe the interpersonal dynamics on the 3rd-grade team?
- How have those dynamics affected the team's work?
- What course of action should Lia recommend to her team members?
- Is it important for teams to have a process for resolving interpersonal tensions between team members? What might this process look like?

## B. Exploring the Dilemma (45 minutes–1 hour)

The book *Difficult Conversations: How to Discuss What Matters Most*[4] demonstrates a framework for how to engage in discussions of controversial or emotional issues. We will use this framework to analyze the case.

### Step 1: Read Handout (5–15 minutes)

In preparation, read the Handout—Difficult Conversations: Resolving Interpersonal Tensions Between Team Members (Figure C1.3).

### Step 2: Choose Characters for a Role-Play (5 minutes)

Participants in this exercise will choose to role-play a difficult conversation between Lia and any of the following characters in the case about the issues below or another that surfaces during the case discussion:

- with Kathy about the *Explorations* reading program
- with Tanya about the leadership on the 3rd-grade team
- with Marie about consistency in expectations and schedules across the team

**Figure C1.3    Difficult Conversations: Resolving Interpersonal Tensions Between Team Members**

---

PREMISE: **Each difficult conversation is really three conversations.**

1. *The "What happened?" conversation*
   - The truth assumption (I am right; you are wrong—even though it's really about perceptions.)
   - The intention invention (We assume we know the intentions of others; when we're unsure, we usually decide others' intentions are bad.)
   - The blame frame (We can't get beyond blaming and can't understand how we all contribute.)

2. *The "Feelings" conversation*
   - Difficult conversations don't just involve feelings. They are about feelings.
   - Ignoring feelings is like staging an opera without the music.

3. *The "Identity" conversation*
   - What does this say about me?
   - Am I competent? A good person? Worthy of love?

---

Adapted from Stone, D., Patton, B., & Heen, S. (1999). *Difficult Conversations.* New York: Penguin Books.

## Step 3: Divide Into Groups (10–15 minutes)

*Preparation for Role-Play—Part A*

- Divide the group in two.
- Group A will prepare to play Lia and collaboratively complete the Handout—Preparation Notes for Role-Play: Lia (Figure C1.4)
- Group B will choose to play either Kathy, Tanya, or Marie and collaboratively complete the Handout—Preparation Notes for Role-Play: Others (Figure C1.5).
- Once the preparation forms are completed, *one person* in Group A will assume the role of Lia and take the perspective of her character. In Group B, *one person* will play Kathy, Tanya, or Marie and take the perspective of her character.
- When playing their roles, the participants should keep in mind the issues stated in the list above for each character.

*Preparation for Role-Play—Part B*

- All other participants in each group—those not playing a role—will act as observers, taking notes during the role-play so they can give specific feedback, tied to the data, when it is over.
- One observer can be a timekeeper, authorized to "pull down the curtain" when the role-play appears to be repeating itself, or when three to five minutes have elapsed, whichever comes first.

## Figure C1.4   Worksheet—Preparation Notes For Role-Play: Lia

**Transforming a Difficult Conversation into a Learning Conversation**

You are: Lia

| What Happened? | | | Feelings | Identity Issues |
|---|---|---|---|---|
| **Multiple Stories** What's **my** story? | **Impact/Intent** My intentions: Impacts on me: | **Contribution** What did I contribute to the problem? | What are the feelings engendered for me around this conversation? | How does what happens or what might happen in this conversation threaten my identity? |
| What's **her** story?* | Other's intentions:* Impacts on the other:* | What (from your perspective) did she contribute?* | | Specifically, when I think about the leadership and authority relationships involved in this difficult conversation, what challenges or identity issues come up? |

*Try to get into the other character's side of the story, and try not to fall into some of the common traps of the Intention Invention.

"Jack's Preparation Notes" from *Difficult Conversations* by Douglas Stone, Bruce M. Patton and Sheila Heen, copyright © 1999 by Douglas Stone, Bruce M. Patton, and Sheila Heen. Used by permission of Viking Penguin, a division of Penguin Group (USA), Inc. and by permission of International Creative Management, Inc.

## Figure C1.5   Worksheet—Preparation Notes for Role-Play: Others

**Transforming a Difficult Conversation into a Learning Conversation**

You are (choose one): ____Tanya  _____ Kathy  _____ Marie

| What Happened? | | | Feelings | Identity Issues |
|---|---|---|---|---|
| **Multiple Stories** What's **my** story? | **Impact/Intent** My intentions: Impacts on me: | **Contribution** What did I contribute to the problem? | What are the feelings engendered for me around this conversation? | How does what happens or what might happen in this conversation threaten my identity? |
| What's **her** story?* | Other's intentions:* Impacts on the other:* | What (from your perspective) did she contribute?* | | Specifically, when I think about the leadership and authority relationships involved in this difficult conversation, what challenges or identity issues come up? |

*Try to get into the other character's side of the story, and try not to fall into some of the common traps of the Intention Invention.

"Jack's Preparation Notes" from *Difficult Conversations* by Douglas Stone, Bruce M. Patton and Sheila Heen, copyright © 1999 by Douglas Stone, Bruce M. Patton, and Sheila Heen. Used by permission of Viking Penguin, a division of Penguin Group (USA), Inc. and by permission of International Creative Management, Inc.

- Referring to the Handout—Difficult Conversations (Figure C1.3), observers in both groups will take note of the three types of conversation . . .
  - o The "What happened" conversation
  - o The "Feelings" conversation
  - o The "Identity" conversation

. . . and seek to identify which of the three different kinds of conversations may be taking place during the role-play.

### Step 4: Role-Play (3–5 minutes)

The role play is a three- to five-minute (difficult) conversation between Lia and the other character chosen. Lia and Marie, for example, may talk about the inconsistency in expectations and schedules across the team.

### Step 5: Feedback (6–8 minutes)

Observers provide specific feedback to the characters, addressing—when possible—the underlying issues revealed in the role-play conversation.

### Step 6: Discussion and Debriefing (6–8 minutes)

Discussion and debriefing should include framing the issues using the Difficult Conversations handout (e.g., What are the three conversations here? What are the identity issues for each party?)

## C. Reflect and Connect (10 minutes)

Think about a time when you had to make a decision but felt caught between two opposite positions expressed by fellow team members.

- How did you approach making the decision?
- Did your decision have any consequences for your relationships with other members of the team? If yes, how did you handle those consequences?

## D. What Do We Do Now? (1 hour)

Moving toward a learning conversation, how does *your* team discuss what matters most? You might want to use the following prompts to develop your own case, a challenging interpersonal interaction to begin to apply your learnings from the Difficult Conversations activity.

1. Discuss participation patterns in team meetings. Who usually talks more? Who usually talks less?

2. Discuss why this tends to happen, and invite people to share how they feel about participating in team meetings and why.

## Step 1: Review Handout

Once again, read the Handout—Difficult Conversations (Figure C1.3), noting the three conversations that are part of every difficult conversation.

## Step 2: Divide Into Groups

Divide the group in two. Using the Difficult Conversations frame, think about a challenging interaction that has confronted your team (e.g., not coming prepared for meetings, participating only minimally at meetings, dominating the conversation, not completing assignments). For example, Group A is annoyed that some people come unprepared; Group B defends that they come unprepared due to all the other demands teachers have that are more closely related to students.

## Step 3: Complete Worksheet

Participants in each group collaboratively complete a blank Worksheet—Preparation Notes for Team Conversation Activity (Figure C1.6) for each side's perspective. Participants identify why the conversation matters and the key elements of the likely response they anticipate.

### Figure C1.6   Worksheet—Preparation Notes for Team Conversation Activity

**Transforming a Difficult Conversation into a Learning Conversation**

You are (choose one): ____Tanya ____ Kathy ____ Marie

| What Happened? | | | Feelings | Identity Issues |
|---|---|---|---|---|
| **Multiple Stories** What's my story? | **Impact/Intent** My intentions: Impacts on me: | **Contribution** What did I contribute to the problem? | What are the feelings engendered for me around this conversation? | How does what happens or what might happen in this conversation threaten my identity? |
| What's his or her story?* | Other's intentions:* Impacts on the other:* | What (from your perspective) did she contribute?* | | Specifically, when I think about the leadership and authority relationships involved in this difficult conversation, what challenges or identity issues come up? |

*Try to get into the other character's side of the story, and try not to fall into some of the common traps of the Intention Invention.

"Jack's Preparation Notes" from *Difficult Conversations* by Douglas Stone, Bruce M. Patton and Sheila Heen, copyright © 1999 by Douglas Stone, Bruce M. Patton, and Sheila Heen. Used by permission of Viking Penguin, a division of Penguin Group (USA), Inc. and by permission of International Creative Management, Inc.

## Step 4: Choose the Observers

- Once the preparation forms are completed, choose *one person* from each group to be the observer. The *other members* in each group participate in the role-play.
- The observer in each group can be the timekeeper, stopping the role-play after three minutes.
- Referring to the Handout—Difficult Conversations, observers in both groups will take note of the three types of conversation . . .
  - The "What happened" conversation
  - The "Feelings" conversation
  - The "Identity" conversation

. . . and seek to identify which of the three kinds of difficult conversations may be taking place during the role-play.

## Step 5: Role-Play

During the role-play the observers take notes so they can give specific feedback, tied to the data, when it is over.

## Step 6. Feedback

Observers provide specific feedback to the people in the role-play, addressing—when possible—the underlying issues that the group acknowledged in their preparation. General discussion and debriefing should include framing the issues using the Handout—Difficult Conversations (e.g., What are the three conversations here? What are the identity issues for each side?)

## CASE 2. Surface Collaboration or Dynamic Interdependence?

Key Concepts: Mutual Accountability, Leadership, Task Focus

## The Nashton School

Located in a large midwestern city, the Nashton School is a K–5 school that serves over 900 students, of which 32 percent are African American, 34 percent are White, 24 percent are Asian, 8 percent are Hispanic, and 2 percent are Native American. Scoring in the top 2 percent of all schools within this large urban district on standardized tests has earned the Nashton School many awards.

At the beginning of the school year, there was a transition of principals. The new principal, Eileen Cunningham, took over after spending several years at a nearby district school. Many teachers were excited about the change in leadership because they hoped that the new principal would be able to weed out some teachers who were "just showing up to receive a paycheck." One of the principal's strongest beliefs was that teachers should be empowered to take on leadership roles within the school. From leading professional development sessions to volunteering to participate in various leadership teams, the principal felt that teachers were at the core of school improvement. She quickly moved to implement grade-level teams and weekly common planning times across all grades.

## The Team of 5th-Grade Teachers

**Malia Hayes** is a 10-year veteran and winner of a many teaching awards. This is her first year at the 5th-grade level.

**Jasmine Moradian** is a fourth-year teacher whose class of 15 students includes five with IEPs (Individual Education Plans). She is dyslexic and has been overwhelmed as the sole provider of special education services for her children since the beginning of the year.

**Edith Klimas** left a job in business and is a first-year teacher recently graduated from the district's two-year residency program.

**Lanna Catricks** is a second-year teacher.

**Kevin Alexander**, a third-year teacher, is quiet and says little during meetings, knows he needs help, and asks other teachers to provide him with resources. He spends his time during meetings typing meeting notes.

**Jim Renales**, the math coach, is not a member of the team. He has been a math coach for four years and typically visits each grade-level team on a monthly basis.

## August 25: Launching the Team

On a warm afternoon in late summer, this newly formed team of five 5th-grade teachers at the Nashton School gathered in too-small chairs around a makeshift conference table cobbled together from a hodgepodge of student desks. Four of the teachers were in the early stages of their careers; one was a 10-year veteran. Excited about their new adventure, they were there to convene their first official team meeting of the year. Earlier that morning, the team had participated in a goal-setting workshop in which they had identified three long-term goals that the team could work on together, which they agreed would help each of them teach more effectively.

Together, they would (1) collaboratively plan for social studies, (2) look at student work (especially writing), and (3) collect instructional resources to share among the team. Their challenge was to become a solid, effective team—interdependent and mutually accountable for work that would actually improve the quality of teaching and learning at their grade level.

It was agreed that working toward these goals would be the focus of the team's weekly common planning time. Their first assignment as a team was to establish team norms and a format for leadership. Four norms emerged: Remain positive, stay focused, work efficiently, and handle conflicts quickly. To address the issue of team leadership, they took the most veteran teacher's suggestion—although with some initial resistance—that they rotate the roles of facilitator, note-taker, and timekeeper on a monthly basis so that each team member would have a chance to practice facilitating throughout the year. They also decided that half of every fourth meeting would be reserved for a team "tune-up," a time for reflecting on the team's process.

## September 3: Mapping the Terrain

For this first meeting, Jasmine—who had been open about her challenges as a dyslexic learner—got things started, reminding everyone that the purpose of the meeting was to take an in-depth look at curriculum maps. Lanna, a teacher early in her career, passed around copies of a one-page curriculum map for September.

"This shows how I plan to do the first 20 days of Reader's Workshop and social studies," she announced. As the team looked it over, she explained further, "I went through and matched my lessons to the state curriculum frameworks. I didn't put math on here because we have the pacing guide for Everyday Math, and writing is missing because I have some questions about how we want to structure it."

Malia, the team's veteran, nodded approvingly. "I think this looks great. It's similar to what I normally do. Since I taught fourth grade last year, I have some writing resources we used that I can share. And I was wondering, does anyone have the *History Alive* teacher's edition I could borrow? I can't seem to find it."

Edith nodded. "I think I have it. It might have gotten moved into my room when they waxed the floors."

"I was thinking that we could rotate responsibility for making the monthly curriculum maps," offered Lanna. "I'll do October if we can talk soon about what should be included. What does everyone else think?"

As a first-year teacher, Edith was clearly relieved to have a curriculum map to help her get started. "This is absolutely wonderful. This breaks it down so I know exactly what I need to focus on. This is great!"

Lanna looked to the others. "What does everyone else think?"

Malia waited for others to chime in. When no one did, she added, "I like it because a shared curriculum map addresses the issue of continuity across the grade level without making it too structured or making us teach the same thing at the same time in the same way." Jasmine nodded approvingly, but Kevin remained silent and pushed slightly back from the table, typing notes on his laptop.

Lanna stared at him and finally asked, "Kevin, what do you think?" He looked up and nodded his assent. "OK then, we'll put on the calendar to do the October map in two weeks." Jasmine wrapped up the meeting, and the teachers headed back to their classrooms to arrange furniture, organize materials, and hang posters for the fast-approaching first day of school.

## September 17: Digging Into Data

Jasmine called the meeting to order about 10 minutes late because the art teacher hadn't shown up to take her kids on time. Edith was heating up her lunch in the microwave, and Malia was hanging "All

About Me" posters in the hallway. "OK, the principal is requiring Jim to come in twice this month to go over State Test math data. So Jim, take it away."

As the math coach for the building, Jim was one of the few remaining coaches from the district's battalion of literacy and math coaches created as part of a five-year reform plan that had been mostly phased out over the past couple of years due to increasing budget constraints. Last year's principal, a longtime veteran of the school system, had managed not only to keep class sizes below 17 in the elementary grades, but also to protect her full-time math coach and provide a stipend for a part-time literacy coach despite cuts, a circumstance the new principal was pleased to inherit.

For Jim's first visit to the team meeting, he prepared an item analysis packet and score summary for each team member and facilitated a dense 45-minute review of the current 5th-graders' performance on the 4th-grade State Test.

"Today we're going to go over the State Test data and do some item analysis for the children you have in front of you now. For each item on the test, use the provided grid to compare the percentage of students whose answers were correct in their current class to the rest of the school and the district." Malia and Lanna began filling in the grid while Jasmine and Edith asked for clarification on Jim's directions. Kevin flipped through the packet, set it aside, and went back to typing on his laptop.

Jim had been through this process with two other grade levels that day and continued matter-of-factly. "Now let's look at the five most-missed items. We'll start with Number 8. Only 22 percent of our students answered this one correctly. Take a minute to work on this problem, and then we will think about what might be causing the common errors. Finally, let's think about how to teach that concept, because the kids in front of you don't know it."

The team became engrossed in the protocol and got through three items before Jasmine looked up at the clock and hastily adjourned the meeting so that teachers could rush to pick up their students from art, science, music, and gym in time for dismissal. As team members scrambled to gather their things, Jim left them with a final directive: "The next thing to do is look at the curriculum map to flag the units where you can work in some reteaching of concepts that many students missed last year."

Walking back to her classroom, Lanna thought about how the structure of the math program, the specific assessment data available, and the leadership of the coach created dynamic conditions for looking at student work and thinking about instruction based on student performance. She wondered what her teammates would do to address the gaps uncovered in the session with Jim. They didn't have time to discuss that at the meeting, so Lanna decided to check in with Edith, her neighbor, at some point in the coming week. Jim's long session had bumped a couple of agenda items. Most notably, they hadn't even had time to work on their curriculum map for October, which was just two weeks away.

They also hadn't agreed on a persuasive essay prompt that the team would use as a grade-level-wide benchmark, which Lanna had planned to give tomorrow. Now they would have to brainstorm and agree over email or put it on the agenda for next week. Either way, she would need to plan something else for tomorrow's Writer's Workshop. She felt less confident about teaching writing than math. The team seemed to be wandering off track, and stepping back into her classroom, she felt overwhelmed.

At the following week's meeting, the team took five minutes to look over a list of persuasive essay prompts Kevin brought. These were suggestions for benchmark assessments as a gauge of students' readiness for the State Test. It was agreed that all the 5th graders would have 45 minutes to write letters to the principal meant to persuade her either for or against requiring school uniforms. Each class would complete the benchmark assessment in the next few days, and teachers would then bring two student writing samples to the next meeting to score and discuss as a group.

## October 1: Preparation, Complication, Frustration

The day before the meeting, Malia, the October meeting facilitator, allotted 20 minutes at the top of the agenda to discuss the writing benchmark and considered how she would lead that section of the meeting. She wanted to make sure that everyone was on the same page when it came to scoring the benchmark essay and, in response to a request Lanna had made as they dismissed their students a couple of days ago, planned to share copies of a rubric in "kid language" that she liked to use when scoring writing. She thought about which rubric to use and decided on a simplified *6 Traits Writing Rubric.*

The morning of the meeting, Malia went to each teacher individually to collect writing samples and made enough copies for everyone. At 12:40, the official meeting start time, only Malia, Kevin, and Edith had arrived in Malia's room for the meeting, so they chatted informally until Lanna came four minutes later.

As Lanna sat down, Malia began, "I'm not sure where Jasmine is, but we have a packed agenda. Is it OK with everyone if we go ahead and get started?" Malia passed around the packets of essays she had prepared. "How would you like to go through these?"

While everyone flipped through the packet, Lanna suggested, "Can we take a few minutes and just read them?"

Malia responded favorably, "OK. After that, let's read one of the essays from the packet and talk about how we would score that essay for each trait on the rubric." Jasmine arrived while everyone was reading. "I'm sorry I'm late. I had an important parent phone call about a behavior problem. I've been trying to reach her for a couple of days and she finally called back."

A couple of minutes later, Malia selected the third essay in the packet for the team to review. It was not the best essay, but it was clearly not the worst, either. The team spent 15 minutes analyzing the essay trait by trait.

Jasmine, whose class of 15 students included five with IEPs, lamented more than once that the essay they had chosen to review reflected a much higher level of writing than most of her class had. "The kids in my room can't even get a sentence down. I don't know how they are supposed to write a five-paragraph essay on the State Test. There's no way they'll be able to do it."

Lanna empathized. "I know. I've spent two weeks just trying to get them to write a paragraph." This wasn't actually true—Lanna's class was actually doing very well and was just where they should be at this time of the year, but she wanted to be sympathetic to Jasmine, who was clearly struggling. At the same time, the team didn't seem to want to spend time solving Jasmine's problems.

"Then you're way ahead of me," said Jasmine. "In my room we're still working on sentences. Subject. Verb. I'm not kidding. Have you seen these essays?" Jasmine held up her stack of benchmark essays and dropped them on the table with exasperation.

Malia let the essay conversation continue about 10 minutes longer than the allotted time, owing to the late start and what she believed could be a productive discussion. She brought the conversation to a close by saying, "Even though we only got through one essay today, we had a really good conversation and that should help us when scoring the rest of our students' essays. We'll look at more next week. Could we say that for next week, everyone brings the resources they use to teach persuasive writing? Be sure and bring enough copies for everyone."

They followed the remainder of the agenda efficiently, but reflecting later, Malia felt frustrated by the late start and the nagging feeling that they didn't get much accomplished. In addition, parts of the essay conversation suggested that rather than holding common definitions, the team had a range of interpretations of the traits of good writing. Malia suspected this had a lot to do with each teacher's experience and expertise. She thought Jasmine was probably the weakest while Lanna, a popular and charismatic teacher, had won a composition award in college.

In addition, last week two different parents had confided in Malia that they had concerns about their child's progress in Edith's class. As a parent, Malia sympathized with the parents' concerns about a first-year teacher, but she also remembered her first year and felt a sense of duty to help Edith along the Writer's Workshop continuum. But as much as Malia wanted to help Edith, she had accepted a student teacher to mentor and couldn't spare much time outside of the weekly meetings. Once again, Kevin was withdrawn during the entire meeting, so Malia had no way to gauge where Kevin stood with writing instruction.

She shifted to thinking about the following week's already crowded agenda. The math coach would be back to discuss a schoolwide problem-solving initiative, and they needed to schedule time for an update from the Instructional Leadership Team. Plus, they needed to work out the details of College Day. For College Day, teachers planned that students would research colleges and make pennants of the ones they hoped to attend for a hallway bulletin board. Teachers would wear T-shirts from their alma maters, and students from various local colleges would be guest speakers in the morning. She worried they couldn't possibly have enough time after the math coach's presentation to spend on scoring more essays and sharing writing resources.

Although Malia was an experienced teacher, and excellent by all accounts, this was her first year at the 5th-grade level and she was hopeful others on the team could provide her with some resources for teaching persuasive writing. Three of the teachers had taught 5th-grade last year. While typing up the agenda, which left only 15 minutes at the end for continuing the work started today, Malia decided that she couldn't wait until next week's meeting if she planned to stay on target to get through persuasive letters in two weeks and move on to biographies. She would ask Lanna for materials after school. Lanna seemed always to be up to date with her work and on top of each problem raised by the team.

## October 8: Crowded Agendas

The next week's meeting was again dominated by the math coach facilitating a long review of extended response items, and

Ms. Cunningham, the principal, stopped in to give an overview of a program she was considering for next year. She needed feedback from the teachers to determine whether to move forward. Since the math student review went over its allotted time, and the principal interjected with an unplanned segment, this meeting, like previous ones, ran long. With just 15 minutes left, Malia asked, "Lanna, can we postpone the Instructional Leadership Team update until next week so we can get to event planning for College Day?"

"Yes, it looks like we have to," agreed Lanna. Malia and Lanna were both disappointed, realizing that this would also mean skipping over the continuation of the persuasive writing conversation from last week. Malia said, "I don't know about you, but I don't know if I can look at any more student work today. Those math extended response items were long and intense. Does anyone object to pushing the review of more student essays to next week as well?"

Jasmine was surprised. "Student essays? We were supposed to bring more student essays? I thought we were supposed to bring packets of things we use to teach persuasive writing, so I brought these." She passed around 12-page packets of worksheets.

"That's what I had already prepared," interjected Lanna, who indicated a stack of manila folders and began to pass them out. In them she had compiled various graphic organizers, a couple of lesson plans, and a list of websites.

"Right. Yes, definitely pass those out. Does anyone else have anything?" Malia said. Kevin shook his head. Edith, who often boasted about her collection of instructional resources, had neglected to bring them.

Malia clarified, "We were going to share some resources and also look at student essays, but we don't have time to discuss writing at all because College Day is next Thursday and we have to get things organized for setup, cleanup, schedules, and the bulletin board. We have about 10 minutes left."

Kevin listened as the team quickly made plans and assigned roles for next week. His mind wandered a bit, which he allowed, knowing Jasmine would send out a detailed schedule that would tell him everything he needed to know about College Day the day before it happened. He was annoyed at having to listen to Jim go on and on for so long, especially after having had him observe Kevin's math lesson earlier in the day. Kevin didn't like to be watched teaching in the first place, and felt that Jim's comments had not been as kind as they could have been. In addition, he had already heard the principal's spiel about the new program because she had invited him to the original meeting.

As for teaching persuasive writing, after the last meeting Kevin had called a friend of his family's, a well-respected teacher at another school, and asked him to point him in the right direction for working on grammar skills, which he noticed were atrocious in his students' benchmark essays. He was particularly pleased that he and Malia had begun to collaborate more on projects with their classes. He found that if he stayed a couple of days behind Malia, she was more than happy to pass resources his way and show him examples of what her students had done. As a third-year teacher, Kevin found he benefited from Malia's experience. His mind snapped back to the present, and he nodded that he'd be happy to set up chairs in the library before school. He also offered to hang pennants in the hallway, given that he stands a lanky head and shoulders above the rest of the team. He could tell from Malia's slump and grumpy face that she was getting tired of leading meetings, and he began to dread his turn in two weeks.

## February 4: Finding a Rhythm

After winter break, the team agreed to push back the start time of the weekly meeting by 10 minutes to give team members time to heat up lunch and make a quick parent phone call, and to accommodate long transitions to specials. From Jasmine's perspective, meetings had become so busy and teachers were inundated with so much work that no one really minded making them a few minutes shorter. By Jasmine's second turn at facilitation, she felt the group had become better at owning their agendas and managing "outsiders." When the speech pathologist stopped in during this meeting and expressed that she would like to meet with the team a few times to address some ways to use technology to help students who struggle with executive function, Jasmine responded, "Could you clarify what you would like to accomplish and how long you would need?"

"Sure," responded the therapist, "I was thinking I could share some ways to use technology to help students who struggle with executive function. I also wanted to share some graphic organizers."

"That would be great. How long would that take?" Jasmine asked.

"Maybe 45 minutes in a couple of upcoming meetings."

"Our agendas are packed the next few weeks, but how about a 30-minute slot in two weeks, and another two weeks after that? Would that work for you?"

"I would really like more time, but if that's all you can give, I'll make it work."

After this brief interruption, the meeting continued following the agenda efficiently. Jasmine felt particularly satisfied when the team's work was cut and dry, when the current day's agenda could be checked off, and when next week's agenda was laid out well in advance. She relished the feeling that the 5th-grade ship was sailing smoothly.

## May 4: Maximum Efficiency

As Edith was about to start the meeting, Jasmine jumped in. "I know this isn't on the agenda, but did everyone see the email from 4th grade about when they reserved the field for Field Day? I think if we are going to do a Field Day we should plan it before any other grades reserve facilities and schedule their times." With nods of agreement, the team began planning the last big event of the year. In under 30 minutes, the team calendared the event, invited—and confirmed!—a local lacrosse team to do a complimentary clinic with the kids, reserved the field, and communicated their plans to the principal, who passed through and approved them on the spot.

To Edith, this felt like a good use of their collective time. It made the whole team look good. She thought back to October, when the principal gave them kudos several times for making College Day a success. When the teachers realized how much students thrived on these special days and enjoyed interacting with the other 5th-grade classes, they made a point of creating other opportunities for students to interact across classrooms. The 5th-grade Halloween party involved making each classroom a rotation station for making crafts, frosting cupcakes, playing ghost tag, and listening to scary stories. "Reading and Math Across the Nashton Days" brought parents and community members to the school to see literacy and math instruction in action.

All of these involved the coordination of volunteers, refreshments, activities, photography, parent communication, and all other variables and details. Even though this wasn't one of the original goals of the team, Edith was proud of these accomplishments because in each instance, it felt like they were truly working together to make something good happen for students. They were getting positive support from the principal and the team's highly visible successes were acknowledged in the school.

Malia, however, remained frustrated with the team process. In the course of planning special events and accommodating the rotation of visitors, the monthly curriculum map idea had fallen by the wayside. So had another of the early plans—a weekly rotation where one team member would be responsible for bringing one resource to share with the team.

## May 18: Reflections

Throughout the year, the team had periodically engaged in 30-minute team reflection sessions called "tune-ups." As the year came to a close, individual team members shared many things that had worked well. They also shared their major challenges. Malia confessed her ongoing frustration with the team's process.

"Our weekly meetings are hit or miss," she complained. "We started out with three goals: collaborative planning for social studies, looking at student work, and collecting resources to share with one another. Social studies planning comes up once or twice a month, but the conversation lasts only about 10 minutes here and there. At this point, that's OK since this year the state scrapped plans to test 5th graders in social studies due to its budget crisis. But looking at student work—other than the math reviews led by Jim—essentially also happens just once or twice month, by 5 to 10 minutes of informally passing around some student artifacts while describing a lesson that went really well. Only on a few occasions did we spend more than 30 minutes looking at student writing samples. Did we learn anything from that?"

Edith answered, "But we have so much else to do, and I feel like we are really good at some things, like planning events."

"Well, yes—we're really good at planning events," Malia replied, "but that's just logistics. We haven't written a single lesson plan together. How could we have channeled our 'magic touch' for event planning into planning units or collecting and sharing teaching resources? I don't feel like we've achieved the deep collaboration we envisioned at the beginning of the year."

Lanna agreed, adding, "Things just seem to take us too long and we get sidetracked. Remember last month, when we experimented with that protocol for providing a teacher with feedback on tailoring instruction to meet a specific need evidenced in a piece of student writing? When we did that, I was really amazed at the amount of quality, focused feedback we could provide each other. And we did that in just 12 minutes. Why haven't we been able to do more of those?"

*********************************************************************

## CASE 2—Guide to Analysis

### Surface Collaboration or Dynamic Interdependence?

**Key Concepts: Mutual Accountability, Leadership, Task Focus**

This teaching case explores the work of a teacher team struggling with the norms established by the traditional culture of schools and teaching, and the lack of team leadership.

---

### Your Facilitator

**Wait!** It would be very, very difficult to gain any appreciable benefit from your expenditure of time and energy by attempting to conduct this analysis and its series of exercises without a facilitator. You *need* to appoint someone (it can be a team member) as a designated facilitator. This is not necessarily your team leader. This person will not be your "boss." But this person *will* be responsible for:

- Copying and distributing to all participants copies of the Case and Case Analysis and all handouts
- Organizing role-plays (appointing time keepers and observers, where indicated)
- Moving the process along and staying on track

**Psst! Facilitators:** Read all the activity directions as if they applied to you.
**Psst! Team members:** You, too.

---

### Materials Needed

Enough printed copies of the following to distribute to all team members:

- The Case and Guide to Analysis
- Worksheet—Action Planning and Goal Setting
- Chart paper and markers

Full-size reproducibles of worksheets and handouts are available on the companion CD-ROM.

---

NOTE: In all Case Analyses presented in this book, we have suggested (strongly) that all meetings need a facilitator. And in a box at the beginning of each Case Analysis—such as that found below—we provide tasks for the facilitator. However, in this Case Analysis we have gone a step further by appending a Facilitator's Guide for those facilitators who might want to gain new skills in meeting facilitation (and where team norms permit), to guide the very beginning of the Case Analysis sections: Establish the Facts of the Case and Case Analysis Questions. We hope this is helpful.

## A. Analyzing the Case

### Step 1: Read the Case (20 minutes)

Distribute the teaching case, and have all team members read it through, underlining or highlighting pieces of information that they think are significant to understanding the case.

### Step 2: Establish the Facts of the Case (10–15 minutes)

As a whole group, make a list on chart paper of the significant *facts* of the teaching case. Include what you know about each team member. Try to withhold judgment, inferences, or evaluation, and come to agreement about what happened.

> **Very Important:** When we say *facts* we mean just that—you must stick to the facts ONLY. There is a huge temptation, when analyzing other teachers' interactions, for teachers to voice *opinions* such as "She talks too much during the meeting" or "She's not a very good teacher." These are not *facts*, and negative comments such as these are counterproductive. The group should consciously steer away from such comments and instead either ask questions such as "Does she allow other voices to be heard?" or offer statements based on *evidence* such as "She says _____, but then she does _____."
>
> If teachers feel they will be attacked for opening up their practice for other teachers to view, they simply will not do it. Making practice public is a risky proposition, and part of your challenge as a case analyst is to pretend that the teachers you are talking about are right there in the room with you.

### Step 3: Case Analysis Questions (20 minutes)

Discuss the following questions. For each question, identify the evidence that leads to your response. (You do not have to address every question.)

*About the Team*

- How would you define the team's overarching purpose?
- What are the team's strengths?
- How would you describe how this team works together?
- How and when do team members rely on one another, if at all?

- What factors (structural, cultural, or interpersonal) affect this team's level of collaboration?
- What supports could have helped the team reach its goals?

### About the Individuals

- What could Malia, Lanna, or other members of the team have done to be more proactive with the team?
- What is it like for Edith to be a new teacher, learning to teach, on this team?
- How would you react to Kevin's behavior?

### About the School

- What is the appropriate role for the principal in this situation? (How might she have best supported the success of this team?)
- What understandings about teaching and learning to teach undergird the culture of this school?

## B. Exploring the Dilemma—A Mutual Accountability Activity

### Step 1: Read the Following Section (5 minutes)

Our definition of *mutual accountability* is drawn from the work of Katzenbach and Smith,[5] which proposes that mutual accountability in teams is

> the sincere promises we make to ourselves and others, promises that underpin two critical aspects of teams: commitment and trust. . . . Mutual promises and accountability cannot be coerced any more than people can be made to trust one another. Nevertheless, mutual accountability does tend to grow as a natural counterpart to the development of team purpose, performance goals, and approach. Accountability, then, provides a useful litmus test of the quality of a team's purpose and approach. Groups that lack mutual accountability for performance have not shaped a common purpose and approach that can sustain them as a team.

We would add to this definition:

> In teams with mutual accountability, team members assume responsibility for team tasks and have the *authority* to hold each other responsible for tasks they have assumed.

## Step 2: Decision Points (15 minutes)

An opportunity to revise history: Invent alternative moves for the individuals on the team.

- Review the case with a partner, and underline where the decision points are in the case.
- Are there any points during the process where decisions were made that could have been made differently in order to have achieved mutual accountability in the team?

## Step 3: Role-Play (15 minutes)

Explore whether a strategic intervention has the potential to improve accountability within the team.

- What were the "sticky" issues in the case?
- Choose one of the sticky issues and role-play a possible intervention that any of the teachers might make at any of the decision points you've highlighted. Choose at least three participants to play the teachers in this role-play. The other participants will be observers. Does someone emerge as the teacher leader?

# C. Reflect and Connect

A research study on teacher teams[6] revealed that in each of the teams studied, teachers were able to hold each other accountable for *noninstructional* tasks. That is, they could successfully complete administrative and logistical tasks necessary for the team to function as a unit within the school. However, when individuals attempted to move the team toward *sustained work on instructional tasks*, there was an observable reluctance among the teachers to perform tasks efficiently and at a high level, and an unwillingness for teachers to hold each other accountable for the effective completion of those instructional tasks.

## Step 1: Take on the Role of Edith, Jasmine, Lanna, or Kevin (5 minutes)

Role-playing one of these four characters, how might you respond to the following?

"We're really good at planning events," Malia replied, "but that's just logistics. We haven't written a single lesson plan together. How could we have channeled our 'magic touch' for event planning into planning units or collecting and sharing teaching resources? I don't feel like we've achieved the deep collaboration we envisioned at the beginning of the year."

## Step 2: Apply the Analysis to Your Team (15 minutes)

Using any insights gained from Step 1, facilitate a conversation around the following questions.

- Why might it be easier for team members to be mutually accountable for logistical and managerial tasks than for instructional tasks?
- When thinking about your own team, do team members appear to better understand the more immediate, concrete, and visible consequences of not completing tasks such as scheduling field trips or setting up bulletin boards? If so, why do you think this is the case?
- How might your team develop ways to hold one another other accountable for the completion of both instructional and non-instructional tasks, while acknowledging the difficulty of mutual accountability?

## D. What Do We Do Now? (40 minutes)

Here's what you could do next to make your team as mutually accountable as it *could* be:

1. Collaboratively create a teaming action plan, prioritizing one or two goals that you plan to address over the next few months.

2. For each goal, try to answer the following questions. (Do not omit this step! It is crucial to realizing your goals.)

   - What would be different in your team if you made progress?
   - What gets in the way of progress? Cultural issues? Structural issues? Other?
   - What strategies might you use to make progress?

3. After discussing the questions above, complete the Worksheet—Action Planning and Goal Setting (Figure C2.1).

**Figure C2.1   Worksheet—Action Planning and Goal Setting**

Team: _____

Date: _____

| What is the goal? | What are the action steps? | Who is responsible for each step? | When will each action be complete? | Notes |
|---|---|---|---|---|
|  |  |  |  |  |
|  |  |  |  |  |
|  |  |  |  |  |
|  |  |  |  |  |

# A Facilitator's Guide

### Establishing the Facts of the Case and
### Examining Case Analysis Questions

## Step 1: Important Facts of the Case

- Five 5th-grade teachers:
    - Malia       10-year veteran
    - Jasmine    fourth-year teacher, also dyslexic
    - Edith       retired from business, just graduated from district program
    - Lanna       second-year teacher
    - Kevin       doesn't say anything during meetings, calls his friend for help, dependent on other teachers to do his work, types notes during meetings and emails them later
    - Jim          math coach

- First year for new principal
- Team meets 90 minutes a week
- Work on curriculum maps started at beginning of year but seems to get lost
- There isn't a team leader, so roles rotate among the five people
- Principal has mandated that Jim come to team meetings twice a month
- Team can't always stick to agenda
- Team has norms: remain positive, stay focused, work efficiently, handle conflicts
- Kevin is just sitting there at every meeting and they don't call him on it, though they agreed to handle conflict
- Originally they set out to look at student work, then they planned to do curriculum mapping

---

NOTE: This is a guide, using Case 2 as a model, that facilitators might develop for the other cases in the book. By creating such a guide, facilitators give themselves an opportunity to play out the scenario of the case presentation in advance of teaching it. Such an activity can help provide facilitators with a better understanding of the "Facts of the Case" and "Examining the Case Analysis Questions," allow them to mentally check off points when they are made by participants, suggest important points that might have been missed, and push the participants to think more deeply about particular elements of the case.

- Team is good at planning events
- The further the team got away from their purpose, the further away they got from staying on task
- It appears that teachers on the team lack agency

---

NOTE: There are many more possible answers.

## Step 2: Examine Case Analysis Questions

- How would you define the team's overarching purpose?
  - Develop social studies curriculum for all members of the team
  - Learn about looking at student work
  - Align curriculum by mapping the curriculum

- What are the team's strengths?
  - Veteran teacher with excellent teaching
  - A group of young new teachers who are eager, have a range of experience, and for the most part are not brand-new to the grade level
  - Team has collectively decided upon their goals
  - Predetermined team roles are rotated
  - Commitment to do the best for their students

- What challenges does the team face?
  - Difference in strengths of teachers
  - Inability to communicate their true opinions about each other (e.g., teachers have opinions of the teacher with the special ed kids, and they're unable to confront her)
  - Specialists who arrive late, making teachers late for meetings
  - Other priorities that take precedence over "team work" (e.g., phone calls from parents)
  - Meetings start late, agenda may or may not be completed, items are given short shrift

- What were the obstacles that prevented the team from reaching its original goals?
  - There is a constant stream of specialists (e.g., math coach arrives once or twice a month, interrupting the flow of the team's agenda; speech pathologist)
  - School's special events that take time and energy and are praised more than anything this team does with its curriculum
  - Poor communication among the teachers

- o Different standards for student achievement
- o Teachers didn't know how to create a leader out of a facilitator
- o Most veteran teacher didn't feel that she could or should be the facilitator

- How might you describe the way the team operated?
  - o Teachers function individually in their own classrooms with intermittent collaborative work on noninstructional tasks
  - o Efficiency with logistics; everything else gets short shrift (e.g., curriculum maps)
  - o No initial goals are realized

- Are there indications that the teamwork is shaping the quality of what the teachers do with students in their classrooms? If not, why not?
  - o No indication; they complain about the person with the special ed kids, but no one helps her
  - o No one seems to learn from the expertise of the veteran, highly celebrated teacher
  - o The new teachers are worried that they may or may not be doing things right (e.g., Lanna never really learns how to do the essay; she's frustrated)

- What supports could have helped the team reach its goals?
  - o One teacher taking the lead
  - o Principal support could have made sure that specialists arrived on time and important instructional items were addressed

### About the Principal

- What could the principal be doing in the long term to support all teacher teams?
  - o Principal participates in the learning of what makes a powerful team—learning team skills, the value of teams, so that that she can be an educational leader in team development and the work of the team.
  - o Principal helps teachers become accountable for their time— that they learn to function with their own authority.

### Decision Points

- Examining this case, are there any points during the process where decisions were made that could have been made differently in order to have achieved a more favorable outcome? Mark these places in the case for discussion. For example:

o To address the issue of team leadership, they took the most veteran teacher's suggestion—although with some initial resistance—that they rotate the roles of facilitator, note-taker, and timekeeper on a monthly basis so that each team member would have a chance to practice facilitating throughout the year.

o Jasmine called the meeting to order about 10 minutes late because the art teacher didn't show up to take her kids on time. Edith was heating up her lunch in the microwave, and Malia was hanging "All About Me" posters in the hallway.

o Most notably, they hadn't even had time to work on their curriculum map for October, which was just two weeks away.

o "This is not the first time Jasmine has complained about what her special ed students can't do," Malia thought to herself. "That's unfortunate coming from someone with a learning disability who has overcome many challenges herself. Is she just frustrated, or does she really believe they can't do it?"

o Malia felt frustrated by the late start and the nagging feeling that they didn't get much accomplished.

o Malia decided that she couldn't wait until next week's meeting if she planned to stay on target to get through persuasive letters in two weeks and move on to biographies. She would ask Lanna for materials after school.

o Student essays? We were supposed to bring more student essays? I thought we were supposed to bring packets of things we use to teach persuasive writing, so I brought these." She passed around 12-page packets of worksheets.

### About the Individuals

• What could Malia have done to be more proactive with the team?

o Instead of expressing frustration intermittently throughout the year, she could have expressed her frustration earlier and made the suggestion that she take the lead. She knew early on that it didn't matter that she was new to this grade level, that it wasn't the grade level that mattered, and that she had pedagogical expertise.

o Did she need more authority to do this?

o Was there a role for the principal?

o Without principal support would the other teachers have vetoed this suggestion?

- What is it like for Edith to be a new teacher, learning to teach, on this team?
  - o No one volunteers to help her.
  - o She appears isolated, defensive (e.g., expresses certainty that her kids cannot do the work, walls herself off, doesn't ask for help).

# CASE 3. Can't Follow the Leader

Key Concept: Building Leadership Capacity for Teacher Teams

## Reflections on a Team Meeting

Staring at the blank screen on her home computer, Karen Monk thought back to the 6th-grade team meeting on March 11. While things had run smoothly for the first half hour, Karen recalled feeling as if her "leadership voice" was heard more often during that time than those of the three 6th-grade teachers who were present. The team had accomplished its first two objectives: analyzing students' recent social studies work with conflict and reviewing details about afterschool prep sessions for the upcoming statewide exam. But Karen wondered if they had accomplished these goals because the team worked smoothly together or because her strong focus on making sure the discussion was productive and efficient was stifling the ideas and contributions of team members, Laurie, Stephanie, and Amelia. They had been able to move forward at a steady pace, but Objectives 3 and 4, completing the month's Instructional Calendar and discussing the details of the next week's lesson plans, were not reached or even talked about.

Reflecting on why this could have happened, Karen recalled that she had purposefully left the last 25 minutes of the one-hour meeting open so that the three teachers could speak in a more relaxed and unconfined manner about their upcoming instructional lessons. Her hope was that this would allow the team members the opportunity to naturally facilitate a productive discussion—especially Laurie, the most veteran teacher and now officially the new team leader (this was a "transitional" year). Hopefully, Karen would gradually pull back and be a resource for the team instead of the "driver" of the meetings.

The grant that had provided Karen with the position of literacy coordinator and team leader of the 6th-grade was about to run out, and she knew that she would not be there to perform that function next year. She wondered how she could directly and indirectly help build the team members' leadership capacities during their common planning sessions. Could she leave the meeting wide open and allow the teachers to talk about whatever they wished? Could she ask Laurie to plan this week's agenda and assign roles to the other teachers? As she rose to get herself a cup of tea, Karen knew she was in for an evening of thinking deeply about this problem.

## Ravenswood Middle School

Located just outside a medium-size southwestern city, Ravenswood Middle School is a Grade 6–8 school with a 500-student body that is racially, culturally, educationally, and socioeconomically diverse: 49% African American, 35% Latino, and 16% Caucasian. Over half the student population receives free or reduced-priced lunch. The school prides itself on recruiting and retaining excellent teachers who strive to improve their practice in the service of student learning.

To accomplish this, Ravenswood's principal, Margo Asante, provided grade-level teams with numerous opportunities for collaboration throughout the week to discuss their benchmark skills, instructional calendars, instructional action plans, and lesson plans in a structured and detailed manner. While the agendas that were used and actions that took place during these one-hour meetings were flexible, Principal Asante strove to ensure that team meetings were consistently rooted in the process of collaborative inquiry.[7]

Principal Asante's goal was that teams of teachers would eventually be able to lead themselves through the collaborative inquiry process, and she understood that for teachers to become efficient and effective collaborators they needed time and support. Four years ago, with funding from a grant, she had created the position of half-time literacy coordinator/team leader for the 6th-, 7th-, and 8th-grade language arts teams. The coordinator/leader was to work individually with each grade-level team to analyze data, plan curriculum, develop lessons, and improve instruction. Knowing that she needed an experienced and personable teacher to take on these roles, Principal Asante looked to her own staff to find someone with the curricular expertise and leadership background that was needed to be effective in these roles. She looked no further than Karen Monk.

## Karen Monk

With six years as a classroom teacher and experience as an English Department chair in an Oregon middle school, Karen had come to Ravenswood with a great resume and strong recommendations. Her previous work had given her the background to create and revise curriculum, mentor teachers, and lead teacher teams. Now in her fourth year at Ravenswood, Karen held numerous positions while continuing to do what she loved most: teaching 7th grade.

Karen created agendas, crafted meeting objectives, and accumulated student data. While leading team meetings and coaching teachers through the collaborative inquiry process was at the center of her work, Karen did her best to utilize the "gradual release of responsibility model"[8] with teachers she worked with so there could be a smooth transition to new leadership on each team. Karen's plan was to "model" leadership in the beginning of the year and then, when the new leader was appointed, "provide guided practice by co-planning and co-facilitating the move toward independent team leadership." The goal was that team leaders would eventually plan and implement team meetings and functions without her leadership.

Karen was pleased with the success she had achieved so far with the 7th- and 8th-grade teams, but her thoughts had been preoccupied with the persistent struggles that engaged the 6th-grade language arts team and the fact that she had yet to fully release the team to work independently. She hoped her work with the team was helping them grow and improve, but she was also aware that her strong leadership style might be hindering the team's "organic" development.

## The 6th-Grade Language Arts Team

At Ravenswood, 6th grade was seen as a vitally important year. While the students received instruction in science, social studies, Spanish, the performing arts, and physical education, the bulk of class time was dedicated to building literacy and mathematical skills. With Laurie, who had taught at Ravenswood for six years; Stephanie, who was new to Ravenswood but had taught for four years prior; and Amelia, who was completely new to classroom teaching, the 6th-grade language arts team's makeup was somewhat different than other grade-level teams Karen had worked with. Karen felt that the team had a steep learning curve because only Laurie was familiar with Ravenswood's collaborative inquiry process, while the other teachers were much more comfortable with the "autonomous, closed-door" model.

Karen was pleased that these three teachers shared a commitment to hard work and a passion for their students and the school. The team rarely bickered or had confrontations, and this allowed her the opportunity to be open and honest with them about their work together and their independent work in the classroom. Karen, Laurie,

Stephanie, and Amelia had developed a relationship of respect, trust, and a shared vision for their work together, but Karen had doubts about whether these teachers could work productively without her leadership and guidance.

Though she had large amounts of exposure to the members of the 6th-grade team, Karen's goal of gradually releasing them to more independent work took more time than she had envisioned. This meant she had to devote a good portion of the team's common planning time to basic logistics, dealing with questions like "Who will make the Reader's Workshop copies for next week?"

## Laurie Willemier

Laurie had been a 6th-grade teacher at Ravenswood for six years. While, in her own words, it "took two to three years" to fully grasp the importance of collaboration and utilizing data, Laurie now believed the time she spent working with other teachers was essential to her growth as a teacher and her impact on students' learning.

Since by title and experience she was the lead teacher of the 6th-grade team, Laurie had worked both formally and informally with Karen throughout the year to plan and create each week's meeting agendas and monthly retreats. At the beginning of the year Laurie and Karen had co-facilitated these meetings, but after the first month Laurie realized this was not working out as successfully as they had wanted. Stephanie and Amelia were new to Ravenswood, its curriculum, and the collaborative process, and Laurie believed her focus as lead teacher should not be on facilitating meetings, but on being the best teacher and planner she could be in order to help Stephanie and Amelia do their best.

"Having to analyze data and teach a whole team how to do the collaborative inquiry process when they're struggling with it—although I think they're really working hard—this is a real challenge for me," said Laurie during one of her sessions with Karen. "Being both a facilitator and a participant . . . I don't know, is this making things more nonproductive for the team?"

Laurie wondered what would happen next year when Karen, who was "so strong in facilitation and leadership, but also very strong in content knowledge," wouldn't be present. She worried about this because she had witnessed and participated in numerous meetings where Karen "stepped back" or was not present, and these meetings were noticeably different than those planned, facilitated, and orchestrated by Karen. Laurie believed the "meetings are still productive, but people relax and we talk more about the day-to-day specifics than the deliverables, data, and larger goals that we are supposed to talk about." But while she knew and believed that she should be the one to keep the team focused when Karen eventually stepped back, she continued to struggle with her role as invested teacher and team leader. "It is hard to transition from colleague and friend to leader—to be an invested participant and leader" she admitted, and wondered if the team could ever be as "professional and productive" with her as their sole leader.

## Stephanie Armundsen

Although she had bought into the collaborative inquiry process like Laurie, Stephanie wished the 6th-grade team had more opportunity to discuss their day-to-day work: "When Karen is not there it becomes less focused on data and a bit more about practical talk, more about our day-to-day work, but this can be a huge help for us because it gives us some time to get into specifics." Stephanie really appreciated that Karen had tried to accommodate the team's need for what she referred to as "practical talk," and she acknowledged that Karen's leadership had helped the team's production and growth. "Karen always plans the agendas, and it is always very tightly organized. At the same time, I do think that maybe leadership could be more shared."

## Amelia Joutras

In her first full-time teaching position, Amelia believed the work she completed with Karen and her fellow team members was essential to her teaching practice: "Our team's work is critical to my work in the classroom. The entire curriculum that I teach, almost all of the lesson activities are commonly taught in all of the 6th-grade classrooms. We essentially teach the same curriculum, which is based on the analytical planning and work that we do together."

From the outset Amelia "has always taken the back seat on literacy plans" because she used Laurie's curriculum. This absence of responsibility was purposeful because Principal Asante, Karen, and Laurie wanted Amelia to focus first and foremost on the work she did in her classroom with her students. To help Amelia, Karen observed and coached her on English, social studies, and Reader's Workshop instruction, while Laurie co-taught English with Amelia twice a week. Amelia appreciated this consistent support because "at the beginning of the year, and still now to some extent, I feel I have the least amount of experience as a literacy teacher."

Because work on the team had been "critical" to her teaching and professional growth throughout the year, Amelia had valued the structure and productivity resulting from Karen's leadership.

## 6th-Grade Team Meeting, March 11

At 1:07 p.m., Karen sat at the table in the library with copies of the meeting agenda, the 6th-grade team's current action plan, and Ravenswood's list of essential literacy skills in piles in front of her. As she got up from her chair to project March's Instructional Calendar on the overhead, Laurie, Stephanie, and Amelia walked into the library and greeted Karen with an enthusiastic "hello."

Karen quickly walked the teachers through the day's agenda: "As you can see we are going to take a few minutes at the beginning to go over some logistics, then spend around 20 minutes doing some data analysis and adjusting the Instructional Calendar for March, then you all will have some time to talk about what is coming up in English and Reader's Workshop. Sound good?" The other members of the team all nodded and Karen immediately jumped in and reminded them about the next few weeks' afterschool prep sessions for the statewide exams. She then led the team in a 20-minute analysis and conversation about student data the team had brought to the meeting on "identifying conflict in the text." Prompting all the team members to participate, and chiming in with supporting comments, instructional suggestions, and constructive feedback, Karen helped the team accomplish the meeting's second objective.

Feeling as though they had gotten through the first two objectives of the meeting, Karen paused the group at 1:35 by asking, "Would it be more beneficial for you to talk some more about specifics and finalize some of next week's and the following week's plans? I'll sit back and be a resource, and you all can facilitate."

The teachers nodded, and Laurie and Amelia said, "That would be great."

Stephanie asked Karen, "Would now be a good time for me to take five minutes to talk to Laurie and Amelia about a new student council I'm working on creating for next year?" Karen said, "OK." Stephanie asked Laurie and Amelia if they could think of any students from their classes whom they would want to nominate. The two started writing down names, and for five minutes the three teachers talked about who should and should not be nominated from the 6th grade.

Noticing the clock, Karen walked over to the table, picked up copies of the Instructional Calendar, and handed them to the three teachers, saying, "So let's make sure that you all really talk about the particular skills and how you are going to work them into the lesson plans for the next two weeks. I'll let you take the lead on this since you are knee deep in it right now. Let's start on the second page of the document."

Amelia started off and asked, "What are we going to do with conflict in social studies? Are we going to do that this week or should we stay with Westward Expansion?"

"My kids aren't done with Westward Expansion, but I can design a wrap-up lesson that involves conflict," replied Stephanie.

Feeling as though Amelia's questions were too specific, Karen, from behind the librarian's desk and the computer, asked, "Could you do an activity from the ranchers' perspective—what the ranchers were wrestling with? What makes the conflict more real for them?"

"Yeah," said Stephanie. "We could possibly have them role-play what is going on with that. Will we do skimming for author's purpose before that?"

"In my class it seems to me the focus should be topic sentences, text structures, then author's purpose," offered Amelia.

"There are lots of strategies for talking about author's purpose. I've been using a lot of previewing and summarizing for that in my class," said Laurie. Then, taking a few minutes, while Amelia and Stephanie listened, Laurie described how today's English lesson had gone for her students.

"Yeah, those are good for finding specific evidence," declared Stephanie. "But what else should we really push them to look for, besides headings?" There was a slight pause.

Karen put forward a question: "Maybe it should be more about previewing and less about skimming the whole document?"

Laurie replied, "Um . . . yeah, we need to think about the difference between skimming and previewing. Doing more modeling of skimming and practicing of skimming would be good."

Aware that they only had five minutes before the bell rang, Karen asked Laurie, "Will you quickly go over some things you want Stephanie and Amelia to know about English and Reader's Workshop?"

"OK, we are going to introduce types of conflicts," responded Laurie, "with maybe a think-pair-share. I also have a conflict card game that we could use, and we could role-play types of conflict. The first days of the week will be different types of conflict." Laurie then proceeded to describe role-plays she had used in the past, and Amelia concurred, saying, "Those sound great!"

Moving toward the table, Karen added, "The third lesson on the Instructional Calendar looks like it could be a summary of the characters' conflict and bring in some real-life examples." Laurie nodded, and the teachers picked up their materials when the bell rang. Karen thanked everyone for their time, and Laurie, Stephanie, and Amelia thanked Karen as they moved out of the library and headed back to their classrooms. Laurie paused before leaving, wondering if she had been contributing enough.

## Ready to Be Released?

With a cup of tea in hand, Karen sat back down at her computer, ready to create the agenda for next week's meeting. She believed that creating an agenda with a combination of focused and structured work and open discussion would allow the team to be efficient, while also giving the teachers an opportunity to talk about their daily instruction. She had hoped that by leading the beginning of the meeting and then serving as an observer and supporter, she would be putting gradual release into action.

She agonized whether doing a more deliberate job of striking a balance between leading and supporting would allow her to remove fully the "leadership mask" she had been wearing with the 6th-grade team since the beginning of the year. Would she be able to take off the mask permanently, or would she have to put it on and take it off depending on Laurie's leadership proficiency? As she struck the first letter on her keyboard, Karen hoped she could soon conclude the release process with Laurie, Stephanie, and Amelia.

\*\*\*\*\*\*\*\*\*\*\*\*\*\*\*\*\*\*\*\*\*\*\*\*\*\*\*\*\*\*\*\*\*\*\*\*\*\*\*\*\*\*\*\*\*\*\*\*\*\*\*\*\*\*\*\*\*\*\*\*\*\*\*\*\*\*\*\*\*\*\*\*\*\*\*\*\*

## CASE 3—Guide to Analysis

### Can't Follow the Leader

**Key Concept: Building Leadership Capacity for Teacher Teams**

This case addresses the issue of developing leadership capacity and transferring team leadership to a team member.

---

**Your Facilitator**

**Wait!** It would be very, very difficult to gain any appreciable benefit from your expenditure of time and energy by attempting to conduct this analysis and its series of exercises without a facilitator. You *need* to appoint someone (it can be a team member) as a designated facilitator. This is not necessarily your team leader. This person will not be your "boss." But this person *will* be responsible for:

- Copying and distributing to all participants copies of the Case and Case Analysis and all handouts
- Organizing role-plays (appointing time keepers and observers, where indicated)
- Moving the process along and staying on track

**Psst! Facilitators:** Read all the activity directions as if they applied to you.
**Psst! Team members:** You, too.

---

**Materials Needed**

Enough printed copies of the following to distribute to all team members:

- The Case and Guide to Analysis
- Handout—Leadership Development Strategy
- Worksheet—Expectations and Objectives
- Handout—Protocol for Problems of Practice
- Chart paper and markers

Full-size reproducibles of worksheets and handouts are available on the companion CD-ROM.

---

## A. Analyzing the Case

### Step 1: Read the Case (15 minutes)

Distribute the teaching case, and have all team members read it through, underlining or highlighting pieces of information that they think are significant to understanding the case.

## Step 2: Establish the Facts of the Case (10–15 minutes)

As a whole group, make a list on chart paper of the significant *facts* of the teaching case. Include what you know about each team member. Try to withhold judgment, inferences, or evaluation, and come to agreement about what happened.

---

**Very Important:** When we say *facts* we mean just that—you must stick to the facts ONLY. There is a huge temptation, when analyzing other teachers' interactions, for teachers to voice *opinions* such as "She talks too much during the meeting" or "She's not a very good teacher." These are not *facts*, and negative comments such as these are counterproductive. The group should consciously steer away from such comments and instead either ask questions such as "Does she allow other voices to be heard?" or offer statements based on *evidence* such as "She says _____, but then she does _____."

If teachers feel they will be attacked for opening up their practice for other teachers to view, they simply will not do it. Making practice public is a risky proposition, and part of your challenge as a case analyst is to pretend that the teachers you are talking about are right there in the room with you.

---

## Step 3: Case Analysis Questions (15 Minutes)

Discuss the following questions. For each question, identify the evidence that leads to your response. (You do not have to address every question.)

- What is this case about?
- Principal Asante and Karen believe that the "gradual release" method (modeling, guided practice, independent practice) is a good way to develop Laurie's leadership capacity. What challenges does Karen face with this model? How do you account for these difficulties?
- What role could Principal Asante have played in supporting Karen as she faced the challenge of transitional leadership?
- There seems to be a tension between using team meeting time for (a) the Ravenswood Middle School Collaborative Inquiry process and (b) planning daily lessons and developing class activities. As a team leader, what steps would you take to alleviate this tension and improve productivity for Ravenswood's teachers?

## B. Exploring the Dilemma (10–15 minutes)

Though Karen would not teach this way in her 7th-seventh grade class, she is using the following teaching model with Laurie[9]:

> Teacher to learner: *"I did it, now you do it alone."*
> There is little opportunity for scaffolded instruction.

It is common knowledge that mentoring promotes new teacher development and improved teaching performance. Just as mentors create supportive environments and learning opportunities for new teachers, it is also essential that we create learning environments for team leaders to develop skills, gain knowledge, and problem-solve issues of team facilitation and leadership.

Compare the above "sink or swim" strategy with the Leadership Development Strategy (Figure C3.1), which includes scaffolding and coaching as a method for teaching effective leadership.[10]

## C. Reflect and Connect (20 minutes)

In order to be an effective team leader, certain fundamental skills are assumed to be necessary:

- Facilitating effective meetings
- Resolving conflict
- Problem solving
- Giving feedback

Re-reading the case, underline places in the text where you see examples of Karen's attempts to teach Laurie leadership skills. What assumptions does Karen make about both the teaching of leadership skills and how teachers learn them?

Using the Leadership Development Strategy as a guide, what suggestions would you make to Karen to develop Laurie's leadership?

1. _____

2. _____

3. _____

4. _____

**Figure C3.1    Leadership Development Strategy**

**Mentored Learning to Lead Team Meetings**

| Phase I | | |
|---|---|---|
| **Clarify your expectations for novice team leader** | | |
| **Role of Experienced Team Leader** | **Role of Novice Team Leader** | **How?** |
| Communicate expectations in ways that are<br><br>• Direct<br>• Specific<br>• Repeated<br>• Modeled<br>• Tenacious | • Listen<br>• Question | Launch the mentor relationship<br><br>• Open communication<br>• Setting boundaries<br>• Expectations<br>• Establish routines for working together |
| **Phase II** | | |
| **Model what effective team leaders do to get results** | | |
| • Explain decisions made during meeting<br>• Be transparent about leadership moves | • Observe<br>• Question | • Team leader invites novice to observe a meeting or show video of a meeting and explain leadership strategies |
| **Phase III** | | |
| **Guided Practice: Ensure appropriate supports are in place to enable success** | | |
| • Make suggestions<br>• Acknowledge strengths<br>• Analyze leadership strategies after the team meeting | • Apply learning<br>• Self-evaluation | • Co-facilitate meetings<br>• Provide feedback after meetings |
| **Phase IV** | | |
| **Independent Practice: Engage in a constant cycle of practice and feedback** | | |
| • Set goals<br>• Evaluate<br>• Coach as needed | • Initiate<br>• Experiment<br>• Acknowledge and value mistakes | • Novice invites experienced team leader to meeting or videotapes meeting and brings to team leader for subsequent analysis<br>• Together, explore critical, perplexing, controversial issues that arose |

# D. What Do We Do Now?

To facilitate the development of team leadership capacity, form a study group focused on building skills for leading effective teams and meetings.

Figure C3.2   Worksheet—Expectations and Objectives

**Expectations**

1.  What expectations do you have for yourself as the team leader?

2.  What expectations do you have for people who are participating in the meeting?

3.  How do you communicate these expectations to the team members?

**Objectives**

1.  Write your objective for a team meeting that you have regularly.

2.  What reason will you give your team for your objective?

3.  How will you communicate your objective to your team?

4.  Read your objective to your study group colleagues. Get feedback on whether it describes what teachers should know or be able to do after the meeting. Revise.

## Step 1: Identify Expectations and Objectives

Begin by having aspiring team leaders fill out the Worksheet—Expectations and Objectives (Figure C3.2). Then follow Question 4 of the Objectives section by having team leaders discuss their objectives with colleagues in the group.

## Step 2: Address Some Typical Challenges of Assuming Team Leadership

Read and discuss the following challenges:

- Lack of process with team members
- "Sink or swim" mentality for learning leadership skills
- Responsibility is given without real authority
- Those who are "led" don't own the new leadership

### Strategies for Novice Team Leaders

1.  *Always have a set agenda for meetings,* give it to the team at least a day before, and stick to it. Don't waste time having a meeting with nothing to discuss.

2.  *Be the first to admit when something isn't working,* and actively listen to suggestions from other team members about solutions. Ask for help (as specifically as possible) when you need it.

3.  *Have the team establish norms for meetings* at the very beginning of the year. It might sound trite, but people do like to have expectations made clear to them—and when they do, they can reference the

norms when it appears that they are not being adhered to (see Chapter 5).

4. Depending on your situation, remember that when it comes to team member relationships, *you are their peer, not their supervisor.* If there's a serious problem, it's your principal's job to handle it, not yours.

5. *Be the spokesperson and cheerleader for your team* with the administration. Be the first person to let the principal know when someone on your team, other than yourself, has done something wonderful in the classroom. Also be the first one to step up and support a teacher who needs help from the administration.

6. *Always be professional.* No matter how other team members behave, never say a thing to one member that you wouldn't say to the entire team. For that matter, don't say anything to the administration about someone that you wouldn't say directly to that teacher.

## Step 3: Facilitate Ongoing Study Groups to Address Problems of Practice

Remember: teaching the skills is only the first part. A constant cycle of practice and feedback is the best way to learn a new skill.

Have novice team leaders get together every few weeks to discuss the issues they may be having with their new skills. Consider having novice team leaders bring a specific problem of practice to the team leader meeting, using the Protocol for Problems of Practice (Figure C3.3).

### Figure C3.3   Protocol for Problems of Practice

1. **Presentation** (5 minutes)

   The presenter will present clearly and succinctly an incident or situation for which she or he would like help. The presentation will finish with a question to focus the discussion.

2. **Clarification** (5 minutes)

   The group will ask questions to clarify the situation. This is not a time for suggestions or judgments.

3. **Restatement of the question** (1 minute)

   The presenter will restate the question based on the clarifying questions.

4. **Brainstorm** (15 minutes)

The group will discuss the question. The presenter will listen and take notes on helpful comments and suggestions but is NOT part of the discussion.

5. **Sharing** (4 minutes)

The presenter will share those ideas that seem useful to her or him. Other ideas may be fine, but the sharing is from the presenter's perspective only.

As a participant, you must:

- Stay focused on the issue and question while drawing from your own knowledge and experiences.
- Not try to engage the presenter in the conversation.
- Help to assure that all members of the group feel comfortable speaking and have a chance to speak.

Adapted from McDonald, J. P., Mohr, N., Dichter, A., & McDonald, E. C. (2003). *The Power of Protocols: An Educator's Guide to Better Practice.* New York: Teachers College Press.

## CASE 4. Good Intentions Aren't Enough

Key Concept: Teacher Autonomy Challenges Alignment of Curriculum in a High School Math Team

# Doing the Math

Lisa Jackson sat in her classroom, listening to the chatter of her AP Calculus students working on their homework problems, while she prepared for tomorrow's Algebra II team meeting. She had students in her classroom almost every day after school, and she was so impressed by their dedication to the difficult work that she was giving them. When she joined the William McKinley High School faculty eight years earlier, the AP math program was teetering on the edge of being disbanded. Now, her course had 15 students and she was preparing for the launch of an AP Statistics program in the upcoming year. She was proud of what she had accomplished, both in her AP Calculus classes and in her Algebra II classes. The students were moving faster, covering more material, and showing more enthusiasm for the topics. But now the department chair was calling for a specific alignment of lessons within the Algebra II curriculum, and she was worried. She sighed to herself. She believed in teamwork, but now she wasn't sure if it was the best way to approach aligning the Algebra II curriculum. Lisa wanted to make sure that any curriculum changes preserved the rigor that she felt was so important. She wondered if it would be worth it to just rewrite the curriculum on her own. Would the team do better than she could do on her own?

## Lisa Jackson

Lisa was a highly dedicated teacher. She spent hours after school each day researching new teaching strategies and developing interesting, accessible lessons. She knew that most of her students were convinced that they were just "bad at math," and she was determined to find ways to prove that they were more able than they realized. Lisa had been educated at a fine midwestern university, and she had been drawn to teaching because of the challenge and her strong belief that all students deserved a chance to realize their potential. She loved mathematics, had majored in it in college, and was always working to instill that passion in her students. She was married but had no children of her own and often joked, "I spend more time with my 150 'school children' than most mothers!"

Lisa was one of the few white teachers in the math department. Although her eight years of teaching experience put her in the middle of the department in seniority, she often felt that she had to prove that she really cared about her (mostly minority) students. Several of the faculty members had grown up together and knew the parents and grandparents of the current students. Lisa had a lot of respect for the hard work of the other four teachers on the Algebra II team. Although she did not have many close friends at the school, she did not have any enemies either. As a result, she worked mostly by herself, although she had recently started informally mentoring Liliana, a second-year teacher who was teaching Algebra II for the first time. They ate lunch together once a week to plan lessons and talk about the material, although Lisa was usually able to do more complex lessons and cover more subjects than Liliana.

## The Algebra II Team Gets Their Marching Orders

A month earlier, at the bimonthly math department meeting, the discussions about curriculum alignment had already begun. But today, just as school was ending for the day, the Algebra II math team at McKinley was filtering into department chair Alfonso Rivera's office for a special team meeting to discuss curriculum alignment. By 3:10, most teachers were seated and ready to start the meeting. Lisa was the last to arrive. "Sorry guys!" she said as she slid into a seat. "One of my AP kids had a homework question, and I didn't want to send him away because we have a test tomorrow."

Alfonso smiled at her. "Don't worry about it, Lisa. Your dedication is what makes you a star!" Meryl Kingsley, the most veteran Algebra II teacher, flashed her a smile as well, but Lisa thought she saw a few teachers grimace at Alfonso's comment.

"Good afternoon, everyone," Alfonso began. "We all have a lot of work, so I'll try to run through this quickly. I've received word from above that central office is not happy to see that we're all teaching different things. Students sometimes have their schedules changed mid-year and find out that their new class is doing something completely different than their old class. Also, we're still having trouble with test scores and administration thinks that part of it might be that we aren't covering everything that we're supposed to."

"But the problem is that the kids are coming to us so far behind!" Frank Smith exclaimed. "I have to spend the first two months reviewing Algebra I because the kids don't know it. What am I supposed to do about that?"

"I hate to say it, but I agree with Frank," Meryl echoed. "I know these kids are capable, but they're coming out of middle school so far behind. Shirley and I have been working together for 30 years, and we've never had kids coming to us with so little knowledge before. We've had to completely readjust our expectations. Fifteen years ago, we were getting through the whole book. Now, we're lucky to get through half."

Alfonso replied, "Actually, Meryl, you and Shirley are a great example of team curriculum planning. I can go back and forth between your rooms and you're always on the same page, same activity. That's what we're looking for! I just need the whole Algebra II team to be doing it."

At this point, Lisa looked concerned. "I think we can get through a lot more than we are currently getting through. I got through most of the book last year, although I didn't necessarily cover it all in depth."

Alfonso interrupted. "This is a conversation for you guys to have in your regular team meeting. I don't care what you decide, as long as you cover the standards and are roughly doing it in the same way. In two weeks, there'll be a department meeting in individual subject areas, and you should come out of it with a course outline that you can all follow. OK! It's 3:45, so I have to let you go. Any quick questions?"

Liliana spoke, ignoring the glum faces of the teachers who were already packing their bags. "I teach three different subjects—which meeting should I go to?"

Alfonso hesitated. "Um, whichever one you teach the most sections of. And that goes for anyone else in that position. All right folks, have a great night! See you tomorrow!"

Lisa packed up her things, making small talk with those around her. As Meryl and Shirley passed her, she smiled at them. "Hey! Maybe we can save some time by sharing our current outlines ahead of time. Then we can just work on aligning them at the meeting."

"Good idea," Meryl said. "I'll have that to you later this week." She rolled her eyes at Frank's empty seat. "But don't expect to get anything from Frank. You know, these aren't his people. He doesn't really care how they do. He's not about to do anything extra to help them. See you tomorrow, sweetie." Lisa nodded uncomfortably, but couldn't help wondering if Meryl had ever had similar thoughts about her. She waited for Liliana, who was engaged in conversation with other teachers.

"Hey, Lisa!" said Liliana, catching up with her. "Sorry to keep you waiting! I hate that I only get to go to one meeting. I wish I could go to all of them. At least I know that with you on the team, the Algebra II curriculum will be good. You always have such great ideas." Lisa smiled but was inwardly worrying about how many of her ideas she would be able to implement.

# William McKinley High School

William McKinley High School is an urban comprehensive high school with 1,100 students and 110 teachers. The students are primarily African American or Latino. Many of the students required extra support, as 26% of them are on IEPs and 15% are LEP (limited English proficient). Almost half of the students speak Spanish as the primary language at home. McKinley failed to meet AYP (Adequate Yearly Progress) for the past five years, and as a result the math and English departments were under pressure from the district to find ways to raise test scores. Despite their efforts, only 26% of McKinley students passed the high-stakes math test last year, while 30% passed the language arts portion. After several years of budget cuts and teacher layoffs, the staff were at an all-time low in terms of morale and pride in their work.

## Alfonso Rivera

Alfonso had been the math department chair at McKinley for 15 years. He immigrated from the Dominican Republic at the age of 10 and had been inspired by the kindness of his own teachers during his first years in the American school system. He entered teaching in hopes of being that inspirational teacher for the next generation of students. When he started as department chair, he had been excited about having control over textbook selection as well as how best to spend the discretionary funds on supplies for the classrooms. Now, he felt that most of his job consisted of relaying information from the administrative team to his teachers. He thought that a lot of their initiatives were good ideas, but just didn't find himself getting excited about it in the same way. A stellar teacher, Alfonso had been named "favorite teacher" by two of the past five senior classes, yet he had never had another math teacher observe his classroom. His time was increasingly filled with paperwork, whether it was compiling materials orders or filling out data spreadsheets, but he seemed to have less authority to make decisions. He was thinking about stepping down and recommending that Lisa fill his role, but he was still unsure about her ability to work alongside other teachers rather than doing her own thing.

## Meryl Kingsley and Shirley Williams

Meryl and Shirley, both African American and with strong ties to the surrounding community, have been friends since they were both 10th graders at McKinley 40 years earlier. They had started teaching at McKinley 30 years ago and, as the youngest members of the department at that time, had worked closely together in planning and navigating the political conflicts in the department. They had continued to work as a team throughout their careers. At this point, they were almost always lumped together by the rest of the department as "MerylandShirley." They ate lunch together every day and talked over their students and lessons, as well as their personal ups and downs. Meryl and Shirley felt that, in their many years of teaching, they had seen most fads come and go. They had chosen what they felt were the best pieces of the different movements to keep, while ignoring the rest. At this point, they felt that they had almost perfected their teaching strategy.

## Frank Smith

Frank had been teaching at McKinley for 15 years. After several years of working as a mathematician for a government office, he decided he needed a career change. He returned to school and earned his teaching degree, and had been teaching at McKinley ever since. Frank knew his content well, but he had been dismayed to find that his students were less capable then he had expected and that the school rarely had the funds to support the large-scale projects he had envisioned doing with the students. After putting the time and money into changing careers, he could not afford to do so again, so Frank had resigned himself to finishing out his career as a high school math teacher. Health problems had caused Frank to miss over 30 days of school last year, and he wasn't sure how many more years he would go before retiring.

# Algebra II Team Meeting

Lisa, Meryl, Shirley, and Frank pulled desks together in Lisa's room and sat down. Lisa pulled out copies of her course outline. Meryl and

Shirley passed around copies of their current outline. Frank shrugged. "Hey, whatever you guys want to do is fine with me. Let's get this meeting done with. I want to go home." Lisa felt frustration rising inside, but she kept quiet. She spread the three course outlines in front of her. As she had expected, hers was much different than the other two. Hers covered twice as many chapters and included several projects throughout the year.

"I like that you're so determined," Meryl remarked to Lisa, "but I just don't think the rest of us can keep that pace. Maybe we can add some of your projects into our outline and all follow that?"

"But if we do that, they'll never be prepared for AP!" cried Lisa. "I know they're behind already, but if we let them get even further behind, they have no chance at the higher levels. I've come up with some ways to review Algebra I while still teaching Algebra II topics. Let me show you." Lisa turned to her desk to find her lesson plans from September, but Frank interrupted her.

"Why are we even bothering? I know it looks good to have AP classes here, but let's be real. Even the kids in *your* class aren't doing well on the test. It's just a show. You're a great teacher, but you're trying to get more out of these kids than they have to give. Some of them can handle it, but most can't. We shouldn't be building our curriculum so that your kids have a shot at passing the AP test. Most of these kids won't go to college. You know I love pure mathematics, but we need to be giving them real-world applications, not theories."

Shirley and Meryl exchanged a glance. "Of course you think so, Frank," muttered Shirley. She then spoke more clearly. "The thing is, Lisa, there's no tracking anymore. Everyone's together, and that makes it harder than it used to be. We don't have the chance to push the bright kids along anymore because we have to bring the weak ones up. I like how you think, but I just don't think it's our first priority. Our first priority needs to be giving kids a solid background in Algebra so that they will actually pass the state test and have a better shot at doing well on the SATs. Once we get scores up, we'll have more leeway to do some more challenging things."

"But I really think that this is something that we could all do!" Lisa countered. "It's not so hard, once you get the hang of it. Liliana has been working some of my ideas into her classes, and it's gone really well."

"Look, we don't all have the time you have. If we're going to do the same thing, we need to make it something that we can all do," said Frank. "I like Meryl's idea. Let's do that. Are we done?"

"No, we're not done!" exclaimed Lisa. "This is important, and I don't want to just blow it off. I can rewrite my outline so that it's something that you can all handle. I'm even willing to make all of the tests and plan the projects. I just don't want to have to teach less because we all have to be together."

"But, Lisa," said Meryl gently, "you can't do all of that forever. We need to come up with something that works for all of us. It was easier when only the brightest kids took Algebra II because most of the kids didn't go to college anyway, but now we're supposed to prepare everyone for college, and that's not easy. I know these kids, and I know what they need. They need a solid background, not necessarily something that moves so fast they have trouble understanding it. There's time for calculus in college. You're a great teacher, and I wish I had your energy, but I don't anymore. I can't keep up with the schedule that you have yourself on."

"I understand," said Lisa calmly, "but if I can do it, I don't see why I shouldn't."

"Well, we have to get the curriculum aligned," said Frank. "Hey, I have to run. Can you guys just leave a copy of whatever you decide on my desk? See you later!"

As Frank walked out, Liliana walked in. "Hey, guys!" she said. "The Algebra I meeting turned into a war zone, and I don't think much will get accomplished today. I decided to escape and see how your meeting is going. How's it going? Did you come up with something?"

Lisa, Meryl, and Shirley exchanged glances, unsure of how to answer.

\*\*\*\*\*\*\*\*\*\*\*\*\*\*\*\*\*\*\*\*\*\*\*\*\*\*\*\*\*\*\*\*\*\*\*\*\*\*\*\*\*\*\*\*\*\*\*\*\*\*\*\*\*\*\*\*\*\*\*\*\*\*\*\*\*\*\*\*\*\*\*\*\*\*\*\*\*\*\*\*

# CASE 4—Guide to Analysis

## Good Intentions Aren't Enough

**Key Concept: Teacher Autonomy Challenges Alignment of Curriculum in a High School Math Team**

This teaching case examines the situation of the Algebra II teaching team in a high school math department. The team is charged with the development of an aligned Algebra II curriculum that all the team members will use faithfully. One team member advocates writing a more rigorous, demanding curriculum than is currently being implemented. The other team members, for a variety of reasons, are reluctant to take on the entirety of the challenging task presented by this individual teacher.

---

### Your Facilitator

**Wait!** It would be very, very difficult to gain any appreciable benefit from your expenditure of time and energy by attempting to conduct this analysis and its series of exercises without a facilitator. You *need* to appoint someone (it can be a team member) as a designated facilitator. This is not necessarily your team leader. This person will not be your "boss." But this person *will* be responsible for:

- Copying and distributing to all participants copies of the Case and Case Analysis and all handouts
- Organizing role-plays (appointing time keepers and observers, where indicated)
- Moving the process along and staying on track

**Psst! Facilitators:** Read all the activity directions as if they applied to you.
**Psst! Team members:** You, too.

---

### Materials Needed

Enough printed copies of the following to distribute to all team members:

- The Case and Guide to Analysis
- Handout—Islands Activity Guide
- Handout—Islands of Strength Diagram
- Handout—Team Action Plan Diagram
- Handout—Directions for Islands Activity
- Worksheet—Islands Activity Diagram
- Handout—Protocol for Viewing Video Clips
- Handout—Protocol for Examining Student Work
- Chart paper and markers

Full-size reproducibles of worksheets and handouts are available on the companion CD-ROM.

# A. Analyzing the Case

## Step 1: Read the Case (15 minutes)

Distribute the teaching case, and have all team members read it through, underlining or highlighting pieces of information that they think are significant to understanding the case.

## Step 2: Establish the Facts of the Case (10 minutes)

As a whole group, make a list on chart paper of the significant *facts* of the teaching case. Include what you know about each team member. Try to withhold judgment, inferences, or evaluation, and come to agreement about what happened.

---

**Very Important:** When we say *facts* we mean just that—you must stick to the facts ONLY. There is a huge temptation, when analyzing other teachers' interactions, for teachers to voice *opinions* such as "She talks too much during the meeting" or "She's not a very good teacher." These are not *facts*, and negative comments such as these are counterproductive. The group should consciously steer away from such comments and instead either ask questions such as "Does she allow other voices to be heard?" or offer statements based on *evidence* such as "She says _____, but then she does _____."

If teachers feel they will be attacked for opening up their practice for other teachers to view, they simply will not do it. Making practice public is a risky proposition, and part of your challenge as a case analyst is to pretend that the teachers you are talking about are right there in the room with you.

---

## Step 3: Case Analysis Questions (20 minutes)

Discuss the following questions. For each question, identify the evidence that leads to your response.

- What are the key educational issues in this case?
- The Algebra II team has been charged with revising its curriculum so that all the teachers' lessons are aligned and differentiated in order to meet the learning needs of all students. Different members of the Algebra II team have different curricular expectations of their students. Given these differences, describe the position of each teacher regarding her or his students and their academic potential, as well as the teacher's rationale for her or his view of the purpose of the curriculum.

- This case illustrates the tension between teacher autonomy and collective responsibility (that is, when teachers no longer regard the students in their own classes as "my" students, but rather see the entire team's students as "our" students). How is this tension played out on the team?

## B. Reflect and Connect

This case raises two challenges that confront teams:

- Teacher autonomy vs. team coherence
- The development of common content expectations and unit and lesson alignment for a high school course

For many teachers at all levels, teacher autonomy is a particularly desirable aspect of their work. Even when teachers use a common curriculum or textbook, they regularly exert their autonomy and their power to control the implementation of the curriculum.

Since the principal and the department head's jobs are frequently "undoable,"[11] teachers are left to their own devices, and the supervision of teachers' work is rarely conducted with any frequency or depth. Thus, it is difficult to implement and monitor a common set of standards for student achievement, and teachers' expectations for the academic challenges given to students can vary depending on each individual teacher's academic expectations.

When mandates come from "on high" to develop a common curriculum, teachers' autonomy is threatened and each teacher's expectations of her or his students are exposed.

### Group Activity: Creating Islands of Strength in a High School Math Team

The Islands Activity is an exercise for finding healthy opportunities for change in a situation that feels, to the participants, as if they were islands of individual strengths, surrounded by rough waters (sometimes inhabited by sharks) and only loosely connected by the dynamics of established relationships. The activity does not deny the size, depth, or complexity of competing and conflicting factors, such as low expectations for underachieving children, poor group process in the faculty, lack of leadership, and so on. However, by identifying how individual **strengths** may contribute to team success, the Islands Activity is explicitly *counter*intuitive. There is agreement that while difficult conditions may exist, this exercise emphatically states that teachers should *not* talk about the negative aspects of those conditions.

The purpose is to address an agreed-upon team task by focusing all attention on the "islands" of possibility that are the "dry land" on which you want to build. This exercise is a conscious effort to *name* the islands and to forcefully stop participants from returning to endlessly describing or complaining about negative conditions. There is a shared assumption among the team members: "We have the capacity, given the potential that exists within the team, and the positive connections that already exist within the team, which—once identified and named—become the solid dry land upon which teachers can make positive changes in our team."

## Step 1: Distribute and Review Materials (5 minutes)

Distribute and briefly review the materials provided, including the Islands Activity Guide (Figure C4.1) and the Islands of Strength Diagram (Figure C4.2).

## Step 2: Study and Discuss the Activity Guide and Diagram (20 minutes)

Introducing and reviewing the Islands Activity concept takes a certain amount of study. Looking at these handouts together and thinking about how the Islands Activity is applied will help get team members accustomed to the notion of how it works.

As a team, study the guide and the graphic, and have a conversation using some of these discussion points:

- Prioritize individual and team strengths.
- Do you see strengths depicted here that you disagree with?
- What do you think could be learned from this activity that might be applicable to *your* team?

## Step 3: Explore a Possible Next Step for the Algebra II Team (25 minutes)

A reading of this case and a subsequent analysis, plus engaging in the Islands Activity, should reveal the fact that this Algebra II team has a number of inherent strengths going for it. As a team, something to wonder about is: why, at the end of the case, did this team seem unable to achieve the goal given to them by their department chair:

## Figure C4.1   Islands Activity Guide

### A Narrative for the "Good Intentions Aren't Enough" Case

TEAM GOAL: To develop an Algebra II curriculum that is aligned throughout the department. It must be differentiated, address students' needs, and raise the achievement level of all students in heterogeneous classrooms.

ACTIVITY: Identify individual Islands of Strength that could, if appropriate bridges were built, support the goal of an aligned curriculum.

ACTIVITY GOAL/OUTCOME: While individual teams are stronger or weaker than others, all teams have inherent strengths (Islands of Strength) that could help them achieve identified team goals.

**Engaging in this activity can help you and your team build self-awareness in order to uncover *your* team's strengths that will allow the formation of an action plan similar to the one that could have helped the team in Case 4.**

#### 1. The Islands

Each person on this team is an island—an Island of Strength. The islands are surrounded by rough water with few bridges between them. Most of the islands are disconnected from one another, as far as their strengths are concerned, but some bridges are in place.

**Lisa:** An 8-year veteran teacher who develops rigorous curriculum for all students

**Strengths:** Has created a rigorous, innovative curriculum; has also developed new lessons

**Liliana:** A new, young teacher who has tried lessons from Lisa's curriculum

**Strengths:** Is enthusiastic, energetic, and willing to try new things; has enjoyed success trying new curriculum

**Meryl and Shirley:** A long-functioning, well-respected duo who work collaboratively with their lessons aligned

**Strengths:** Expert teachers familiar with existing curriculum; are using an aligned curriculum; have already written a curriculum that other teachers find acceptable

***Meryl:*** Very supportive of Lisa; wants to add several of Lisa's projects throughout the year so that all the teachers can do them

***Shirley:*** Wants to give all students a solid background in algebra, raise scores for SATs

**Frank:** A 15-year veteran who likes Meryl's idea for trying several of Lisa's ideas; wants to build in real-world applications

**Strengths:** Good content knowledge, highly qualified; will do whatever the group decides

**Alfonso:** The long-time math department chair
**Strengths:** Respects the collaboration of Meryl and Shirley as well as the creative, rigorous work of Lisa

#### 2. Team Strengths

In addition to individual Islands of Strength, some strengths are shared; they're owned by the team as a whole.

- Three teachers have written curricula acceptable to all members.
- One teacher has extended the existing curriculum with new lessons and specific projects.
- All teachers have content knowledge.
- The team has a significant number of combined years of teacher experience.
- The teachers are willing to work together.
- The team has a novice teacher who is enthusiastic.

#### 3. Existing Bridges

**Lisa to Liliana:** A mentor-mentee relationship with mutual respect and Liliana's willingness to try Lisa's curriculum.

**Lisa to Meryl:** Meryl wants to add several of Lisa's projects throughout the year to benefit all the students and teachers.

**Lisa to Meryl and Shirley:** Shirley is willing to follow Meryl's lead in adopting Lisa's initiatives.

Using data from the case, do you see where the team could have used opportunities to build other bridges?

### Figure C4.2 Islands of Strength Diagram

Task: Align Curriculum for Algebra II Team That Addresses the Needs of Heterogeneous Classes
**(ISLANDS OF STRENGTH)**

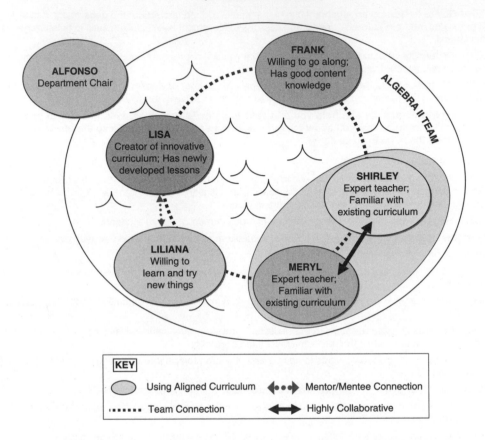

an aligned math curriculum that serves all students? Could a well-thought-out action plan have helped them reach that goal?

Distribute and briefly review the Team Action Plan Diagram (Figure C4.3).

Let's assume that it would be feasible, by examining a possible scenario illustrated by the Team Action Plan Diagram, for the team to (theoretically) have followed these steps:

1. Clarify the task (Circle No. 1 on diagram)

First, the Algebra II team had to understand that the goal of aligning an Algebra II curriculum that addressed all the learning needs of a heterogeneous class was simply too big a job to be accomplished all at once. In fact, it should have been viewed as a multiyear project.

*The success of achieving a large goal depends on first breaking it down into a sequence of smaller, more realistically achieved tasks. Eventually, when each step is accomplished in sequence, the larger goal is reached.*

**Figure C4.3    Team Action Plan Diagram**

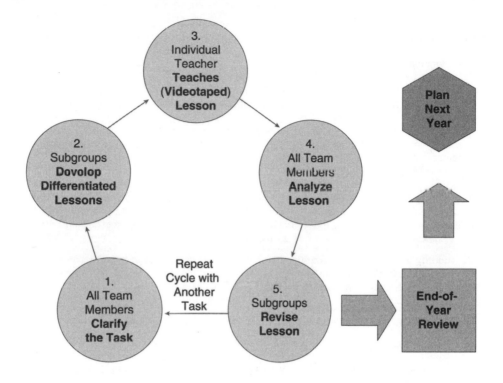

2. Develop differentiated lessons (Circle No. 2 on diagram)

The team decided its first task would be to develop differentiated lessons—benchmark lessons in selected units of the Algebra II curriculum, one unit at a time, beginning with some lessons developed by Lisa. In subgroups they developed one or two differentiated lessons for a unit that met the learning needs of all students in the classes.

3. Each teacher teaches the same new lesson (Circle No. 3 on diagram)

Each team teacher then taught *the same, new, collaboratively developed, differentiated lesson.*

4. Analyze (Circle No. 4 on diagram)

The team realized that a good way to deepen their understanding of how to teach one of the two differentiated benchmark lessons in the unit was to encourage one of the team's teachers to teach the lesson and then present it formally to the team. This can be done in several ways; we offer two possible protocols (Figures C4.6 and C4.7) in the Create Your Own Action Plan section.

### Figure C4.4   Directions for the Islands Activity

The purpose of the Islands Activity is to make participants aware of the potential for positive change by recognizing positive aspects of any situation, ignoring intuitive (negative) responses to complicated situations, and deciding to proceed in a manner that is often counterintuitive (positive), creating the possibility for change.

A challenging, conscious effort to *name* the islands, and to forcefully stop participants from returning to descriptions of the "rough water," can yield a dozen or more "islands" of sane, healthy, aspects that—once identified and named—can be the "dry land" onto which you scamper when you feel like you're about to drown in the rough water.

**Begin the activity** by drawing a circle or oblong shape on a large piece of chart paper. This circle, which should stretch almost to the edges of the paper, represents the rough water of problems for the team members around a specific goal. (For an example of how this could look, see the accompanying Islands Activity Worksheet Diagram)

1. **Identify a goal.** Decide on one rough watery area that needs landfill (the sooner the better). What do you want to accomplish? Visualize the end result of this activity. The goal of the Islands Activity is to project into the future with the goal of "selling hope" and helping participants visualize what it would look like to actually solve a problem.

2. **Identify positive and useful specific elements** that are unique to this situation (the islands: people, structures, or artifacts that are key to finding a solution to the problem). Place the names of these elements in smaller circles within the large circle.

3. **Do not debate** whether something or someone is or isn't a "real" island. If there might be some dry land, the task is to name it and locate it now for possible use later.

4. **Remind** the participants that the frequent intuitive response is to describe endlessly all the negative aspects of the rough water. ("You think that's bad, let me tell you what happened yesterday"). The Islands Activity is explicitly *counter*intuitive. It begins by agreeing that there is toxicity and difficulty in every problem, but we are intentionally *not* talking about all the bad aspects of the rough water.

5. **Identify the bridges or landfill that can be created in order to connect the islands.** Recognize that bridges can be built to improve the island-to-rough water ratio so that the dry land-to-rough water ratio becomes progressively more positive. How do these islands move the group forward on the assigned task?

6. **Decide how you can connect the islands.** Cluster the individuals who could create a positive island. This cluster can then become a subgroup that can work to improve whatever situation the participants have identified. As the participants add the most obvious islands and create bridges between them, they will have proven that every situation is *not* 100 percent rough water. As the group finds a dozen or more identified islands, additional islands will naturally emerge.

7. **Make a list of the tasks that must be completed** for the Island Activity and its goals to be accomplished.

8. **Be sure to end the exercise** with the group of participants in agreement on the plan and the particular tasks that each person will accomplish in order to be ready to implement the results of the Islands Activity.

9. **Establish two monitors** who will hold the participants accountable for the tasks they have developed: one to look at the product, the other to keep track of the process of the group as it progresses through the tasks.

10. **Review and adjust.** At one team/department meeting each month, reassess the list of tasks as well as the progress the group has made toward the set goal. Revise and improve plans.

NOTE: Throughout the islands process it is important to cultivate allies and advocates outside of the team itself. Acquiring the support of the department head and, if possible, the principal should enhance the effectiveness of the team's work.

**Figure C4.5    Worksheet—Islands Activity Diagram**

Task: _____

**(ISLANDS OF STRENGTH)**

Name_____
Strength_____

Name_____
Strength_____

Name_____
Strength_____

Name_____
Strength_____

Name_____
Strength_____

The Islands of Strength graphic example that was provided with the case study included islands, dotted lines, arrows, and circles to denote individual strengths and team connections. As you develop your own model, feel free to use these same symbols or to create your own as you label the Islands of Strength or the qualities of connection in your task

**Figure C4.6    Protocol for Viewing Video Clips**

**1. Previewing**

<u>Host Teacher Presentation</u> (7 minutes)

- Describe ways in which the lesson supports the team goal.
- Briefly describe your students and the context in which the video was filmed.
- Briefly describe the level of student engagement and understanding of the content in the unit.
- What learning goals did you have for your students?
- What goals did you have for yourself? Examples:
    - Integrating special education students into discussions
    - Being clear about learning goals by talking to students about them and revisiting these learning goals during the lesson
    - Improving classroom discourse

- Focus question for feedback: What would you like us to pay attention to as we watch the video clip?

*(Continued)*

(Continued)

---

2. **View the Video (10–15 minutes)**

3. **Postviewing (15 minutes)**

<u>Non-Host Teachers</u>

Respond to the host teacher's focus question as well as some of the following suggested prompts:

- What pedagogical techniques does the teacher use?
- How are students grouped for instruction?
- What do the students do in the lesson discussion, and what does their communication suggest about their understanding?
- How does the teacher assess student understanding?
- How is the lesson differentiated?

*The host teacher may take notes, but should not interject.*

<u>Host Teacher</u> (10 minutes)

- Respond to the group, and pose any new questions you may have.

<u>All Teachers</u> (10 minutes)

- Respond to any new questions/comments raised by the host teacher.
- Brainstorm positive and constructive implications for future work.
- How will <u>each team member</u> adjust his or her practice as a result of the observation?

---

## Figure C4.7 Protocol for Examining Student Work

---

1. **Introduction** (5 minutes)

   Discuss ways in which the student work supports the team goal.

2. **Presentation** (5 minutes)

   Presenter has an opportunity to share the context for the student work:

   - Information about students and class: How does this lesson fit into the unit?
   - Assignment that generated the student work, context for the assignment
   - What are some approaches you anticipated students would take?
   - Student learning goals: What are the underlying ideas?
   - Samples of student work (one strong, one average, one weak)
   - Evaluation format (scoring rubric and/or assessment criteria)
   - Focusing question for feedback

   Participants are silent; no questions are entertained at this time.

3. **Clarifying questions** (5 minutes)

   Participants have an opportunity to ask clarifying questions. (Clarifying questions are matters of fact.)

4. **Examination of student work samples** (10 minutes)

(Participants should use the Student Work Analysis Recording Sheet.)
   Participants look closely at the work, taking notes on where it seems to be in tune with the stated goals and where there might be a problem. Participants focus particularly on the presenter's focusing question.

The presenter is silent; participants examine work silently.

5. **Warm and cool feedback** (10 minutes)

Participants share feedback while the presenter is silent and takes notes.

- Warm feedback: how the lesson meets desired goals.
- Cool feedback: may include disconnects, gaps, or problems. Participants offer ideas or suggestions for strengthening the work presented.
- Comments are primarily focused on the questions of the presenter.

6. **Reflection** (5 minutes)

The presenter addresses the comments, ideas, and questions he or she chooses while participants are silent.

7. **Debrief** (5 minutes)

Team members comment on the experience. How did the protocol help achieve the goals?

| Student Work Analysis Recording Sheet | | |
|---|---|---|
| **Student** | **Evidence** | **Interpretation** |
| | | |
| | | |
| | | |

5. Revise (Circle No. 5 on diagram)

Based on their examination of the artifacts, the teachers revised their lessons, noting aspects of the lessons that worked well or didn't accomplish the lessons' goals, and considered how to further revise for the following year.

6. Review and plan ahead

At the end of the year the team had created a set of lessons within the unit that could be increased the following year. Units would include more differentiation, and the teachers' units—collaboratively designed—would be aligned with each other.

## C. What Do We Do Now?

### Step 1: Apply the Islands
### Activity to Your Team (1 hour)

Now, with your own team, apply what you've learned from this exercise. Distribute the Directions for the Islands Activity (Figure C4.4) and examine the Islands Activity Diagram Worksheet (Figure C4.5).

- The first six directions should be done collaboratively, and one person should record the islands on large chart paper.
- For Number 7, use a few other large sheets of chart paper, consider the connections made between islands on the chart, and develop the tasks and a timeline for implementing the island strategy.
- Remember that Numbers 8, 9, and 10 are critical for the success of this team activity. Clearly understanding the group and individual tasks, holding each other accountable for the team's work, regularly monitoring the team's islands implementation, and developing advocates within school administration will either make or break this optimistic, positive, doable strategy for improving your team productivity.

### Step 2: Create Your Own Action Plan (30 Minutes)

Revisit the Team Action Plan Diagram used to describe what the team in the case could have done to achieve its goal of implementing an aligned curriculum, along with the steps the team members executed on the way toward reaching the goal. To help support this activity, we offer two possible protocols that could be used (see Figures C4.6 and C4.7).

Realize that every team is different, and every team has different goals/tasks and strengths. However, no matter what your goal, you must do the following:

- **Start small** by breaking down the larger goal into a sequence of doable tasks.
- **Clarify the task** you choose as the first in your identified sequence of tasks.
- **Develop a plan** to execute the next step in the sequence . . . and the next . . . and the next.

- **Analyze and revise** as you go along.
- **Review progress and plan ahead** to the next sequence in the path toward your goal.

Developing the Team's Islands of Strength

## CASE 5. A Principal's Dilemma: The Challenge of Change

Key Concepts: Administrative Leadership and Resistance to Change

## Team Turbulence

Footsteps could be heard coming down the hall from two classrooms away, and Natalie Rhodes knew who it was, and that there was going to be trouble. She didn't want to deal with it, but what could she do?

"Hi, Natalie," said Patricia as she came in the door. "I noticed your math chart on my way to lunch yesterday and was wondering why I didn't get a copy."

"Oh, the math chart? Jennifer gave me that copy. I know she has it on her computer . . . you could ask her," replied Natalie.

"Well, I'm not too comfortable asking her," Patricia admitted. "Could you possibly see about getting me one? Thanks so much, I need to go get my kids from PE."

"Boy, I really hate this," Natalie mumbled. "Patricia always wants all of our efforts and doesn't want to put in any work on projects. Jennifer will be upset and complain but will give her a copy. I'll never hear the end of it. And if she doesn't get what she wants, she'll complain to Ms. Tarrant, who already spends needless time trying to mollify Patricia and help our team work together and coexist peacefully."

It was true. The principal and assistant principal were well aware that teams at Oceanside Elementary were struggling. Administration had tried to inject a model of grade-level teacher teaming that had been implemented in schools all around the country, believing that closer collaborations between teachers would lead to improvements in teaching practice and efficiency. "Why is this happening?" asked Alana Tarrant, the assistant principal. "We can't continue to have squabbles like this. What could we do to build a community so that everyone can feel that they are a part of a winning team of great teachers?"

## The School and its Leaders

Built in 1960 and located in a stable neighborhood peripheral to a sprawling urban complex on the west coast, Oceanside Elementary School has approximately 650 students from Pre-K to 6th grade and serves a predominantly Hispanic student body; 80% are considered economically disadvantaged. Many students have parents and older siblings who also attended Oceanside.

## Cynthia Brent

Since her arrival as principal eight years ago, Mrs. Brent had been experimenting with various initiatives for the purpose of building a strong professional learning community. She had a like-minded administrative partner in her assistant principal, Alana Tarrant, who had been a teacher at Oceanside for seven years before being hired as assistant principal three years ago.

## Alana Tarrant

Unlike many assistant principals, Ms. Tarrant did not play the disciplinary role of "chief enforcer," instead being entrusted with curricular and school organizational responsibilities. As a former Oceanside teacher, she believed herself to have a deeper understanding of the school culture than her principal, and because of that her advice and counsel were valued by Mrs. Brent.

Before the arrival of Mrs. Brent and Ms. Tarrant, the culture of Oceanside had always been a campus atmosphere of a family of educators, but both principal and assistant principal felt that more collaboration among teachers would help promote professional development and lead to teachers' personal and professional growth. After their first year together, the administrative duo reorganized faculty and made major changes in grade-level assignments. Some teachers who had formerly taught one grade level were moved to a different grade level, with the philosophy that learning new curricula and preparing new materials from time to time would keep teachers "fresh" in their approaches to teaching. Teachers were also grouped into grade-level teams.

# A 3rd-Grade Team

## Natalie Rhodes

An Oceanside teacher for five years, Natalie was motivated to learn as much as she could and to try new concepts. She was always willing to help and contribute, and was eager to accept an assignment as team leader. Her nature as a high achiever enhanced her success at team leadership when grade-level teams were instituted, and she found common teaching ground with a fellow 3rd-grade teacher, Jennifer Sanders, someone who seemed to have similar teaching philosophies.

## Jennifer Sanders

Jennifer found her six-year experience at Oceanside (including student teaching) to be an asset because her established relationship with administration eased her transition from student teaching to full-time teacher. Her outspoken personality made her controversial among some teachers, but Natalie admired this attribute and the two became fast friends.

## Patricia Fox

Patricia had been a teacher at Oceanside for four years; during that time she, as well as other teachers, was moved to new grade levels. This was very difficult for her and she took the administrative decision personally, not seeing it the way it was viewed by administration, as a productive new concept. She felt that as the "new" transferred teacher in a new grade level, she should receive additional support or that others should at least share the materials she needed.

# An Attractive Solution Arrives by Mail

It was early in the summer when Ms. Tarrant received an invitation to participate in a professional development workshop designed to help school administrators build leadership in teacher teams. She was painfully aware of the problems teachers were having at Oceanside: the numerous instances of teachers complaining about cliques forming on the campus, "favorites of administration" always being picked to do things, and the never-ending behind-closed-door meetings with teachers about their colleagues not pulling their weight with their grade-level team. Convincing Mrs. Brent that she should participate in the workshop was not difficult.

During the training, the assistant principal's head was exploding with the onrush of new ideas—the information she was being given on how to build a culture of teachers as leaders, how teachers could talk to each other and really listen to one another and form teams that were more collaborative. The training was exactly what Ms. Tarrant believed she and the school needed. How was a culture of teacher leaders going to be built? How could a school get away from the cliques, and everyone be able to truly appreciate the great things each of them had to offer? The book *Difficult Conversations*[12] was recommended as a foundation for helping with the process, and she made a note to buy it when she returned to school. As the training progressed, she heard topics such as *everyone is good at something, use what you've got, build trust,* and most importantly, *get administrative support.*

On the plane ride back home, Ms. Tarrant reflected on everything she had just experienced, thinking about what it would take to turn the school in another direction; how the staff would take it would be another thing. She closed her eyes and kept thinking about her 3rd-grade team. She kept going back to the numerous meetings she had with them and the fact that all of them were good teachers, possibly the best in the school, but they hadn't acknowledged each other's talents and didn't seem to be able to solve their inability to function smoothly. She hoped she now had the tools that would begin to make a difference in each of their lives . . . and hers.

Before the new school year began, and with high hopes and aspirations, Ms. Tarrant met with her principal to share her ideas and debrief her on everything she had learned. "Our teachers don't know how to talk to each other," she said. "We have to create opportunities for everyone to be a leader; we have to have them think about what they are best at."

When learning of Ms. Tarrant's ambitious agenda, Mrs. Brent looked at her assistant principal with skepticism. "Um . . . this looks like an awful lot for teachers. I see your big picture, but do you really think this isn't too much?"

In reality, Ms. Tarrant knew it was a challenge, but in her heart she was firm in her intent to follow through with her proposed initiatives designed to turn teacher team members into teacher leaders. She felt she needed something radical enough to get results. Taking a deep breath, she pushed forward. "If this works, the campus as a whole is going to be a better place and we will know that the teachers are able to carry the torch of leaders. And the students will ultimately benefit." Mrs. Brent gave her assistant principal full support and added some more ideas. The two began to plot out their professional development game plan for the teachers.

As the plans unfolded, Mrs. Brent began to feel uneasy but wanted to give her assistant principal all the support she needed in order to help her plans succeed. She knew that a benchmark formula used by change agents was the 30-40-30 proposition. That is, with any proposed organizational change, 30 percent of those offered the change would sign up right away, 40 percent would hold back and take a "wait and see" attitude, and 30 percent would resist or just say no. The trick to achieving a successful outcome was always convincing the middle 40 percent to join the first-adopters. Then, when the organization was at 70 percent versus 30 percent, the naysayers would be in a small minority and the envisioned changes could survive. She wondered how this new initiative would play out.

## Attempt at Transformation

"There's no doubt in my mind that the first thing teachers need to do is just be able to talk to one another," Ms. Tarrant said to the principal. "I've ordered 15 copies of the book *Difficult Conversations* for our first group of team leaders to study. Then, we need to give teachers opportunities to assume leadership roles and feel comfortable with that. The process has to be simple, and so easy that they'll feel confident in taking the plunge as a teacher leader. For example, teachers will be asked to pick the subject area in their grade level that they feel they teach the best. They'll be the expert in that area. During their PLC (professional learning community) planning time, they'll be responsible for coming up with the lesson in that content area and presenting it to their peers. They have to model what the lesson would look like. Before coming to the planning time, teachers will have to have their lesson prepared for the following week to present to the grade level."

The new initiatives were going to be introduced to teachers during their first couple of days of professional development before the beginning of school. Ms. Tarrant had spent many late nights working on the best way to present her vision to the teachers. As she prepared, she kept thinking, "What are they going to say? They are going to feel overwhelmed, and I have to assure them that they will be supported, but most important, that this is going to make a difference in our students' lives . . . Yeah, think positive now, because tomorrow you are going to be the most hated person in the school building."

## Late August

Just back from summer vacation, the teachers sat assembled in the cafeteria for the first day of professional development, and Ms. Tarrant began her PowerPoint presentation to the faculty on the new changes for this school year. The first slide was on the team leader for the grade level. Ms. Tarrant proposed strategies for making teacher leadership improve the workings of the teams. She suggested that teachers pick someone from their grade level to be their team leader and that there would be a small stipend to take on this role. This person would attend monthly meetings with other team leaders. For the first semester their focus was to be on reading the book *Difficult Conversations*, which she would provide. One to two chapters would be assigned per month. As a team they would discuss how these chapters applied to the school and how these situations would help their grade level. Various scenarios were discussed to help deal with difficult conversations. For any teacher reluctant to become a teacher leader, team members would also pick someone from their grade level to be the team facilitator. That person would be responsible for paperwork and timelines being kept up with for the grade level and reminders to keep everyone on track. Even though it was a minimal teacher leadership role, it was still important to the team.

There was murmuring among the teachers. Natalie listened and then said to Jennifer that she didn't want the position of team leader. "I don't feel I could be effective as the team leader. Going into another classroom, observing and making recommendations would be difficult. What do you think?"

"I'm not sold on the concept," Jennifer replied, "but if chosen, I guess I would have no choice but to be the guinea pig."

Natalie laughed. "I believe that is exactly what you will be."

The next slide presented was: "No Homework." There was no murmuring this time, but uproar in the room. Patricia said, "I can't believe this! I know that will not work to the benefit of the student."

"Well, I've heard of new studies that indicate this is a good concept," Natalie said, "and I'm willing to give it a try. Maybe we should find out more about the studies."

Several teachers from other grade levels commented that this leadership role would help organize their grade level to benefit all. When Jennifer asked Patricia if she would like to be grade-level chair, Patricia replied, "I am totally overworked and couldn't possibly fit another duty into my schedule." Jennifer looked at Natalie and both smiled because they knew Patricia would always try to get out of doing any extra work, whatever it was.

Ms. Tarrant emphasized that while this seemed like a lot of new things to grapple with all at once, she told her teachers that if they embraced these new strategies they would find them helpful in establishing team harmony and making teams more efficient. "I know this has really worked in other schools and I really hope you'll give it a try. Let's see how it goes, and please talk to me if you're having any problems. Now we'll take a short break, and then I'll tell you about the rest of the ideas I think you'll be excited about."

During the break, over coffee, Jennifer and Natalie talked about the meeting. "I don't think any of these extra assignments are going to help the problems with our team—or with the problems other teams are having, either," said Natalie. "Sometimes team chemistry works, and sometimes it doesn't. If someone on a team doesn't feel like holding up her end (a reference to Patricia), or doesn't show up on time for meetings, or keeps coming late, what's the point of having a 'leader'? And where is the so-called leader going to find the time to go to these extra meetings with other leaders? And the stipend really doesn't matter very much. Maybe it even makes for more trouble."

Jennifer just shrugged. She was willing to give it a try but wondered what kind of support Ms. Tarrant had planned to help teachers fit into their new roles as teacher leaders. Patricia came over and looked distressed. "I think it could be worth trying . . . I don't know . . . but why is administration making so many of these changes? It seems like just when we get used to a certain routine, something new and different comes down on us. Newer isn't always better."

After the break, Ms. Tarrant revised schedules for some specialists, reviewed whole-school logistics such as a new bus dismissal procedure, and presented some new ideas about how to activate more parent involvement in the school.

Teachers then hurried back to their classrooms to get their rooms prepared for the opening day of school, now just two days away.

By the end of the first week of school—with some coaxing from both Ms. Tarrant and Mrs. Brent—teachers had volunteered to be leaders and the team meeting schedules were arranged. The 3rd-grade team and the other teams in the building obediently read the first few chapters of *Difficult Conversations* and participated in the activities developed by Ms. Tarrant and the team leaders. By and large, the teachers enjoyed the role-playing, but comments like "Does this really help my teaching?" and "The administration must think we don't have enough to do already" were whispered in the hall and the parking lot.

## Professional Development
## Release Day, January

At the beginning of the second semester, Ms. Tarrant introduced the second phase of her new teaming initiative, with her PowerPoint presentation focused on putting what they learned from *Difficult Conversations* into practice. Grade-level teams would pick a content area as a focus. The first PowerPoint slide presented a brief explanation of the plan. Team leaders would go into each teacher's classroom and observe them teaching that area. Both would then meet to discuss positives and negatives of the lesson and how it could improve. Team leaders would have to put into practice those difficult conversations when giving constructive feedback to their team members. During monthly meetings all team leaders from the various grade levels would come back together as a large group and discuss instructional issues without any teachers being identified. These meetings would lead to further discussions about the weaknesses and strengths students were coming with when moving on to the next grade level and how to improve teaching and learning throughout the campus.

The next slide was an explanation of peer observations. As Ms. Tarrant explained, every third Wednesday of the month, teachers had to observe another teacher for 30–45 minutes, looking for best practices to bring back to their classroom. Each month two grade levels were chosen for everyone to observe. This provided each teacher with an opportunity to showcase the great things that she or he could do. It also opened the doors to each other's classrooms. Sixth-grade teachers had to go see 1st-grade teachers teach. First-grade teachers had to go see 6th-grade teachers teach. This allowed everyone to view teaching foundations and long-term performances. Jennifer thought, "Maybe it could be interesting to observe other teachers and their classrooms, but being the subject of observation is not going to be much fun."

Everyone participating was to complete a short worksheet to answer the following questions:

1. What did you observe in the class that you really liked?

2. What did you observe that you could take back and implement in your class?

3. What are your comments for the teacher you observed?

The next slide described the idea of establishing a subject leader for team planning time. To make planning more efficient, teachers were to divide up the content areas, decide upon a leader, and plan the lessons for the following week in only one content area and share it with the other members of the team. This concept could cause headaches for the facilitator. Natalie leaned over to whisper to Jennifer, "I like the idea of this, but if someone doesn't turn in the subject on time, then you have no lesson plan."

"Exactly," replied Jennifer. "This is really going from bad to worse."

The next slide described how several leadership opportunities would be offered. Teachers could present a trainer's professional development best practices or model to the staff; they could also pick a session that they felt would be beneficial in that they could take what they learned back to their classroom and make a difference toward student success. Everyone on the campus would have to attend some sessions because of school initiatives (e.g., technology, Reader's and Writer's Workshop), but more important, their peers were to give these professional development trainings. Ms. Tarrant assured the teachers that this would allow them to feel more comfortable and less hesitant to ask questions. As presenters, teachers would have the advantage of presenting to those who knew the school's strengths and weaknesses in academics.

Teachers had yet another opportunity to become leaders in the school through a technology cadre, open to any teacher who had a passion for technology and could teach it to others or those who just wanted to learn how. Teachers who wanted to take this challenge could receive additional training and then take what they learned back to their grade level and coworkers. They would have to hold training sessions on how to use the new software or hardware. The outcome would be that if faculty or staff had trouble with any part of the technology in their classrooms, they could contact a cadre member. As teachers left the workshop, Ms. Tarrant felt pleased that this school offered so many opportunities for teachers to be leaders. This was not a school where there was a one-stage career; on this campus there was a cadre of teacher leaders all dedicated to improving teaching and learning for all students—focused on student success.

## Assessment?

It was the end of the first year, and Mrs. Brent and Ms. Tarrant were organizing the student test data. It looked like student achievement may have been up and more teachers seemed to be willing to take on teacher leadership roles. Ms. Tarrant and Mrs. Brent were anticipating a wealth of positive data.

There was a knock at their door, and Jennifer walked in. Believing in what the administration was trying to accomplish, she had nonetheless become frustrated because she recognized that many teachers were only begrudgingly going along with the process and were bringing down those who were starting to stand up as leaders. As she sat slumped over on her chair, Jennifer asked, "Can't we just go back to the way it used to be? I'm tired of all the complaining. It's been months since Patricia has turned in a lesson plan on time, even though we always remind her of the deadlines. Yes, I do think it's interesting to look at other teachers' teaching—it does give us a new perspective. But how can we apply that to our own teaching? I really am in favor of the teamwork and the lesson planning, but I am worried about the time spent out of the classroom. We're missing an additional 45 minutes of instruction time every week."

Ms. Tarrant responded, "But haven't you noticed a drop in your student failure rates? Aren't you seeing a gain in student achievement?"

Jennifer pondered this statement. "Well, I understand your point—that giving up 45 minutes of instruction in order to plan quality lessons may be worth the tradeoff—but it's taking its toll. I'm the team leader for our grade level, and I find it very difficult to get everyone to work together and be on the same page. And as everyone gets more tired and overwhelmed, what will be the end result? Are any teachers really happy about this? I hear teachers say that their teaching is suffering and they can't take on all these new tasks . . . and I have to tell you—I don't think I can carry on as a teacher leader, either. The stipend just isn't worth it."

\*\*\*\*\*\*\*\*\*\*\*\*\*\*\*\*\*\*\*\*\*\*\*\*\*\*\*\*\*\*\*\*\*\*\*\*\*\*\*\*\*\*\*\*\*\*\*\*\*\*\*\*\*\*\*\*\*\*\*\*\*\*\*\*\*\*\*\*

## CASE 5—Guide to Analysis

### A Principal's Dilemma: The Challenge of Change

**Key Concepts: Administrative Leadership and Resistance to Change**

This case explores the work of an Assistant Principal as she struggles to address her school's "culture of complaint" by implementing productive teacher teams and optimizing teacher involvement.

---

### Your Facilitator

**Wait!** It would be very, very difficult to gain any appreciable benefit from your expenditure of time and energy by attempting to conduct this analysis and its series of exercises without a facilitator. You *need* to appoint someone (it can be a team member) as a designated facilitator. This is not necessarily your team leader. This person will not be your "boss." But this person *will* be responsible for:

- Copying and distributing to all participants copies of the Case and Case Analysis and all handouts
- Organizing role-plays (appointing time keepers and observers, where indicated)
- Moving the process along and staying on track

**Psst! Facilitators:** Read all the activity directions as if they applied to you.
**Psst! Team members:** You, too.

---

### Materials Needed

Enough printed copies of the following to distribute to all team members:

- The Case and Guide to Analysis
- Handout—Ms. Tarrant's Timeline
- Handout—"Yeah, but . . ."
- Worksheet—Gains and Losses
- Index cards
- Post-It notes in three colors
- Chart paper and markers

Full-size reproducibles of worksheets and handouts are available on the companion CD-ROM.

---

NOTE: This is a case that a principal might want to use with the school leadership team.

# A. Analyzing the Case

## Step 1: Read the Case (20 minutes)

Distribute the teaching case, and have all team members read it through, underlining or highlighting pieces of information that they think are significant to understanding the case.

## Step 2: Establish the Facts of the Case (10–15 minutes)

As a whole group, make a list on chart paper of the significant *facts* of the teaching case. Include what you know about each team member. Try to withhold judgment, inferences, or evaluation, and come to agreement about what happened.

> **Very Important:** When we say *facts* we mean just that—you must stick to the facts ONLY. There is a huge temptation, when analyzing other teachers' interactions, for teachers to voice *opinions* such as "She talks too much during the meeting" or "She's not a very good teacher." These are not *facts*, and negative comments such as these are counterproductive. The group should consciously steer away from such comments and instead either ask questions such as "Does she allow other voices to be heard?" or offer statements based on *evidence* such as "She says _____, but then she does _____."
>
> If teachers feel they will be attacked for opening up their practice for other teachers to view, they simply will not do it. Making practice public is a risky proposition, and part of your challenge as a case analyst is to pretend that the teachers you are talking about are right there in the room with you.

## Step 3: Case Analysis Questions (20 minutes)

Discuss the following questions. For each question, identify the evidence that leads to your response. (You do not have to address every question.)

- What is the problem in the case? Whose problem is it?
- What is the problem from Ms. Tarrant's perspective?
- What issues did Ms. Tarrant hope to address with her initiative?
- What is the problem from the teachers' perspectives?
- What are the assumptions about teacher leadership and the work of teacher teams that Ms. Tarrant makes as she plans her intervention? In what ways do you agree or disagree with these assumptions? What advice would you give Ms. Tarrant?
- If you were Principal Brent, how would you have coached Ms. Tarrant?

## B. Exploring the Dilemma

This case uncovers how the core culture of teaching and learning creates challenges for those who wish to implement change.

### Step 1: Read and React to the Following Views (5 minutes)

We need to understand that, for better or worse, culture is a powerful force and efforts to shape it, change it, or fight it can have serious repercussions.[13] Change is a process, not an event—it is a journey, not a blueprint. Successful projects are divisible; they can be done in steps or phases.[14]

The change process is both difficult and complex, requiring that we take the long view by realizing that change takes time and should not be forced to occur too quickly.[15]

### Step 2: Replay the Case by Critiquing the Timeline (20 minutes)

Ms. Tarrant created a timeline (Figure C5.1) to help her get ready to implement her teaming initiative. Examine the timeline critically. Find specific turning points in the case when you might have made a different move than Ms. Tarrant did (being as specific as possible).

- What problems do you notice?
- What would you have done differently, and why?
- How might this have changed the outcome of the case?
- How would you modify the timeline to create opportunities for success?

## C. Reflect and Connect (40 minutes)

### Analyzing Ms. Tarrant's Leadership as Assistant Principal

Many leaders are good at determining what they want to change but falter in fully examining how to change, deciding when to change, and assessing the consequences of change. "Change-savvy leadership"[16] requires fully understanding the many interrelated factors of successful change, which are identified in the following Change Savvy Leadership Checklist.

**Figure C5.1  Ms. Tarrant's Timeline**

| Impetus | Task | Due date | By whom |
|---|---|---|---|
| Constant teacher complaints | Think about how to build a community so that everyone can feel that she or he is a part of a winning team of great teachers | End of school year | Me |
| Invitation to professional development (PD) | Get principal to fund the PD | June 5 | Me |
| Need to learn basics | Go to workshop for building leadership on teacher teams | June 25 | Me |
| Learnings from workshop | Buy the book *Difficult Conversations* for team leaders | July 15 | Me |
| Implement ideas from workshop with faculty | Meet with principal; get her buy-in | August 1 | Me |
| Importance of changing the bickering culture of school | Develop plan for faculty summer PD | August 10 | Me |
| Make the plan clear and easy to understand | Create PowerPoint | August 15 | Me |
| Initiate teachers | Make Phase I presentation to faculty | August 18 | Me |
| Move plan forward | Make Phase II presentation to faculty | October 15 | Me |
| Measure progress | Assess first year | June 21 | Mrs. Brent and me |

Successful change-agent leaders get that way by taking these steps:

- Entering carefully into the new setting
- Listening to and learning from those who have been there longer
- Engaging in fact finding and joint problem solving
- Diagnosing the situation carefully (rather than rashly)
- Addressing people's concerns forthrightly
- Being enthusiastic, genuine, and sincere about the change circumstances
- Obtaining buy-in for what needs fixing
- Developing a credible plan for making that fix

This case can be examined from the point of view of someone who might be in a position to give Ms. Tarrant some advice on any one of these Change-Savvy Leadership Checklist issues. Now, if *you* were in that position, what would be your advice to her on the issue of "addressing people's concerns forthrightly"? Participants can use that question as the springboard to play the "Yeah, but . . ." game (see Figure C5.2).

**Figure C5.2   "Yeah, but . . ."**

**1. Individual Reflection (5 minutes)**

- On your table arrange a stack of index cards. Distribute three cards to each member of your table group.
- Use these cards to record concerns about the proposed initiative. Please put only one concern on each card. If you have only one concern or more than three, use the necessary number of cards.
- On each card you complete, write a concern (i.e., "Yeah, but . . .") that you would like to address.

**2. Round One (10 minutes)**

- When you have completed your cards, circulate them for two or three minutes at your own table. If, as you read the circulating cards, you find that you really agree with a particular concern, place a small dot on the card and put the card back in circulation. If you don't find the concern listed as one of your main issues, simply place the card back in circulation.
- Read through as many cards as you have time to read.

**3. & 4.   Rounds Two and Three (15 minutes)**

- After three minutes your table group will, at a signal, exchange cards with another table.
- Repeat the circulation process with the new cards, marking dots to indicate a high level of interest in questions posed.
- At the end of three to five minutes you will, at a signal, exchange cards with yet another table and repeat the process.

**5. Collection (10 minutes)**

- Upon completion of this round, place the cards in the center of your table and report the main concerns that are raised by this initiative.
- Record main issues on chart paper so that everyone can see them, and create small interest groups to address these concerns. Teachers may choose the "Yeah, but . . ." that they would most like to tackle.

## Activity: Play the "Yeah, but . . ." Game

In the case you have just read, how do the teachers express their concerns? For this activity, have teachers take on the role of one of the Oceanside teachers (Natalie, Jennifer, or Patricia) and, using their own reading of the case, develop a "Yeah, but . . ." that expresses an individual concern.

| Examples of "Yeah, but . . ." Responses to Ms. Tarrant's Proposed Initiatives | |
|---|---|
| *Initiative* | *"Yeah, but . . ."* |
| For observation: Grade-level teams would pick a content area as a focus. Team leaders then would go into that teacher's classroom and observe her or him teaching that area. | "Yeah, but . . . I don't want someone who doesn't know my kids or my style of teaching telling me how to teach!" |

| For sharing lesson plans:<br>To make planning more efficient, teachers are to divide up the content areas, plan the lessons for the following week in one content area, and share them with the other members of the team. | "Yeah, but…how am I supposed to teach from someone else's lesson plan? They don't know my students like I do!" |
| --- | --- |

# D. What Do We Do Now?

At the end of the day, dissatisfied teachers have the power to obstruct any school reform. A common mistake made by administrators is to try to implement change without first addressing teachers' legitimate concerns by giving them a forum for expression and then finding a way to solve the problems they see in the proposed change.

In this section are two schoolwide activities that can help your faculty become engaged in a proposed initiative.

## Activity 1: Play the "Yeah, but . . ." Game, Again (40 minutes)

This time, using a schoolwide initiative that you yourself propose, give the teachers an opportunity to put it to a "Yeah, but . . ." test. Play the game against your initiative, using the "Yeah, but . . ." worksheet (Figure C5.2). The results could surprise you.

## Activity 2: Examine Gains and Losses (40 minutes)

This exercise will help uncover what you and your faculty believe would be gained and/or lost if your proposed initiative were to be implemented.

Step 1: Distribute Gains and Losses worksheet (Figure C5.3).

Step 2: Think about how the initiative would affect students, teachers, parents, and (if applicable) the school board. In what ways would each of these stakeholders gain from the initiative, and in what ways would they lose? Complete the worksheet individually.

**Figure C5.3   Worksheet—Gains and Losses**

Proposed initiative: _____

| | | |
| --- | --- | --- |
| *The teachers* | Gain | Lose |
| *The students* | Gain | Lose |
| *The parents* | Gain | Lose |

Step 3: Form groups of three or four, and share your worksheets.

Step 4: On chart paper, draw a grid similar to the one on the worksheet, and complete it using the different ideas generated by your group.

Step 5: Each group posts its chart paper.

Step 6: Distribute three colors of Post-It notes; one color will be used for items you agree with, a second color for disagree, and a third color for questions (something that is on a chart that you don't understand).

Step 7: Gallery walk. Ask participants to walk around and read all the charts. Explain that the notes should be placed on items that people agree with, disagree with, or don't understand.

Step 8: Highlight areas of agreement and disagreement. Discuss questions that were raised.

## Next Steps

- Participants receive typed-up lists of the gains, losses, and questions that were generated.
- Revise the initiative; develop an action plan.

Identifying Gains and Losses

# CASE 6. How Far We've Come

**Key Concepts: Conditions of Effective Teams and Sustaining Change in Schools**

Principal Anita Gallardo sat at her desk thinking about everything she'd observed in the teachers' professional learning communities (PLCs) this morning. As she did every week, Anita made her rounds, observing a few minutes of each 90-minute meeting to update herself on the teams' work and offer any assistance they needed. Today, however, much of her observation was spent reflecting on the road the teams had traveled to get PLCs up and running at Stoneridge, a K–8 school. Last week, Anita was asked to create a report for the school board about the six-year process of implementing the teams that, from the beginning, had been formally called *professional learning communities*. Knowing the school board was interested in piloting PLCs at other schools with the hope of seeing improved student achievement throughout the school district, Anita understood that her report needed to be honest and realistic. As she stared at the blank document on the computer screen, she wondered what it would take to embed PLCs as a permanent fixture in the school, thereby sustaining Stoneridge's past successes.

## Morning Rounds

Anita began her PLC visits every Wednesday at 7:30 a.m. Teachers had a full 90 minutes to meet before school started at 9:10. The Wednesday late-start schedule the Newkirk School District had adopted for professional development seven years ago was perfect for the implementation of PLCs.

On this particular day, Anita started with the 2nd-grade team. As she entered the meeting, Marybeth Johnson, a 2nd-grade teacher and the K–2 teacher leader cadre representative, was reviewing the agenda. "Today we need to debrief Susan's math lesson that we observed on Monday and then decide on our next steps."

Susan began, "We also need to preview the lesson Dennis wants to do for our next observation. Sharon is out sick today, so I'll take the minutes for us."

Anita sat in on the meeting for a few more minutes. The team pulled out a protocol for discussing the lesson they had observed

Susan teach. Susan said, "I'd love it if you would specifically focus on how I started that lesson. When the kids were at the rug with me for the direct instruction piece, I thought they got it. But then they went to their seats and I realized they didn't know what to do."

Anita couldn't help but smile at this. Five years earlier, most members of this team hadn't wanted anything to do with observing each other teach. In fact, Susan had been one of the loudest opponents, saying, "If we take all this time to watch other teachers who have different kids, we'll have less time for our own planning." It was amazing to Anita at the time to think that a teacher could describe peer observation as something that might *cause* poor teaching.

As the group began discussing the lesson, Anita excused herself and went to visit the kindergarten PLC. As usual, she found this team huddled over a lesson they were planning. The kindergarten team members liked to maintain the same pace with their work. They said it helped them meet parents' expectations and get through the more rigorous academic curriculum adopted by the district several years ago. Third-year teacher Larry pulled out his lesson plan and said, "OK, so I knew I had to have this ready for today, so I stayed up 'til midnight putting this lesson together. Bear with me, I'm a little tired, but I think I found a way for us to use the book *Make Way for Duck-lings* to teach these phonemic awareness skills." The teachers began reviewing Larry's lesson plan while almost immediately adding their own revisions to it.

Anita then headed up to the intermediate school wing and entered 5th-grade teacher Brian's classroom. Today, the team was poring over assessment data. They had just received the fall assessment results and were looking for patterns in the data. Brian stood at a sheet of chart paper and wrote down the observations teachers were making about the data. "Almost 40 percent of our kids missed the problems dealing with using prepositions in context," said Alicia.

Brian interjected, "Yeah, but that's because we hadn't taught that yet."

Alicia started to respond when Lisa said, "Don't forget, we're just stating our observations right now. We'll shift to discussing them in a minute."

Brian responded, "That's the problem I always have with this discussion protocol. I get that we want to put all of our observations out there before we discuss them in detail, but a lot of times I forget what I want to say later, and we could be missing out on important points."

"I have to say I agree with Brian," said Joan, a veteran teacher. "Discussion protocols are useful, but not if they limit our conversation so much that they halt our discussion."

"I'm just afraid if we don't stick with the protocol we'll end up going off on tangents like we used to do," responded Lisa. "I really don't want to go back to those days."

Roxanne Montgomery, the Grade 3–5 teacher leader cadre representative, had been silent until now. "Well, what can we do to help everyone feel heard, without getting off track?"

The teachers were silent. They looked around or at the floor, but no one had a response. Roxanne then said, "Well, maybe we can adapt this protocol. Can we put in a step somewhere that lets people share thoughts during the observation brainstorming?"

Lisa responded, "OK, don't laugh now, but I actually know of another protocol that could help us with *this* protocol!"

Everyone did laugh, including Anita. Lisa smiled too and said, "OK, OK. Just hear me out. It's like a mini-protocol we can put into this one. After each person brainstorms an observation, we can quickly open it up for others to respond. But each person only gets two chances to respond during the brainstorming round. So once you've used up your two responses, you're done until we move to the full discussion. It's like you only get a certain number of timeouts in a football game."

The team immediately began nodding. "I can live with that," said Brian.

"All right. Let's try it now and see how it goes," said Roxanne.

Anita then turned toward the middle school wing and walked into the 7th-grade PLC. As she entered the room, she heard Joe say, "We've really got to address this, guys. We've got to get our kids ready for 8th grade, and it's not gonna happen if all our time is spent planning the 7th-grade trip."

"Tell me about it, Joe, but there's only so many hours in a day," replied Sylvia.

Joe looked to Anita. "What seems to be the problem?" Anita asked.

Joe responded, "This trip is eating up a lot of our time. We've all taken on a piece of the planning, but between the new bus scheduling system, and parent permissions, and payment and planning with the staff at the camp site, this is just taking too much time. We haven't been able to put together the student work to examine in our PLC time, because we've spent so much time running around trying to get this trip planned."

"I know the new bus scheduling system is a mess, and it's not likely to be streamlined any time soon," said Anita. "What if I handled the buses for you?"

"That would be terrific—it'd be a huge weight off our shoulders," said Joe.

"Consider it done," responded Anita.

"Great," said Joe. "Let's move past this then and get back to our student work samples."

Anita spent the rest of the PLC time visiting the other grade-level teams and the PLC composed of specialists. As she walked down the hall toward her office, she began thinking about how PLCs had developed at Stoneridge over the past six years.

## A History of PLC Development

The development of PLCs at Stoneridge was precipitated by the creation of late-start Wednesdays by Newkirk School District seven years earlier. The 90 minutes of protected time was supposed to be used exclusively for professional development; however, in the first year of implementation, the time was rarely used for that purpose.

That was Anita's first year in the district and her third year as a principal. Not wanting to make too many waves in her first year at Stoneridge, Anita allowed the teachers to plan their own professional development. She also figured that giving ownership to teachers for their professional learning would lead to better uses of their time. She quickly learned that teachers' definitions of professional development varied. Most teachers used the time to work in their classrooms grading papers or preparing for the school day. About halfway through the year, Anita realized that the teachers' only responsibility on late-start Wednesdays was to be present in the building from 7:30 to 9:00 a.m. Even those teams that met during that time, such as the kindergarten team, spent most of their time filling out district paperwork or creating their weekly newsletter.

Anita knew she needed to make a change, but it couldn't come from her alone. So she created the teacher leader cadre. Stoneridge had many informal teacher leaders, and Anita knew she could rely on their experience to help her plan more productive professional development. The teacher leader cadre she developed consisted of three representatives. Second-grade teacher Marybeth Johnson was the K–2 teacher leader cadre member. Roxanne Montgomery was a 5th-grade teacher leader who represented Grades 3–5. And Joe Aguilar was a 7th-grade teacher supporting Grades 6–8. These teachers were selected for their leadership skills, their rapport with other teachers, and their interest in improving the professional learning time in the school. As formal teacher leaders, these cadre members served as mentors to other teachers, and they supported Anita in implementing the school's improvement plan.

It was at a conference that Anita and the teacher leader cadre first learned about the power of teacher teaming. PLCs was one model that they repeatedly heard about. Since PLCs focused on teams of teachers examining their own instruction and their students' performance, Anita and the teacher leader cadre knew PLCs could fit seamlessly with the district's expectations for late-start Wednesdays.

When they returned to campus with enthusiasm for the model, however, they quickly realized there was a lot more to do than just provide a dedicated meeting time. Most important, buy-in from the faculty was required. Anita and the teacher leader cadre first held a professional development meeting to share what they had learned at the conference. While they shared their enthusiasm for the PLC model, they also stressed the importance of shared planning for the late-start Wednesday professional development time. As expected, some teachers initially resisted the idea. Although the faculty got along well, Anita soon realized that they rarely collaborated on their work. Consequently, she incorporated small-group activities into many faculty meetings for the remainder of that first year so the teachers would become more comfortable working with their colleagues. While this alone didn't get her the faculty investment she needed, Anita garnered extensive support by giving teachers multiple opportunities to have input into the development of the PLC initiative.

The teacher leader cadre also took an active role in working with faculty members. In order to equip them for their new roles, the cadre attended training on how to effectively run a meeting and hold their peers accountable for progress in student learning. Rather than acting merely as facilitators mostly responsible for handling logistical issues, the teacher leader cadre served more like mentors to others. They had to learn how to provide coaching and feedback to other teachers who were their peers at the same time. Balancing this responsibility with the need to maintain collegiality required practice. Throughout the spring semester, the cadre members met with each other and with Anita to discuss their work and the support they provided to teachers.

With all of this preparation, Anita and the teacher leader cadre felt they were ready to implement PLCs at Stoneridge at the start of the second school year. At the faculty retreat in August, they laid out the plans for starting PLCs. With buy-in and input from most of the faculty, they began holding regular PLC meetings at the start of the school year. Very quickly, more challenges arose. A few vocal resisters, including 2nd-grade teacher Susan, threatened to derail things. They complained that teachers at other schools in the district were still allowed to work in their classrooms during late-start Wednesday time. Anita even heard rumors that the group was threatening to file a union grievance over the differing job requirements across schools. Many conversations had to happen between Anita and the teachers, between the teacher leaders and the complaining teachers, and between Anita and the district to clarify what constituted legitimate uses of teachers' time during late-start Wednesday professional development. In the end, Anita was pleased with the result, but knew that she would never win everyone over.

At the same time, other challenges arose as the PLCs got off the ground in the second year of late-start Wednesdays. Most noticeably, some teams had a very difficult time operating efficiently. By October of that second year, Anita had different members of the 4th-grade team complaining to her every week about how the others on the team weren't letting them get any work done. And while she didn't hear from every team, Anita still heard reports from the teacher leader cadre about other grade levels. Even her trusted custodian, Eddie, told her he didn't know how she was going to get the 8th-grade teachers to agree on anything.

"They just go round and round about everything, Ms. Gallardo," revealed Eddie. "Sometimes I think they're just talking to the wall, because everyone says their own thing, but they never actually listen to each other."

After hearing this, Anita realized that although she and the teacher leader cadre had told every team they needed to assign roles such as timekeeper and note-taker, they never taught the teachers how to lead their own teams. Anita knew they would gain buy-in by having teachers decide what they discussed in each meeting, but she realized she had never taught them *how* to decide. As a result, Anita and the teacher leader cadre spent several weeks scrambling to provide professional development on how to work as a team while also providing support to the most struggling teams.

By January of the second year of late-start Wednesdays, Anita felt like they were finally starting to get somewhere. The PLCs resembled her initial vision, and it was abundantly clear that the teams at least knew what they were supposed to be doing. That's when Anita was blindsided by her own teacher leader cadre. They didn't threaten anything like the union grievance that the resistant teachers did, but the cadre called a meeting with Anita to address a growing concern.

"Anita, as teacher leader cadre members we've been meeting with all of the other teams since the start of the school year," began Grades 3–5 cadre member Roxanne.

As soon as Anita heard the words "since the start of the school year" she knew what was wrong. "You've never had a chance to meet with your own team, have you?" she interjected.

"No, we haven't," said Roxanne. "We understand that the other teams needed our help, but we also have to be teachers. We have to be a part of our own team."

Anita knew she had to find a better balance for the teacher leader cadre. Alienating them would be devastating to the teams they'd spent so long developing. She agreed to let them devote their Wednesday morning time to their own teams and only call on them as a last resort. Anita then began her "morning rounds" model where she tried to sit in on each team meeting for several minutes. While it only gave her a snapshot of the nine teams, Anita still kept up on the teams' work through their notes, which they turned in to her each week. Finally, by February of the second year of implementation, Anita felt like the teams were functioning.

This cycle continued until they faced another challenge. Looking back on it now, Anita considered it a bump in the road, but at the time she wasn't so sure. As standardized testing season approached in April, the district began requesting teachers to complete many forms and review testing procedures during their late-start Wednesday professional development time. Almost immediately, teachers began complaining about the pink forms that kept appearing in their boxes.

"The district says these are supposed to take us 10 minutes to fill out, but I'd like to see them try to complete these things in 10 minutes," said Max, a 6th-grade teacher.

"And I swear I've filled out this same form twice already!" complained Samantha, a 3rd-grade teacher.

Anita knew this was another roadblock she needed to address, but this time it meant going up against the district. As she looked into it, she learned that not only was the evaluation department giving teachers work to do during late-start Wednesday time, but the curriculum department was planning a series of workshops to take place at the same time for language arts teachers about the newly adopted curriculum. Anita cautiously raised the issue at the next principals' meeting. "I know late-start Wednesdays are for professional development, but when we started this initiative we were told it was for site-based professional development, meaning that it was to be held on-site and decided by the school leadership team," Anita said. Although she was nervous about broaching this subject, she knew she had a point. The superintendent could acknowledge that and say he had changed his mind, or they could work out a solution. Anita was thankful when other principals voiced support for her. In the end, the central administration agreed to find other ways to gather the information they needed and train teachers on the new curriculum. At the end of the second year of late-start Wednesdays, Anita knew her faculty had come a long way, and she was proud of the work they had accomplished together.

PLCs continued to develop at Stoneridge. After two years of teachers looking at student work in team meetings and identifying students for additional support, Stoneridge eventually showed some improvements in its test scores. However, Anita knew she still had some teachers who needed to upgrade their teaching skills. She had teachers who had very little skill in managing their students, and she had others who were strict disciplinarians but did not know how to group students for targeted instruction. She met with her teacher leader cadre about this and was struck when Joe, the Grade 6–8 teacher leader cadre member remarked, "Well, they just need professional development."

"But that's what their PLC is for," replied Anita.

"Well, if you think about it, they're not really getting professional development during Wednesday late-start time," responded Joe. "They may have learned how to look at student work in their teams, but that's all they're doing. No one is showing the teachers how to actually teach those targeted instruction groups they created."

Cadre member Marybeth reminded the group that they had seen sessions on peer observation at the initial conference that sparked their interest in professional learning communities. Anita considered this a turning point as they began their four-year journey to incorporate peer observation into their PLC work. In many ways, Anita felt like she was starting all over again. She had to build buy-in, provide professional development on peer observation, find time for teachers to observe each other teach, and deal with vocal resistance from teachers. It wasn't easy. People like 2nd-grade teacher Susan raised concerns that time spent outside of their own classrooms would be detrimental to their teaching. It took two more years of professional development, coaching, and other work before teachers regularly incorporated peer observation into their teams' work.

In its sixth year of development, Anita felt she could genuinely say PLCs were thriving at Stoneridge, and the results were undeniable. The school's test scores had risen more than any other school in the district. Moreover, she had had no teacher transfer requests in the past two years, which was practically unheard of in the Newkirk School District. Anita was convinced that much of their success was due to the implementation of teacher teams.

## Conclusion

Anita looked at her computer screen and reflected. "There really was a lot more that went into the creation of these teams than I realized," she thought to herself. Based on her observations today, she knew they didn't all run perfectly, but she was still proud of how far they'd come. Yet she couldn't help but wonder, "Will these teams ever be able to run without any oversight on my part? Is that even reasonable to expect? What needs to happen to make them such an ingrained part of the culture here that, if I left, they'd keep going?"

\*\*\*\*\*\*\*\*\*\*\*\*\*\*\*\*\*\*\*\*\*\*\*\*\*\*\*\*\*\*\*\*\*\*\*\*\*\*\*\*\*\*\*\*\*\*\*\*\*\*\*\*\*\*\*\*\*\*\*\*\*\*\*\*\*\*\*\*\*\*\*\*

## CASE 6—Guide to Analysis

How Far We've Come

**Key Concepts: Conditions of Effective Teams and Sustaining Change in Schools**

This teaching case explores the work of a principal in implementing professional learning communities (PLCs) in her school.

---

### Your Facilitator

**Wait!** It would be very, very difficult to gain any appreciable benefit from your expenditure of time and energy by attempting to conduct this analysis and its series of exercises without a facilitator. You *need* to appoint someone (it can be a team member) as a designated facilitator. This is not necessarily your team leader. This person will not be your "boss." But this person *will* be responsible for:

- Copying and distributing to all participants copies of the Case and Case Analysis and all handouts
- Organizing role-plays (appointing time keepers and observers, where indicated)
- Moving the process along and staying on track

**Psst! Facilitators:** Read all the activity directions as if they applied to you.
**Psst! Team members:** You, too.

---

### Materials Needed

Enough printed copies of the following to distribute to all team members:

- The Case and Guide to Analysis
- Worksheet—PLC Events Timeline
- Worksheet—Analysis of Stakeholder Roles
- Worksheet—Scale of Team Effectiveness
- Handout—The Five Conditions of Effective Teams
- Chart paper and markers

Full-size reproducibles of worksheets and handouts are available on the companion CD-ROM.

## A. Analyzing the Case

### Step 1: Read the Case (10 minutes)

Distribute the teaching case, and have all team members read it through, underlining or highlighting pieces of information that they think are significant to understanding the case.

### Step 2: Establish the Timeline (10 minutes)

Draw a timeline on the board (or chart paper; see Figure C6.1). Use the questions below to guide participants in filling in the events in the development of PLCs at Stoneridge. Make sure the timeline includes key events in the development of PLCs from the initiation of the idea until the present time.

- How long ago did all of this work begin in the district?
- What was the first event in the district that led to the PLC initiative?
- What was the next piece of the PLC initiative that Anita put into place?

Continue to complete the timeline by adding events until it is as complete as you can make it. (The goal is to reach an understanding that this was a lengthy and complicated process.)

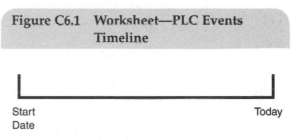

**Figure C6.1   Worksheet—PLC Events Timeline**

Start Date                                                   Today

### Step 3: Examine the Key Players (20 minutes)

Draw a four-column chart on the board (Figure C6.2). Use the questions below to have participants complete it to get a picture of the roles different stakeholders played in implementing PLCs at Stoneridge. Remind participants to cite evidence from the case when making their responses.

- What role did Anita play in developing teacher teams at Stoneridge?

**Figure C6.2   Worksheet—Analysis of Stakeholder Roles**

| Anita | Teacher Leader Cadre | Teachers | District |
|-------|----------------------|----------|----------|
|       |                      |          |          |
|       |                      |          |          |

- What role did the teacher leader cadre play?
- How did the teachers contribute to the development of the teams?
- What did the district do to facilitate this work?

### Step 4: Analyze Team Effectiveness (20 minutes)

Look at the scoring line (Figure C6.3). If you had to grade the teams at Stoneridge on their level of effectiveness on a scale of 1 to 5, what score would you give? (Consider the overall effectiveness of the teams as a group, since there aren't enough data given to grade individual teams.) Draw the scoring line on a chart, then call on three or four participants to come up to the line and draw an X where they would place the teams. You will revisit this scale of team effectiveness later on in this activity.

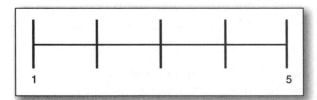

**Figure C6.3   Worksheet—Scale of Team Effectiveness**

Call on participants who gave the teams a high score and those who gave a lower score and ask:

- Why did you rate the teams in this way?
- What criteria did you use to place your X where you did on the scoring line?
- How effective do you think the teacher teams are now, based on evidence in the case?
- Does anyone want to change their ranking after hearing others' responses?

## B. Exploring the Dilemma (15 minutes)

Distribute to each participant a copy of the Five Conditions of Effective Teams (Figure C6.4).

Write a list of the five conditions for effective teacher teams on the board or chart paper, and ask meeting participants the following questions:

- Which of the five conditions do you think is *most* developed among the teams at Stoneridge? (Hear from each participant, and use plus signs [+] as tally marks against the list on the board to record their responses.)

## Figure C6.4   The Five Conditions of Effective Teams

### 1. Task Focus

- Is the team's task well defined and articulated, and does it focus on improving student learning?

The lowest level of development would indicate that the team focuses most of its energies and attention on logistics, or that its goals are not well defined. Or, more critically, that its goals do not have student learning at their center and that their focus is driven by crises or pressing school needs. At the highest level of achievement, the team's focus is proactive and team meetings are directed toward improving the planning and measuring of student progress. Team conversations are dialogues that help team members develop new understandings about teaching and learning. It should also be understood that one of the team's goals is to make clear that teacher learning is an ongoing process in and of itself and that this learning directly contributes to student achievement.

### 2. Leadership

- Does the team encourage leadership by all its members?

A low level of achievement in this area occurs when leadership roles are assumed reluctantly, or forced upon a member, or when leadership is assumed by the strongest or most vocal person on the team. A higher level of functioning occurs when potential leadership roles are distributed so that they are available to all team members in one way or another, and at one time or another. In high-functioning teacher teams, both novice and veteran teachers are empowered to take risks, and individual teacher instructional expertise is valued and utilized by all team members.

### 3. Structures and Processes

- Does the team determine ways to work together to achieve agreed-upon goals?
- Can the team articulate its structure and the team processes it uses to accomplish its goals?

A team cannot function well if its goals are poorly defined or if articulated goals are arrived at merely to satisfy low expectations of the team's abilities to affect student learning. Does the team apportion resources effectively to accomplish its goals? Does the team know how to access and enlist outside expertise? Highly effective teams have a process for deciding if certain tasks are best accomplished by individuals or by the group, and the team *continuously* adapts plans and processes to ensure that the team's focus is on students' learning needs.

### 4. Collaborative Climate

- Does the team promote a working environment that generates trust, communication, and synergy?

It's easy to avoid conflicts by never confronting serious issues and achieve harmony by simply allowing only the more dominant members to have a voice in conversations. Yet successful teams do not shy away from conflict; rather, they understand that there are benefits to be gained from conflict resolution. Teams have to find ways to legitimately and strategically make critiques within the team. Members should be encouraged to directly express their ideas, positions, and feelings, coupled with learning how to listen, react, and integrate different points of view. To encourage constructive arguments, teams could designate a devil's advocate or naysayer, or have a norm that no important decisions are to be finalized before contrary points of view are aired and discussed. These strategies can help teams recognize that seeking to resolve conflicts for mutual benefit is a means to promote team effectiveness. There is a difference between *collegiality*, which is simply a cooperative relationship between colleagues, and *collaboration*, which means working, collectively and successfully, to get the work done.

### 5. Personal Accountability

- Is there an expectation of performance improvement for both the team and the individual?
- Is there any *articulated* expectation of accountability?
- Do team members fail to complete tasks or deliver unacceptable levels of quality?

In a team that is functioning at mid-level, you might expect variable quality, with some assigned tasks completed well. In those teams, individuals may hold themselves accountable, but there is no process in place to hold individuals accountable for accomplishing team goals. In the highest-level teams, all members complete tasks effectively; the team holds all members accountable for their performance; all members share responsibility for the team's success and for the success of all students within the purview of the entire team.

- What evidence is there in the case for your answer?
- Which of the five conditions do you think is *least* well developed among the teams at Stoneridge? (Hear from each participant, and use minus signs [–] as tally marks to record their responses.)
- What evidence is there in the case for your answer?
- After seeing the others' responses, how effective do you think the teams are now?

You might track your answers to look something like this:

Task Focus + – + + – +

Leadership – – + – + +

Structures and Processes – – + – +

Collaborative Climate + + + + + –

Personal Accountability + + + – + +

Scoring Team Effectiveness

It's always important to keep the Five Conditions of Team Effectiveness in mind when assessing how effective any team may be. With that perspective, participants could now revisit the Scale of Team Effectiveness scored earlier and, upon reflection, determine if they might want to revise earlier scores.

## C. Reflect and Connect (15 Minutes)

1. How are the PLCs at Stoneridge like teacher teams you have seen?

2. What aspects of the student work and peer observation model are present in your own setting?

3. What could be gained from implementing such teams in your school? Consider the challenges you might experience along the way.

Refer back to the chart of key players (stakeholders) in Step 3 under *A. Analyzing the Case.*

4. Given all the work each of these people had to do to make the PLCs a reality, how long do you think it would take to implement collaborative teacher teams in your school?

5. What would people in your school have to do to make this happen?

## D. What Do We Do Now? (1 hour)

### Use the Future Protocol (aka Back to the Future)[17]

A good time to use this protocol is in the early stages of creating a plan or project that ultimately will have an endpoint. In this case, using the Future Protocol enables participants to consider how they can develop sustainable teams like the ones described at Stoneridge. By envisioning the ideal scenario as it could look at some point in the future, participants can identify the challenges they may face and the conditions needed to foster lasting change.

Enacting the Future Protocol, participants can work in small groups to envision what a team could look like in their own setting. Groups could envision teams within their grade level, or departments or groups from across a district could envision teams at the district level or teacher teams across schools.

This protocol-driven activity can be used by . . .

- Teacher leaders
- Team coaches
- Principals

- Heads of school
- Directors of professional development

. . . who want to . . .

- Create new teams or
- Improve the effectiveness of existing teams

### Purposes of Protocol

- Envision the future and describe what it would look like in the very best-case scenario
- Initiate discussion about the steps, players, resources, actions, and timelines it will take to be successful.

### Goals

- To expand and clarify the vision of what a group or individual is really trying to accomplish
- To identify opportunities and avenues for focused improvement
- To guide purposeful actions and reduce wasted efforts

### Considerations

- May be presented by an individual or an entire group
- Does not focus on the obstacles, but rather the opportunities . . . stay very positive

## The Future Protocol (Approximately 1 hour)

1. Present what you are trying to accomplish. (5 minutes)

Presenters (either individual or group) share what they are trying to do and how it might look when it is all done.

2. Ask clarifying questions. (5–10 minutes)

If presented by a single person and not a whole group, the rest of the group asks clarifying questions. If a group presents together, there are no clarifying questions.

3. Ask probing questions. (10 minutes)

Participants ask probing questions to further the presenters' thinking about what they want to accomplish. The presenters may choose to answer, think aloud, or quietly consider the questions.

4. Project into the future (using whatever timeline seems appropriate). (10–15 minutes)

Participants thoroughly describe what it looks like, sounds like, and feels like to have accomplished this endeavor. (We recommend the presenters be silent during this phase to allow them to listen more closely to the ideas of others and not feel the obligation to respond.)

- Talk in *present tense.*
- Describe what is in this best-case scenario. Do not yet describe how.
- Focus on the sights, sounds, behaviors, and feelings surrounding this accomplishment.
- Chart Steps 4, 5, and 6 so that all participants can see publicly what is being said.

5. Look "back" from your projected present, and describe how this initiative looked when it started. (5–10 minutes)

- Talk in *past tense.*
- Think about issues, culture, conversations, teacher's work, student achievement, and so on.
- Try to keep examples as concrete as possible.

Continue to chart this conversation. It is helpful to put dates at the top of the chart to identify the time period to which the group is referring.

6. Continue looking back from the "projected present," and discuss how you addressed the starting place and how you moved from that to the projected present. (5–10 minutes)

- Talk in *past tense.*
- Directly relate the previous description of how it looked when it started.
- Consider discussing how, when, with what resources, and by whom.

7. Return to the "projected present" and discuss whether it can get any better than it is or if this as good as it could possibly be. Again, think about how it will look, sound, and feel if it can get even better. (At this point the presenters should be able to participate.) (5 minutes)

8. Presenters share with the group their thoughts about the future and the information they have gathered. (5 minutes)

9. Debrief the process. (10 minutes)

## E. Next Steps

If you've completed the Future Protocol process, you probably have arrived, at the very least, at some philosophical conclusions or guiding principles. But if you want to go further and put those into action, here's a brief summary of what you need to look for as an outcome—a checklist of decisions reached, and actions taken.

You will want to have:

- Defined and articulated your vision of the "should be"
  - ☐ The vision clearly stated
  - ☐ The vision's importance justified

- Set realistic and attainable goals
  - ☐ Long term
  - ☐ Intermediate term
  - ☐ Short term

- Created a blueprint for action
  - ☐ Identified requirements for achieving goals
  - ☐ Decided who will do what
  - ☐ Determined how to coordinate the parts

- Laid out the timetable
  - ☐ Determined how many phases
  - ☐ Assigned responsibility for each phase
  - ☐ Identified milestones for each phase

- Assessed the necessary resources
  - ☐ Financial
  - ☐ Human
  - ☐ Time

# CASE 7. A Vague Destination, No Compass or Map

Key Concepts: Team Leadership and the Role of the Principal as a Facilitator, Motivator, and Supporter

# The 2nd-Grade Team Meeting

Charlene Anderson, the 2nd-grade team leader, stood next to the large easel pad, with marker in hand, and posed the question: "What are some of the typical reading struggles you might see your students having with a lesson you taught last week?"

The teachers around the table sat in silence while Charlene waited. She tried again. "Can we think of a specific example from the past week's lesson that might help us understand why some of our readers are having so much difficulty?"

Harriet Russo commented quickly, "Some of my students get through this text without any problems, and then there are plenty of others who seem to stumble on every word."

Jack Herman let out a loud sigh. "Yeah, it seems like we get more and more low-level students every year. What are they teaching in 1st grade, anyway?"

Charlene tried to press ahead. "Harriet, can you be a little more specific? For your students who struggle with this book, what types of patterns do you see?"

Harriet let out a heavy sigh. "I feel like I spend most of my time with Chris and the nonreaders, and the other students get hardly any attention from me at all."

Esther Cho, a second-year teacher and the youngest and newest member of the team, sat silently, while Jack looked out the window.

Charlene nodded her head and bit her lip. "Well," she said, "I was hoping we could come up with a list of some of the ways in which students were having difficulty with this book and develop some specific strategies to support them." The team continued to sit silently. She wasn't sure how to proceed. "Let me give you an example from my class."

For the remaining 20 minutes, Charlene explained how she worked with a girl in her class whose decoding skills had improved significantly over the past few months. Esther seemed to listen with some interest to her example but said nothing. Charlene could feel Harriet and Jack tune her out.

At the end of the meeting, Charlene suggested that over the next week, the teachers try to list specific reading problems from their students that they'd like to work on problem solving together. While the teachers all nodded their heads, Charlene could feel the skepticism from her veteran teammates as they gathered their things and returned to their classrooms. Another hour-long meeting had passed and little had been accomplished. Charlene herself was wondering whether these meetings were the best use of the team's time and whether she was the right person to lead the team. Jack approached her and said, "I know you mean well, but those kids need the reading specialist to pull them out. We're not equipped to handle these kinds of issues." Charlene sighed and felt helpless. She knew this was what the team believed, and at the same time she knew she was expected to convince them otherwise.

As she walked out into the hallway, she saw that Harriet's class had already moved into their reading groups, and Harriet was in a small group with Chris and the four other boys who made up her lowest reading group. Harriet was leaning forward and trying to listen to Chris, while the other boys distracted themselves with their pencils. These were the moments that Charlene needed to document, so that the team could begin coming up with concrete strategies to work with exactly these students, but her own class sat waiting for her. As Charlene stepped inside her classroom, she wondered what she could do that might move this team's work forward.

## Inclusion at the Buckley School

The Buckley School had a reputation in the community for strong discipline and rising test scores, even though two-thirds of its students qualified for free or reduced-price lunch and there was a growing number of nonnative speakers of English. Buckley had many veteran teachers and a charismatic, take-charge principal, Laura Shea, who was skilled in attracting community partners and grants as well as recruiting talented young teachers.

But a recent dip in the students' scores on the state reading test had marred Buckley's otherwise exemplary results, and Principal Shea was vocal in her insistence that the school take aggressive action to reverse the trend. With the new superintendent's emphasis on more in-class interventions, principals and teachers were being asked to "be creative" about making the best of a shrinking budget for reading specialists. Mrs. Shea felt strongly that investing more resources in early literacy would pay off with better test scores in later grades. "We want to do everything possible to make sure that by the 3rd grade, students feel like they are capable readers. In each class we can identify the students in need of the most support; we simply need to focus and deliver those supports as consistently as possible," she explained.

In late October, Mrs. Shea hired Marianne Bennett as an assistant principal, specifically because she had a strong background in early literacy and had many ideas about creating teacher-led teams that would look closely at student work and develop formative assessments to improve literacy instruction. When she was first introduced to the staff, Marianne caused some anxiety, using statements like "It shouldn't be your kids and my kids; they should all be our kids" and "Collaboration is the key to serving all children well." Charlene had heard these types of sentiments in the graduate program she had recently completed, and it was no wonder, since Ms. Bennett looked like she had just graduated from college. Charlene hadn't seen much evidence of those theories at Buckley; teachers and administrators were always preoccupied with raising test scores or dealing with budget cuts. "Great," Jack groaned under his breath. "Another Ivy League genius to look over our shoulders."

But when she bumped into Ms. Bennett in the hallway, Charlene mentioned her graduate training in reading and it turned out they had taken some of the same coursework on reading interventions. Charlene hoped that Ms. Bennett would bring resources and perspectives to support some of the teachers and students around literacy.

Later that week, when she was called into a meeting with Mrs. Shea and Ms. Bennett, Charlene's first thought was that she was being evaluated. Instead, Ms. Bennett surprised her. "We've received a small grant to expand the 2nd-grade team model so that teachers can work together to develop strategies and supports for our lowest-performing readers. We've received funding so that the entire 2nd-grade team will have an additional prep period each week to discuss best practices and ways to better implement interventions. Mrs. Shea and I felt that due to your background you would be the ideal person to lead the meetings and help your colleagues make sure they're doing everything possible for their lowest readers. You and I can conduct some classroom observations and give your colleagues feedback and suggestions. Of course, you would receive a stipend, and we would provide substitute coverage when you need to be working with other teachers or observing in classrooms. You would report to me to keep me in the loop."

Charlene felt overwhelmed by the offer, but she immediately saw the potential of working together as a team to improve reading instruction. She had been frustrated in the past by teachers whose attitudes reflected low expectations for children who came into the 2nd grade with poor reading skills, but never felt like she could say anything. Now, she could actually offer help to her colleagues like Harriet—good, caring teachers who were feeling overwhelmed by the demand to help those students "catch up." But she had concerns, too. She wasn't the most veteran teacher on the team and she didn't want to be seen as some kind of supervisor or someone who was telling other teachers how to run their classrooms. Charlene took the job, though, saying clearly, "I'm just a regular classroom teacher. Even though I have a master's in teaching reading, I was hired as a 2nd-grade teacher, not a literacy specialist." A few days later, she commented to a friend, "I decided to take the leadership role because I hoped that teamwork might offer teachers support in an environment where there's a lot of pressure to get the scores up. I also felt like we could be doing a better job with our struggling readers and that sharing our experiences and resources might be one way to do that."

## Checking In

A few weeks after she'd accepted the position, Charlene met with Ms. Bennett to discuss the progress on the 2nd-grade team. Charlene said to the assistant principal, "I'm not sure what I'm supposed to be doing. I try to get the teachers to talk about students so we can problem solve, but a lot of times our conversations are for teachers to vent their frustration and complain about wanting more resources or to talk about planning school activities." When it came to student progress, she reported, the team wanted the reading specialist to work with students in pull-out groups or someone from the district to come and test the children for learning disabilities.

Ms. Bennett asked, "What about classroom observations? Have you scheduled them?"

"I've tried," Charlene admitted. "I've observed in Harriet's room once, but none of the other teachers have set up their observations. I can tell that Jack is less willing to do it. He keeps suggesting that next week would be better."

"Well, that's an important part of your role, so be sure to get those scheduled," Ms. Bennett said. They went over Charlene's notes from the meeting and some of her plans for the next meeting. The teachers had some questions about when they could get information about the next round of formative assessments, and Ms. Bennett promised to get them the information. Charlene found herself struggling to report on the content of the meeting and didn't admit to Ms. Bennett the amount of time they had spent talking about the buses for next week's 2nd-grade trip to the Science Museum, and about last week, when they spent so much time discussing the reading books and bulletin board assignments. Throughout the meeting, Ms. Bennett was positive and encouraging, but Charlene left feeling more uncertain about her leadership and this team than she had felt when she walked into Ms. Bennett's office.

## The 2nd-Grade Team

Harriet was a 10-year veteran of the district and someone Mrs. Shea thought of as one of the top teachers in her school. She had deep knowledge of the community's literacy curriculum and taught it creatively and well. Harriet saw the work of the 2nd-grade team as important, but fundamentally she felt that the team was avoiding larger instructional issues. "I think if everyone taught the required curriculum, we would improve our student success," she admitted. "Not everyone on our team is teaching the district-adopted curriculum, which I think is the root of the problem. Some teachers seem to think that they can still teach whatever they want, but then we all are held accountable for the results. I like Charlene Anderson. She's been a good colleague to me, but I'm not sure if she has enough skill to lead this team. I have brought my concerns to Ms. Bennett numerous times about certain members of the 2nd-grade team, but it doesn't seem like much can be done about it." She let out a frustrated sigh. "I guess the best I can do is shut my door and teach."

Jack voiced his take on the team. "I know I'm a good teacher. I've been doing this for a long time and I've seen these programs and dozens like it come and go. I like Charlene, too. I think she's a lot more easygoing than some other people on our team, and I'd like to see her do well. I just don't need anyone looking over my shoulder. I'm not really looking for advice. I know I do some things differently than other people on the team, but I'm not telling them how to teach their students. Like I said, I've been doing this for 25 years now. I think I know how to teach 2nd grade."

Esther had her own thoughts about the team. "I came into this team of veteran teachers and clearly there was a dynamic here, long before me. I am doing my best to learn the curriculum and get my classroom in order, so anything that Charlene or other teachers want to share about how to do that, I welcome. But I'm not trying to get involved in any politics here. When I go to those meetings I feel like there's a lot left unsaid, but I'm hardly in a position to rock the boat. I chat with Charlene sometimes and I know she has a lot of good ideas, but right now those meetings just seem like one more thing I'm adding to my already very long day. Honestly, I could use the time to be doing more lesson planning or communicating with parents."

Charlene was discouraged. "I'm not sure if it's this team, or if I'm not the right person to lead it. There are so many things we could be working on to improve, and I don't like the feeling that this is 'my' issue. I guess I was naïve to think that people would just enthusiastically jump on board and want to talk about their toughest students, but I'm not judging anyone. I want to help and provide more resources, which I thought everyone would want. As for classroom observations, I can't force anyone to do anything. I just don't think we can have real conversations unless we know what's happening in each other's classrooms. I guess I didn't know people would feel so protective. In general, I feel like I'm without a map. I wonder if Ms. Bennett should be running these meetings instead of me. Right now, I'm questioning the whole enterprise."

## Meeting Time

It was a Thursday afternoon, a few months after Charlene had been named team leader. The meeting began, and a few minutes later Ms. Bennett and Mrs. Shea entered the classroom. "I've heard good things from Ms. Bennett about what's happening with this 2nd-grade team, so I came to listen in for a few minutes," Mrs. Shea announced.

The teachers shifted in their seats somewhat uncomfortably. Charlene put on a smile and said, "Wonderful. We're glad you can join us. We've been talking about some of the data from last month's formative assessments and how we might use the information to form reading groups. I've been encouraging teachers to bring some examples of students progressing from one reading level to the next."

"Outstanding," nodded Mrs. Shea.

"Does anyone want to begin?" asked Charlene.

The team looked down at their papers but remained silent. Looking around, Mrs. Shea said, "Perhaps I should give you all some of the background on literacy instruction here at the Buckley School and why this topic is of particular interest to me."

Charlene felt a sudden sense of panic. As Mrs. Shea talked about the recent drop in reading scores and some of the current plans for reform in the district, Charlene wondered what would happen when she finished talking. She glanced over at Ms. Bennett, who offered her a tense smile.

Mrs. Shea was talking about how she felt confident that the experience on this team might result in some powerful problem solving. "I'll present what I've prepared for today," decided Charlene, "and if they all want to sit there in silence, at least Mrs. Shea and Ms. Bennett will see it's not my fault."

Charlene had already begun to frame her explanation of why she no longer wanted to continue as team leader. "Maybe some people just weren't meant to work together," she thought sadly. "I can't force people to talk if they don't want to, and if that's what it takes, they'll have to find someone else to do it."

\*\*\*\*\*\*\*\*\*\*\*\*\*\*\*\*\*\*\*\*\*\*\*\*\*\*\*\*\*\*\*\*\*\*\*\*\*\*\*\*\*\*\*\*\*\*\*\*\*\*\*\*\*\*\*\*\*\*\*\*\*\*\*\*\*\*\*\*\*

## CASE 7—Guide to Analysis

### A Vague Destination, No Compass or Map

**Key Concepts: Team Leadership and the Role of the Principal as a Facilitator, Motivator, and Supporter**

---

### Your Facilitator

**Wait!** It would be very, very difficult to gain any appreciable benefit from your expenditure of time and energy by attempting to conduct this analysis and its series of exercises without a facilitator. You *need* to appoint someone (it can be a team member) as a designated facilitator. This is not necessarily your team leader. This person will not be your "boss." But this person *will* be responsible for:

- Copying and distributing to all participants copies of the Case and Case Analysis and all handouts
- Organizing role-plays (appointing time keepers and observers, where indicated)
- Moving the process along and staying on track

**Psst! Facilitators:** Read all the activity directions as if they applied to you.
**Psst! Team members:** You, too.

---

### Materials Needed

Enough printed copies of the following to distribute to all team members:

- The Case and Guide to Analysis
- Worksheets—Team Planning, Part 1 and Part 2
- Chart paper and markers

Full-size reproducibles of worksheets and handouts are available on the companion CD-ROM.

---

## A. Analyzing the Case

### Step 1: Read the Case (15 minutes)

Distribute the teaching case, and have all team members read it through, underlining or highlighting pieces of information that they think are significant to understanding the case.

## Step 2: Case Analysis Questions (20 minutes)

Discuss the following questions. For each, identify the evidence that leads you to your response. (You do not have to address every question.)

### About the Team

- What are the 2nd-grade team's strengths and weaknesses?
- How would you articulate the team's goal?
- What factors (structural, cultural, or interpersonal) affect this team's level of collaboration?

### About the Individuals

- What could Charlene do to address the particular concerns of Esther, Jack, and Harriet?
- What, if anything, can Charlene ask of her teammates to improve the workings of the 2nd-grade team? What, if anything, can Charlene ask of the school administrators?
- What obstacles are preventing Esther, Jack, and Harriet from participating more actively in team discussions? What would you do to address those obstacles?

### About the School

- What was the process for choosing Charlene as team leader? What are the costs and benefits of that process?
- What is the appropriate role for the principal in this situation? How might she have better supported the success of this team?
- What are the conditions for teamwork at the Buckley School?

# B. Exploring the Dilemma

## The "Triple Threat" to Teacher Leadership at the Buckley School (40 minutes)

Before beginning this section, take a vote on whether Charlene should remain team leader. Record the results.

## Step 1: Read the Following Section

### Persistent Cultural Barriers to Teacher Leadership[18]

1. Protecting autonomy

The belief that teachers have the right to teach as they see fit and that what happens inside their classroom is not related to what goes on in other classrooms.

2. Ensuring egalitarianism

The belief that all teachers are essentially the same, with no teacher being better or having more authority than any other.

3. Reinforcing seniority

The belief that teachers with more years of experience do not need to concern themselves with the problems of teachers with fewer years of experience. Years of experience means that teachers "know what they're doing" and don't need additional suggestions for improving practice.

## Step 2: Review the Case

Identify interactions where one of the three elements of the triple threat is preventing the team from working together productively. After reviewing the case, discuss these questions:

- Do you think Charlene is aware of these cultural barriers?
- Does she try to get around them?
- Why would Charlene be resented as a leader?

## Step 3: Read the Following Section

### Coping Strategies Adopted by Teacher Leaders[19]

Faced with the triple threat obstacles to leadership noted above, teacher leaders often devise coping strategies in order to persist with their work. The three that are identified here are just a few; but when you read them, keep in mind this case and Charlene's challenges as the team's leader. Which strategies, if any, seem to fit?

*Waiting to be drafted:* If they wait until they are "assigned" a leadership position by an administrator, teachers can avoid accusations of seeking more power. Teachers can then attempt to maintain a sense of solidarity with their fellow teachers by making their leadership seem like the result of an administrative ruling. ("It's not my fault. They gave me this job.")

*Working with the willing:* By waiting for teachers to volunteer to work with them, or by working exclusively with novice teachers or trusted colleagues, teacher leaders can avoid the discomfort of working with teachers who have greater seniority or teachers resistant to feedback. While this might provide valuable support to new teachers, it limits the teacher leader's ability to achieve team goals.

*Working side by side:* Teacher leaders can characterize their work exclusively as optional support and resources. Working side by side allows for collaboration and support without feeling authoritarian. However, by limiting or minimizing their authority, teachers can protect their autonomy and can essentially reject interventions that might improve instructional practice for themselves and others. It also undermines any expertise that a teacher leader might bring to her or his position.

## C. Reflect and Connect (30 minutes)

### Evaluating Individual Coping Strategies

Having explored the triple threat to teacher leadership, follow up with a discussion of how most teachers attempt to navigate around these obstacles. Charlene illustrates some of the strategies that teacher leaders employ to cope with persistent cultural norms and ill-defined roles that exist in schools. These strategies are specifically developed to allow teachers to avoid rejection by their colleagues and reduce opposition for their ideas.

Going through the case, identify if and when Charlene attempted to use any of the following common coping strategies:

| Coping strategy | How Charlene used the strategy | Results |
|---|---|---|
| Waiting to be drafted | | |
| Working with the willing | | |
| Working side by side | | |

As you identify Charlene's coping strategies, consider the following:

- Why does Charlene *wait to be drafted* as team leader even though she has wanted to say something before?
- Thinking about the *working with the willing* strategy, whom does Charlene choose to work with and why does she make that choice?
- Charlene says, "I'm not judging anyone. . . . I can't force anyone to do anything." How does that comment reinforce the strategy of *working side by side?*
- What are the benefits and limitations of these coping strategies?

The following statement reflects comments made by several teachers who have studied this case.

> While some of these coping strategies might allow teachers to continue in their roles, the effects of their leadership may be limited, and resources and instructional improvement may not reach the teachers who could derive the most benefit.

In what ways do you agree with the statement; in what ways do you disagree?

## D. What Do We Do Now? (10 minutes)

Review components of the triple threat to teacher leadership. Think about the work of your team, and consider whether any of your team's challenges are a result of the triple threat.

### Leadership and Organizational Support (15 minutes)

This case demonstrates some of the ways in which school leaders overlook cultural norms and append the notion of teams and teacher leadership to an existing compartmentalized school structure, but with poor role definition and inadequate support. Without strong administrative support, clear communication to faculty, and structural supports for collaboration, teacher leaders are frequently doomed to fail before they even begin.

- Consider what interventions individual teachers or teacher leaders are able to make on their own and which need to be handled at the organizational level.
- If you could wave a magic wand, what would you ask from your administrators?
- Brainstorm several ways that teacher leaders and administrators can work together to overcome some of the barriers presented by the triple threat.

Look at this checklist to determine what's in place in your school/ team and what you would like to be in place.

- ☐ A clearly defined goal with clear outcomes that can be used to assess progress
- ☐ An open, transparent, and rigorous process for selecting the team leader

- A schoolwide introduction of the purpose and goals of the team, the team leader, and how the administration plans to support the work of the team
- Direct administrative intervention with reluctant team members
- A form of regular team assessment to reflect on team goals and determine if and how the goals are being met; an agreed-upon system for how to address and solve the problems that the team has identified

Write some recommendations for what you would want to change about the leadership and organizational support in your school. Be prepared to discuss at least one of these suggestions and some initial steps to implement your suggestion. Use the Worksheets— Team Planning, Part 1 and Part 2 (Figures C7.1 and C7.2), to plan your strategy.

**Figure C7.1    Worksheet—Team Planning (Part 1)**

| Date | |
|---|---|
| Participants | |
| Goal | |
| What would be different in our team if we made progress on this goal? | |
| What gets in the way of progress? | Structural issues? |
| | Cultural issues? |
| | Other obstacles? |

**Figure C7.2    Worksheet—Team Planning (Part 2)**

| Intervention/ action | When will this step be implemented? | By whom? | What to bring to the meeting? |
|---|---|---|---|
| 1. | | | |
| 2. | | | |
| 3. | | | |
| 4. | | | |
| 5. | | | |
| 6. | | | |

## CASE 8. The Team That's "Practically Beloved"

**Key Concepts: Leadership, Task Focus, and Mutual Accountability**

Giddy teenagers tumbled into the room, making those noises typical of students entering Ella Tye's 7th-grade ELA (English language arts) classroom.

"Hello, kids!"

"Good morning, Ms. Tye."

Just as most of the desks had become occupied, the principal popped her head through the classroom door.

"Welcome, Dr. Gustason."

"I was hoping I could have a word with you in the hallway," said the principal. "It'll only take a moment."

The room grew silent for a minute. The kids looked from Ms. Tye to Dr. Gustason and tried to measure the seriousness of the situation. Ms. Tye smiled gently at her students and said, "I'll be gone for just a minute."

As Ms. Tye moved toward the doorway, her classroom slowly began to buzz.

## Linwood Middle School

Linwood, a large middle school located in the Northwest, has a student population of 1,200, approximately 70 percent of whom are white, 15 percent Asian, 10 percent African American, and 5 percent Hispanic. Teachers are divided into teams by grade level and assigned to "Pods." Over the years the school has performed modestly well on standardized tests, but with No Child Left Behind and the recently implemented statewide exams, there are increasing worries about indications of not meeting Adequate Yearly Progress (AYP).

Linwood is considered a good place to teach, and the majority of Linwood teachers have been teaching there for at least six years.

## The Hallway

Dr. Gayle Gustason started, "You know, we just finished placing students on teams for next year, and I thought you and your teammates would be pleased to know that Pod 5 was requested more by parents than any of the other 7th-grade pods." Ella's smile grew and spread across her face. The principal continued, "What you five teachers have done for the kids on your team is amazing. I wish everyone in this building could be more like your team. The kids love you, their parents love you, and that makes my job easier. This school would be incredible if more staff members worked together like you guys do. Share the accomplishment with your teammates. You should all be very proud of yourselves. In this town, it's nearly impossible to earn the reputation you people have managed to. You're practically beloved! Keep up the great work!"

Ella blushed. In nine years of teaching, she'd never experienced a moment like this, and after a few slow blinks and a nod she ducked, smiling, back into her classroom. As she had expected, the room buzzed with enthusiastic chatter. Ella leaned casually against the chalkboard's ledge and enjoyed the moment a little longer. In four more days, the year would be over and school would be dismissed for the summer. She knew the kids were excited about vacation, but she also knew that her 7th graders had been coming to class for months excited and ready to learn. In fact, she and her teaching teammates had worked hard to create exactly this type of culture in Pod 5, one of five 7th-grade academic teams in the school.

The team members understood middle schoolers, both the challenges of working with this age group and the enormous energy and excitement that is always close to the surface in every middle school student—energy that could be channeled in positive ways to increase student success in middle school classrooms. The teachers all fervently believed that creating community was the key to good teaching, and they had established, in each of their classrooms, a culture of caring and warmth that was project-based, with innovative projects in each subject area geared to this group's high energy level and eagerness to learn. The students loved the team. They knew that the teachers in Pod 5 understood them, and across the board, students of Pod 5 got good grades. Parents thought highly of the teachers and of the glowing reports that the Pod 5 team teachers had given their children. Now, looking out over her classroom, Ella took a few deep breaths. She swelled with pride. More than at any other time in her career, she felt affirmed, and it felt really great to be a teacher.

## That Afternoon

Room 10 was empty except for four teachers who sat together around a table. It was prepped with chairs for six teachers, but two were still empty. Ella, as the team's leader, looked at her watch and sighed. She was proud of the role she played. Her leadership responsibilities included organizing and chairing team meetings and maintaining intermittent communication about team activities with the principal. She received a small stipend for this work; it wasn't much, but it was enough to make her feel responsible for the smooth functioning of the team.

One o'clock. The team meeting should have started 10 minutes ago. It always frustrated her when people were late, especially the *same* people. "Man, Santorino and Abby are always late. Where are they? I've got good news. Great news actually, and I can't wait to tell you guys." Ella checked her watch again.

"I'll text Santorino and tell him to get in here," complained Ross Lowry, Pod 5's social studies teacher. He pulled out his cell phone and began punching at the keys. Beside him, Nick Scarpone, the special education teacher who worked with all the students with IEPs (Individual Education Plans) in the 7th and 8th grades, sat silently finishing his late lunch, and science teacher George Gilespie was filling out an order form for new textbooks. Gilespie was the curriculum coordinator for the school's science department in addition to being a full-time science teacher. He knew well the stress associated with trying to conduct a productive meeting, and he shared Ella's frustration with Abby Waller, the team's Spanish teacher, and math teacher Paul Santorino's persistent tardiness. In fact, he and Ella had once strategized ways to address this issue, but they eventually both agreed that confronting their colleagues might actually do more harm than good.

Though most team meetings started this same way, with the same two teachers always being late, it never seemed to affect the quality of the team's time together, only its length. Ella's concern for student learning and growth and Gilespie's concentration on curriculum and assessment kept the meeting minutes student-centered and intensely focused. The team members often shared their innovative curricular ideas with each other, and they prided themselves on using their own particular sort of formative assessment to keep track of the students' academic growth. Ross's phone buzzed to life. "Santorino says they're on their way down. Right now," Ross reported. Ella checked her watch again and took a deep breath.

## The Team Meeting

Abby came swooping into the room. "Sorry I'm late. I just got off the phone with a parent." Santorino was right on her tail. He spun through the doorway. Unlike Abby, he offered no explanation for his tardiness as he took the last open seat at the table.

"So, I've got some good news to share with you—*great* news actually." Ella took her job as team leader very seriously, and even though some of her teammates poked fun at her seriousness, they trusted Ella to keep the teacher team members as well as their 120 students on track. Parent teacher conferences were well organized; grade-level field trips went off like clockwork, there were few discipline problems, and the kids were happy.

"Dr. Gustason dropped by my room this morning and told me that the administrative team had just finished assigning students to Pods for next year," said Ella. "They sorted through hundreds of parent requests for placement and, well, we were the most requested team. Dr. Gustason said that we are, in her words, 'practically beloved.'"

Smiles erupted around the table. Lowry and Gilespie high-fived, Santorino fist-pumped, and Abby and Ella laughed at the antics of their teammates. Ella ended the meeting early. It was the end of the year after all, and if anyone had earned a break, they had.

## The Following September

Ella entered the library exactly three minutes before the first full faculty meeting of the new school year was scheduled to start. She couldn't remember the last time she'd cut it this close to being late to a faculty meeting, especially the first one of the year, but she'd gotten sidetracked by an email Dr. Gustason had sent her a half-hour earlier.

"The results are in from the statewide exam. You need to come see me, ASAP." The email made Ella feel anxious. She knew that if it had been good news, Dr. Gustason would have shared it with her face to face. The realization made Ella's stomach drop.

During the meeting, Ella tried to listen carefully, but the principal's email absorbed all her energy. Pod 5 had ended last year on such a high note. Since June, she'd anticipated starting this year at the top, as the most requested 7th-grade team in the school. It had felt hopeful, well deserved, and invigorating. They had been the best in the school last June, and the year had literally just started. What could possibly have gone wrong already? It just didn't make sense. When the meeting ended, Ella jumped up from her seat and headed straight for Dr. Gustason.

"Dr. Gustason, I got your email. Is everything OK? I was wondering if you'd have time to talk right now." The words kind of spilled out of Ella's mouth. She felt embarrassed by how desperate she must have sounded.

Dr. Gustason rubbed her forehead. "Look, Ella, go home. Relax. In the morning, come by my office before homeroom. Pod 5 has got a lot of work to do. You have an action plan to write."

Ella's forehead wrinkled in confusion. An action plan? No way, she thought to herself. "Action plans" were written when "instructional improvement" was necessary. Pod 5 on an action plan? Dr. Gustason had already said she wished more of the staff could be like the teachers on Pod 5. She'd complimented their efforts, even said they were amazing. Heck, she had told Ella to "keep up the great work." Ella was stunned. It just didn't make any sense.

## The Next Morning

Ella sat in a chair outside the principal's office. When Dr. Gustason arrived, Ella didn't wait for an invitation. She followed the principal into her office and settled into a seat. She waited in silence for their conversation to begin.

"Look, Ella," Dr. Gustason finally started, "I'm going to get right to the point. The statewide exam scores for your team are not where they should be. Have you seen them?" The principal slid a thick, stapled packet across to Ella. Dr. Gustason continued, "It's not that the scores are bad, Ella. They're OK, but after last year and all the parent requests for placement, all the compliments and high praise, I had expected so much more from the students on your team. I thought they'd have the best scores in the entire 7th grade. Instead, three other teams at your grade level have better scores than you have. I think we *can* do better. Damn it, Ella, I thought we *would* do better, but now we *have* to. That's the bottom line."

Ella felt sick to her stomach. She had to clear her throat in order to find her voice. "I don't know what happened, Dr. Gustason. I'm not even sure what to say. . . ." Ella examined the data in the packet. She could see that Pod 5's special education students had, as a group, failed to meet AYP in any subject area. This was immediately troubling, but when she looked more carefully, Ella realized that nearly half the students on last year's team had not met AYP. It wasn't just the special education students who were at risk; it was half of all their students who were at risk. Ella's face flushed. She could barely catch her breath.

Dr. Gustason sensed Ella's growing discomfort. "Look, Ella. It's not the end of the world. We're going to be OK if we react with swift and deliberate action. Pod 5 needs a plan for action. Action, Ella, we need action!"

Ella nodded her head in silent agreement.

## The Team Gets the News

Abby and Santorino were late. Again. Ella had had enough. If improvement came with swift and deliberate action, then she was starting today.

"What do you say we just get started?"

Lowry scrunched up his face. Gilespie gave her a quick nod to show support for her decision. Scarpone looked nervous, knowing that this was not the way things were done in Pod 5. Ella took a few deep breaths. She wanted to seem confident, sturdy, and capable.

"So, this morning before school, I met with Dr. Gustason. And the news isn't great. It's our statewide exam scores. They're, well, they kind of . . ."

At this point, Santorino and Abby blew through the door and into the team meeting. "Sorry, sorry, sorry," Abby was full of apologies. Santorino sat down without a word.

Gilespie ignored them both. "They're what, Ella? What's wrong with them?"

Santorino seemed offended, "Wait, you guys started without us? What's up with that?" He looked around for an explanation, but it was like nobody had even heard him.

Abby leaned over toward Lowry and whispered, "What'd we miss? What's going on? Is something wrong?"

Ella responded with frustration. "Yeah, Paul, we did start without you two today. And we'll start without you tomorrow too if you don't show up on time. And yes, Abby, something is wrong."

With an arrogant smirk, Santorino interrupted, "Well, it looks like somebody's forgotten who's the most requested team in the school. Huh, Ella, did you forget?"

Across the table, Gilespie had put his head in hands. Lowry was pushed back from the table and balancing on two chair legs. This type of fighting was unusual for the teachers of Pod 5. It was all very overwhelming for Ella. This is not how she had wanted it to go.

After a few moments' pause, she tried again. "Look, I met with Dr. Gustason this morning before school. It's our statewide exam scores. They're just not where they should be. Almost half of our students failed to meet AYP. Nearly half."

The news was devastating to Gilespie. Ella knew it would be. As curriculum coordinator for science, he was constantly pushing the teachers within his department to use data to improve instruction. But to her surprise, it was Lowry, the social studies teacher, not Gilespie, who spoke first. "What do we need to do, Ella? I mean, what's the first step here? We have to do better."

Ella started to explain, "Well, we have to write an action plan that outlines our—"

"Whoa, whoa, whoa! Are we writing this action plan as a team?" Santorino interrupted brusquely. He grabbed hold of the state exam data packet that Ella had distributed to each member of the team and sorted through the information. He never looked up while Ella continued speaking.

"Yes, we're writing it as a team. That's the idea here. *Our* students are struggling to be successful so *we* come up with strategies to improve instruction, curriculum, and ultimately, student perform—"

"Well, I'll tell you one thing, I'm not agreeing to any action plan. Check the math scores. Most of the kids met AYP, and a few even scored 'advanced.' So there's no way I'm writing any kind of action plan. There's no way I'm doing anything extra."

Santorino had barely finished when Abby added her two cents' worth, "Yeah, I mean, Spanish isn't even on the state exam. Seems like I automatically get a free pass on the action plan."

Nobody spoke. Gilespie looked stunned. Lowry seemed confused. Scarpone had the look of someone who'd just had the wind knocked out of him. Ella tried to think fast.

"Look, Paul," she said, "You might be right. Maybe an action plan isn't the answer, but our students deserve the best, and we're not giving it to them. Do you have a better idea for action?"

After a few moments of silence, Santorino responded, "Yup, I sure do. I'm out of here." Abruptly, the math teacher got up from the table and left the meeting, with Abby right behind him.

## Ella's Predicament

At the end of a long, sleepless night, Ella emailed Dr. Gustason before dawn to ask for an early morning appointment—before the arrival of the kids.

Gustason replied almost immediately. She was an early riser herself, a hard worker who put her all into making her school run well. "What's up, Ella? Sure, come to my office at 7. That'll give us a few minutes to talk." Ella quickly wrote back a "thanks" and started to get ready for her day.

The school hallways were still mostly dark when Ella arrived at Dr. Gustason's office. Dr. Gustason looked worried, and Ella got right to the point. "As I'm sure you'd have expected, Pod 5 was terribly upset yesterday when I delivered the bad news about our low scores—our not making AYP in special ed and the poor showing of 50 percent of all our kids. The problem is, not everyone on the team sees it as *our* problem. Two team members have literally refused to work on an action plan together with the others. Paul Santorino says his kids got great math scores and there's nothing else he needs to do. Abby says she's a Spanish teacher, her subject's not tested, and she doesn't feel she has any responsibility for working on an action plan for the entire team.

Dr. Gustason bristled. "What? I made it clear that this was a directive. Opting out of writing this plan is not their choice. Your entire team has to work on an action plan and that's final! If we say we're a school that's made up of grade-level teams, then every grade level has to act like a team. Mistakenly, I guess, I thought you were a team—my best team. Well, my response to this situation is simple. Your job as team leader is simple. Deliver my message. All of your members *must* take part in the development and implementation of the action plan. We need all of you on board. That's final, and I'll be in to check on the action plan at the end of the week."

Now Ella felt worse than ever. She would seem like a traitor when she delivered the news, and the team's trust in her leadership would surely be shaken. But she and they knew they couldn't disobey orders. Now the trick for Ella was to keep up the goodwill and energy of the team at the same time as two of the team members had just been overruled by the principal. They would feel betrayed and sure that they as professionals should not be treated this way.

Ella headed down the hallway. The lights in the building were all on now, and teachers were greeting each other, cups of coffee in hand, heading toward their classrooms. A new school year had begun. There was excitement in the air, but not for Ella.

What would she do now?

\*\*\*\*\*\*\*\*\*\*\*\*\*\*\*\*\*\*\*\*\*\*\*\*\*\*\*\*\*\*\*\*\*\*\*\*\*\*\*\*\*\*\*\*\*\*\*\*\*\*\*\*\*\*\*\*\*\*\*\*\*\*\*\*\*\*\*\*\*

# CASE 8—Guide to Analysis

## The Team That's "Practically Beloved"

**Key Concepts: Leadership, Task Focus, and Mutual Accountability**

This case addresses the issue of a team that is highly regarded by parents and administration; however, their students receive surprisingly low scores on the standardized state test.

---

### Your Facilitator

**Wait!** It would be very, very difficult to gain any appreciable benefit from your expenditure of time and energy by attempting to conduct this analysis and its series of exercises without a facilitator. You *need* to appoint someone (it can be a team member) as a designated facilitator. This is not necessarily your team leader. This person will not be your "boss." But this person *will* be responsible for:

- Copying and distributing to all participants copies of the Case and Case Analysis and all handouts
- Organizing role-plays (appointing time keepers and observers, where indicated)
- Moving the process along and staying on track

**Psst! Facilitators:** Read all the activity directions as if they applied to you.
**Psst! Team members:** You, too.

---

### Materials Needed

Enough printed copies of the following to distribute to all team members:

- The Case and Guide to Analysis
- Worksheet—Rubric for Grading Student Writing in All Content Areas
- Worksheet—Teamwork Tracking Chart
- Worksheet—Team Action Plan
- Chart paper and markers

Full-size reproducibles of worksheets and handouts are available on the companion CD-ROM.

# A. Analyzing the Case

## Step 1: Read the Case (10–15 minutes)

Distribute the teaching case, and have all team members read it through, underlining or highlighting pieces of information that they think are significant to understanding the case.

## Step 2: Establish the Facts of the Case (10 minutes)

As a whole group, make a list on chart paper of the significant *facts* of the teaching case. Include what you know about each team member. Try to withhold judgment, inferences, or evaluation, and come to agreement about what happened.

---

**Very Important:** When we say *facts* we mean just that—you must stick to the facts ONLY. There is a huge temptation, when analyzing other teachers' interactions, for teachers to voice *opinions* such as "She talks too much during the meeting" or "She's not a very good teacher." These are not *facts*, and negative comments such as these are counterproductive. The group should consciously steer away from such comments and instead either ask questions such as "Does she allow other voices to be heard?" or offer statements based on *evidence* such as "She says _____, but then she does _____."

If teachers feel they will be attacked for opening up their practice for other teachers to view, they simply will not do it. Making practice public is a risky proposition, and part of your challenge as a case analyst is to pretend that the teachers you are talking about are right there in the room with you.

---

## Step 3: Case Analysis Questions (20 minutes)

Discuss the following questions. For each question, identify the evidence that leads to your response. (You do not have to address every question.)

### About the Team

- What are the team's goals?
- How would you describe the way the team works together?
- What are the team's strengths and weaknesses?
- Do team members rely on one other or feel accountable to one another? If so, in what ways?

- How does the team spend its meeting time?
- What beliefs about students are revealed in the team members' talk?
- How honestly and nondefensively do they deal with one another?

### About the Individuals

- How would you describe Ella's role as team leader?
- What does this case tell you about the role of the principal in this school?
- How might Ella have reacted to the principal's demands?
- If you were Ella's leadership coach, what suggestions would you make?

## B. Exploring the Dilemma (30 minutes)

Collaborative work across curriculum areas does not come easily to middle or high school teachers. Why should it? Middle and high school teachers have had a laser-like focus on their own subject areas for well over a century, indeed since the advent of middle and high schools. Why should a science teacher feel any responsibility for the students in her or his middle school science class when they are in their English language arts classes? Why should a math teacher whose students might receive high test scores feel accountable for the same students' low scores in English language arts? And even if middle or high school teachers did admit that cross-area collaboration might improve all their students' work, how many teachers would even know how to make the leap to collaborative work?

But the word is out that collaboration does make a difference, and middle and high schools are beginning to recognize that cross-area teams working together on a common academic thread—or high school departments using a common curricular focus, usually literacy, across all departments—can enable the school to make enormous progress.

When middle school cross-area teams of teachers in Memphis, Tennessee, put their heads together and combined their pedagogical expertise, they improved the learning of *all* their students. Indeed, there were clear gains in test scores in both reading and math.[20] This phenomenon has now been replicated in other states where teams of teachers from different subject areas work collaboratively.

## The "Hedgehog Concept" as a Model for Middle School Teams

The most convincing rationale for working in collaborative teaching teams comes from the world of business. Jim Collins, whose best-selling book *Good to Great*,[21] demonstrates how team collaboration improves the work performance of American corporations, uses a powerful metaphor to drive this idea home. He calls it the "hedgehog concept," and he uses it to describe how work teams, looking inwardly and collaboratively to improve their own work, gain momentum and increasing success. He begins with a comparison between the behavior of two common field animals—foxes and hedgehogs. Foxes see the world in all its complexity; their eyes are everywhere. Hedgehogs, on the other hand, stay close to home and work cleverly and in an entrepreneurial manner to use their strength from within on one common task to help them survive. While Collins uses the hedgehog concept to describe the success of teams in business, it is clear that the same concept can work in middle and high schools. It's about mobilizing the existing energy and working strategically. It's about looking inward and working together.

The enormous untapped potential of teachers working together can be unleashed when an entire grade, department, or even school works together toward a common goal. In 2010 the *New York Times* reported on a large urban high school in Brockton, Massachusetts, where, 10 years earlier, a group of teachers had lobbied the principal to create a "school restructuring committee."[22] Its goal was to provide a focus for all departments so that all students would improve. The school had been a dismal failure; before 2001 only a quarter of its students passed statewide exams and one out of three students dropped out. Yet by 2009 Brockton High School (the largest public school in Massachusetts) had outperformed 90 percent of all Massachusetts high schools. The common focus was literacy. All departments, from the science department to the math department and even the physical education department, were directed to use this common focus to improve the school.

Bob Perkins, chair of the math department at Brockton High, described how he used a writing lesson in his Introduction to Algebra II class:

> He wrote "$3 + 7^2 - 6 \times 3 - 11$" on the board, then asked students to solve the problem in their workbooks and to explain their reasoning, step by step, in simple sentences.

"I did the exponents first and squared the 7," wrote Sharon Peterson, a junior. "I multiplied 6 × 3. I added 3 + 49, and combined 18 and 11, because they were both negatives. I ended up with 52 − 29. The final answer was 23."

Some students had more trouble, and the lesson seemed to drag a bit.

"This is taking longer than I expected, but it's not wasted time," Mr. Perkins said. "They're learning math, but they're also learning to write."

The hedgehog concept can work equally well in both high schools and middle schools, challenging cross-area teams or departments to depend on each other and mobilize their strengths. Thus middle school teams can strengthen all the teachers' knowledge by strengthening core knowledge through sharing prior knowledge and best practices to build a stronger foundation. And high schools—with, for example, a shared curricular focus on literacy—can be transformed, literally.

## Questions for Discussion After Reading the Hedgehog Concept

1. Thinking about your own team dynamics, do you operate more like foxes or hedgehogs? Give examples.

2. What challenges would your team face if you were to adopt the hedgehog concept?

3. One recent study noted that middle schools where teachers collaborate across curriculum areas

   > have successfully improved student performance when they have also had a common decision-making vision. Students in middle schools do not just experience one teacher, they experience an entire program with a climate that can either invite them in or push them out and either promote learning or hinder it. Consistency [and] coherence . . . for a sustained period of time are required for success.[23]

Discuss this excerpt by considering the following questions:

- Does it ring true for you?
- How would you implement a program with consistency and coherence to improve your students' test scores?
- Might your team benefit from a more collaborative approach to student learning even if it takes more time?

# C. Reflect and Connect (20 minutes)

Role-play and subsequent analysis helps uncover and illuminate issues that may be lying just under the surface but are difficult to bring forward.

## Part 1: Use a Role-Play to Clarify the Issue

### Step 1: Structuring the Role-Play (5 minutes)

We suggest a role-play to highlight this common dilemma on teams.

This role-play takes place during a pivotal scene that occurs at the end of the case, when two team members refuse to take part in the development of the principal-mandated action plan because of their particular situations. They do not agree that they need to be part of any activity that would make all the team members accountable for all the team's student progress.

The characters:

- Ella Tye: English language arts teacher and team leader with responsibility (but no authority) for holding the team accountable for its work
- Paul Santorino: math teacher whose students' state test scores are high and who doesn't see any reason to work with his colleagues on developing an action plan for the team
- George Gilespie: science coordinator, science teacher, and active member of the team
- Ross Lowry: social studies teacher who values the team and takes an active role in meetings
- Abby Waller: Spanish teacher and full member of the team (Spanish is considered an academic subject in this school) whose students do not take state tests and thus feels that collaborative team work does not affect her

*The setting:*

The principal has just informed Ella that the team has received surprisingly low scores on its state tests, and she expects an action plan for team improvement as quickly as possible. Ella is being held responsible for making this happen.

Ella and two other team members, Lowry and Gilespie, agree that the task must be done. The two other members of the team, Santorino and Waller, are unwilling to participate in this team-wide effort.

Here, in short, is the section of the case where the issue arises:

(Santorino says) "Well, I'll tell you one thing, I'm not agreeing to any action plan. Check the math scores. Most of the kids met AYP, and a few even scored 'advanced.' So there's no way I'm writing any kind of action plan. There's no way I'm doing anything extra."

(Waller adds) "Yeah, I mean, Spanish isn't even on the state exam. Seems like I automatically get a free pass on the action plan."

The goal of the role-play is to convince the two members that their input will be essential for the success of the team and to suggest ways in which they might lend their expertise to the success of the team.

### Step 2: The Use of an Observer

During the role-play an observer takes notes so that she or he can give specific feedback, tied to the data, when the role-play is over. The observer is also the time-keeper, authorized to "pull down the curtain" when the role-play appears to be repeating itself, or when three minutes has elapsed, whichever comes first.

### Step 3: Feedback (6–8 minutes)

The observer provides specific feedback to the mock team, addressing—when possible—the underlying issues that the presenters shared in the meeting.

### Step 4: Discussion and Debriefing (6–8 minutes)

Discuss and debrief the issues using the quote about middle schools that appears at the beginning of this section of the case (e.g., What good points do each of the characters make during the role-play? How have the team leader and the two advocates for the action plan made their case? What were their successful moves, and what other moves might they have made that would have gotten the two reluctant teachers "on board"?)

## Part 2: Apply the Analysis to Your Team (15 minutes)

Discuss the following:

- What characteristics of the team in this case are similar to your team? What are the differences?

- Do all your team members feel accountable for the success of all the team's students?
- How are curricular and instructional decisions made in your team? Does every member of the team have a voice in the decisions that are made? Does your team have an overall vision of curriculum and instruction for your grade level?
- In what ways might your team begin to hold each other accountable for the instructional work of each team member for the benefit of all the team's students?

# D. What Do We Do Now?
# (45 minutes for discussion;
# 45 minutes to complete an action plan)

Is there a chance that students in your class would be more successful if they mastered a new literacy skill? When the Brockton High School teachers met, they determined that to successfully adopt the literacy focus, every content area would teach the following:

- Take notes
- Explain one's thinking
- Argue a thesis and support one's thinking
- Compare and contrast
- Write an open response
- Describe an experiment, report one's findings, and report one's conclusion
- Generate a response to what one has read, viewed, or heard
- Convey one's thinking in complete sentences
- Develop an expository essay with a formal structure

## Discuss With Your Team

Can teaching literacy skills become the responsibility of every teacher on the team regardless of her or his specialty or content area? What are the challenges—and the benefits?

If your discussion points to more benefits than challenges, here are ideas about how to proceed:

1. At a team meeting, consider how writing might be a way to work effectively together. We suggest writing because it is more measurable than reading and therefore a potentially effective entry point.

2. Brainstorm the kinds of writing that individual teachers do in their subject areas.

3. Teaching literacy skills can become the responsibility of every teacher on the team regardless of content area.

4. Should you decide to take this on, you might use as your guide the Rubric for Grading Student Writing in All Content Areas (Figure C8.1) developed by the teachers at Brockton High School.

5. Highlight the work of one subject area teacher per month so that every few weeks students receive the same literacy lesson using different content. The format of the lesson should be the same; the context is different.

6. Individual teachers assess using the team/schoolwide rubric.

7. Monthly, the team collaboratively examines student work and suggests ways to improve the instruction. Often there are inconsistent expectations in different content areas for writing. The standardized rubric ensures consistency of rigor, regardless of content area.

A Teamwork Tracking Chart (Figure C8.2) can help your team stay on track as it works on its cross-area collaboration.

If your team decides to commit to this complicated initiative—focusing on writing skills across all content areas, offering an immediate opportunity for improvement—you will need an action plan (Figure C8.3). You can use the same one found in Chapter 5.

This is not easy work, and much of it will be new to teachers collaborating in teams. But it will help to keep this guiding principle in mind:

*Student achievement will rise when teams focus thoughtfully and relentlessly on improving the quality of instruction.*

## Figure C8.1   Rubric for Grading Student Writing in All Content Areas

| Content | Form | |
|---|---|---|
| **8**<br>• Response contains a clear thesis and insightfully answers all parts of the question.<br>• Response provides relevant and specific textual evidence.<br>• Explanations of evidence are clear and accurate, and demonstrate superior understanding of the material. | **4**<br>• Response contains sophisticated and effective use of transitions and strategic repetition, indicating complete control of the material.<br>• Response is logically and effectively organized in its thesis, paragraphing, and sequencing of examples.<br>• Response contains clear sentence structure with few or no errors. | **Legibility**<br><br>**1:** Easy to read<br><br>**0:** Difficult to read |
| **6**<br>• Response contains a clear thesis and adequately answers all parts of the question.<br>• Response provides relevant but general textual evidence.<br>• Explanations of evidence are mostly clear and accurate, and demonstrate good understanding of the material. | **3**<br>• Response contains adequate but simplistic use of transitions and strategic repetition.<br>• Response is organized in its thesis, paragraphing, and sequencing of examples.<br>• Response contains clear sentence structure with no distracting errors. | |
| **4**<br>• Response contains a thesis but only partially answers the question.<br>• Response provides a mix of accurate and inaccurate textual evidence.<br>• Explanations of evidence are vague and/or demonstrate limited understanding of the material. | **2**<br>• Response contains some inappropriate use of transitions and strategic repetition.<br>• Response demonstrates lapses in the organization of its thesis, paragraphing, and/or sequencing of examples.<br>• Response contains lapses in sentence structure that interfere with the clarity of thought. | |
| **2**<br>• Response contains a thesis but only minimally answers the question.<br>• Response provides insufficient and/or largely inaccurate textual evidence.<br>• Explanations of evidence are unclear and/or demonstrate minimal understanding of the material. | **1**<br>• Response contains incorrect or inadequate use of transitions and strategic repetition.<br>• Response reflects minimal organization of its thesis, paragraphing, and/or sequencing of examples.<br>• Response contains major errors in sentence structure. | **Length**<br><br>**1:** Sufficient<br><br>**0:** Insufficient |
| **0**<br>• Response is incorrect.<br>• Response contains insufficient evidence to show understanding of the material.<br>• Response is off-topic and/or contains irrelevant content. | **0**<br>• Response contains no evidence of transitions and strategic repetition.<br>• Response reflects no organization.<br>• Response contains little to no evidence of sentence structure. | |
| **Evaluated by: Self     Peer     Teacher     (Circle One)**<br><br>**Comments:** | | **Scoring**<br>13–14 = Advanced<br>11–12 = Proficient<br>8–10 = Needs Improvement<br>0–7 = Failing<br><br>_____ **Total Score** |

NOTE: This rubric was developed by the teachers of Brockton High School, Brockton, Massachusetts. Used with permission.

**Figure C8.2   Worksheet—Teamwork Tracking Chart**

| Month | Date that the presenting teacher's lesson plan will be distributed to all team members | Date that the lesson will be presented | Date that student work will be examined at the team meeting |
|---|---|---|---|
| October | | | |
| November | | | |
| December | | | |
| January | | | |

**Figure C8.3   Worksheet—Team Action Plan**

| What is to be accomplished? (List action steps.) | Who is responsible? | When will action be complete? |
|---|---|---|
| 1. | | |
| 2. | | |
| 3. | | |

# References

## Foreword

1. Bryk, A., & Schneider, B. (2002). *Trust in schools.* New York: Russell Sage Foundation; Edmondson, A. (2002). The local and variegated nature of learning in organizations: A group-level perspective. *Organization Science, 13,* 128–146; Goddard, R., Hoy, W. K., & Woolfolk Hoy, A. (2004). Collective efficacy beliefs: Theoretical developments, empirical evidence, and future directions. *Educational Researcher, 33*(3), 3–13; Hackman, J. R. (2002). *Leading teams: Setting the stage for great performances.* Boston: Harvard Business School Press.

2. Bransford, J. D., Brown, A. L., & Cocking, R. R. (2002). Teacher Learning. In J. D. Bransford, A. L. Brown, & R. R. Cocking (Eds.), *How people learn: Brain, mind, experience, and school* (pp. 190–205). Washington, DC: National Research Council.

## Chapter 1

1. Hoffman, N. (1981). *Woman's "True" Profession: Voices from the History of Teaching.* Old Westbury, NY: Feminist Press

2. National Commission on Excellence in Education. (1983). *A Nation at Risk: the Imperative for Educational Reform.* Retrieved from http://www2 .ed.gov/pubs/NatAtRisk

## Chapter 2

1. Cromwell, S. (2004). Team teaching: Structure an effective team and develop a strategy that works for you. *Education World.* Retrieved from http://www.nea.org/tools/13413.htm

2. National Commission on Teaching and America's Future. (2008). *Learning Teams: Creating What's Next.* Retrieved from http://www.nctaf.org/ documents/NCTAFLearningTeams408REG2.pdf

3. Moffet, C. (2000). Sustaining Change: The Answers Are Blowing in the Wind. *Educational Leadership, 57*(7), 35–38.

## Chapter 3

1. Janis, I. L. (1982). *Groupthink: Psychological Studies of Policy Decisions and Fiascoes* (2nd ed.). New York: Houghton Mifflin.

2. Stone, D., Patton, B., & Heen, S. (1999). *Difficult Conversations.* New York: Penguin Books.

3. Wooley, A. W., Chabris, F., Pentland, A., Hashmi, N., & Malone, T. W. (2010). Evidence for a Collective Intelligence Factor in the Performance of Human Groups. *Science, 330,* 686–688.

4. City, E. A., Elmore, R. F., Fiarman, S. E., & Teitel, L. (2009). *Instructional Rounds in Education: A Network Approach to Improving Teaching and Learning.* Cambridge, MA: Harvard Education Press.

5. McKnight, K., & Carlson-Bancroft, A. (2008). *Analysis of Instructional Talk in Teacher Workgroup Meetings.* Retrieved from http://pearsonlt.com/article-lt-facilitates-richer-instructional-discourse

6. Little, J. W. (1982). Norms of Collegiality and Experimentation: Workplace Conditions of School Success. *American Educational Research Journal, 19,* 325–340.

7. Boles, K. (2009). *A Study of Instructional Talk in Teacher Teams.* Chicago: Spencer Foundation.

8. Cooperating to Cut Bypass Deaths. (1996, March 20). *New York Times.* p. C13.

9. City, E. A., Elmore, R. F., Fiarman, S. E., & Teitel, L. (2009). *Instructional Rounds in Education: A Network Approach to Improving Teaching and Learning.* Cambridge, MA: Harvard Education Press.

## Chapter 4

1. Wallace Foundation. (2008). *Becoming a Leader: Preparing School Principals for Today's Schools. New York: Author.* Retrieved from http://www.wallacefoundation.org/SiteCollectionDocuments/WF/KnowledgeCenter/Attachments/PDF/becoming-a-leader.pdf

2. Wallace Foundation (2011). *Shared Leadership: Effects on Teachers and Students of Principals and Teachers Leading Together—Learning From Leadership.* Retrieved from http://www.wallacefoundation.org/pages/1_2-shared-leadership-learning-from-leadership.aspx

3. Troen, V., & Boles, K. C. (2003). *Who's Teaching Your Children? Why the Teacher Crisis Is Worse Than You Think and What Can Be Done About It.* New Haven, CT: Yale University Press.

4. Adapted from Saphier, J. D. (1995). *Bonfires and Magic Bullets. Making Teaching a True Profession: The Step Without Which Other Reforms Will Neither Take nor Endure.* Carlisle, MA: Research for Better Teaching.

5. National Association of State Boards of Education. Retrieved from http://www.nasbe.org/leadership/leadership-continuum/teacher-leadership/overview

6. Adapted from a working document on teacher leadership standards developed by the Teacher Leadership Exploratory Consortium, Educational Testing Service, Princeton, NJ (June 2010).

7. Ibid.

## Chapter 5

1. Robbins, S. P. (1974). *Managing Organizational Conflict: A Nontraditional Approach*. Englewood Cliffs, NJ: Prentice Hall.

2. Heifetz, R., & Linsky, M. (2002). *Leadership on the Line: Staying Alive Through the Dangers of Leading*. Boston: Harvard Business School Press. (pp. 51–55)

3. Adapted from Tuckman, B. W. (1965). Developmental Sequence in Small Groups. *Psychological Bulletin, 63*, 384–399.

4. This team assessment tool was created by Don Clark and is used here with his permission. It is available for free download at http://www.nwlink.com/~donclark/leader/teamsuv.html

5. Woodcock, M. (1989). *Team Development Manual* (2nd ed.). Surrey, UK: Gower. (pp. 19–20)

6. Used with permission of Doug Kilmister, principal, Pittsfield Elementary School, Pittsfield, NH.

## Chapter 6

1. Husock, H. (2000). *How to Use a Teaching Case*. Cambridge, MA: Harvard University, Kennedy School of Government Case Program. Retrieved from http://www.ksgcase.harvard.edu/uploadpdf/teaching_case.pdf

## Chapter 7 (Cases)

### Case 1

1. U.S. Department of Education, Office of Elementary and Secondary Education, Student Achievement and School Accountability Programs. (2006). LEA and School Improvement Non-Regulatory Guidance. Retrieved from http://www2.ed.gov/policy/elsec/guid/school improvementguid.pdf

2. For more information about progress monitoring, view the information available at http://www.studentprogress.org/default.asp

3. Fullan, M. (1993). *Change Forces: Probing the Depths of Educational Reform*. London: Falmer Press.

4.  Stone, D., Patterson, B. M., & Heen, S. (1999). *Difficult Conversations: How to Discuss What Matters Most*. New York: Penguin Books.

## Case 2

5.  Katzenbach, J. R., & Smith, D. K. (1992). *The Wisdom of Teams: Creating the High-Performance Organization*. New York: McKinsey.

6.  Boles, K. C. (2009). *A Study of Instructional Talk in Teacher Teams*. Chicago, Spencer Foundation.

## Case 3

7.  David, J. (2008/2009). Collaborative Inquiry. *Educational Leadership*, 66(4), 67–88. Collaborative inquiry is the core professional development model embedded in the belief that powerful learning occurs when teams of educators intentionally collaborate to evaluate the effectiveness of their classroom instruction. The collaborative inquiry cycle begins with the determination of critical skill objectives and the setting of measurable goals for student achievement. From there, teachers incorporate research-based best practices into their instructional plans and assessment designs. They then implement the instructional and assessment plans, grade and analyze assessment results to identify gaps in achievement, interpret results to determine potential causes of these gaps, and finally adjust instruction and/or revise curriculum to ensure that all students achieve mastery of the essential skills. This cycle is iterative and ongoing with the goal of sustained, systematic, and demonstrable progress over time.

8.  Routman, R. (2003). *Reading Essentials: The Specifics You Need to Teach Reading Well*. Portsmouth, NH: Heinemann.

9.  Fisher, D., & Frey, N. (2008). *Better Learning Through Structured Teaching: A Framework for the Gradual Release of Responsibility*. Alexandria, VA: Association for Supervision and Curriculum Development.

10. Adapted from Routman, R. (2003). *Reading Essentials: The Specifics You Need to Teach Reading Well*. Portsmouth, NH: Heinemann.

## Case 4

11. Troen, V., & Boles, K. C. (2003). *Who's Teaching Your Children? Why the Teacher Crisis Is Worse Than You Think and What Can Be Done About It*. New Haven, CT: Yale University Press.

## Case 5

12. Stone, D., Patton, B., & Heen, S. (1999). *Difficult Conversations: How to Discuss What Matters Most*. New York: Penguin Books.

13. Deal, T., & Peterson, K. (1999). *Shaping School Culture: The Heart of Leadership*. San Francisco: Jossey-Bass.

14. Fullan, M. (2001). *The New Meaning of Educational Change*. New York: Teachers College Press.

15. Sparks, D. (n.d.). Thirteen Tips for Managing Change. Retrieved from http://www.ncrel.org/sdrs/areas/issues/educatrs/leadrshp/le5spark.htm

16. Herold, D. M., & Fedor, D. B. (2008). *Change the Way You Lead Change: Leadership Strategies that REALLY Work*. Stanford, CA: Stanford University Press.

### Case 6

17. Murphy, S. (2002). *Future Protocol, a.k.a Back to the Future*. Retrieved from http://www.nsrfharmony.org/protocol/doc/future.pdf

### Case 7

18. Johnson, S. M., & Donaldson, M. L. (2007). Overcoming the Obstacles to Leadership. *Educational Leadership, 65*(1), 8–13.

19. Ibid.

### Case 8

20. Cassellius, B. (2006). Using Relationships, Responsibility, and Respect to Get From "Good to Great" in Memphis Middle Schools. *Middle School Journal, 37*(5), 4–15.

21. Collins, J. (2001). *Good to Great: Why Some Companies Make the Leap . . . and Others Don't*. New York: HarperBusiness.

22. Dillon, S. (2010, September 27). 4,100 Students Prove "Small Is Better" Rule Wrong. *New York Times*, p. A1. http://www.nytimes.com/2010/09/28/education/28school.html

23. Cassellius, B. (2006). Ibid.

# Index